Script into Performance

SCRIPT INTO PERFORMANCE

A Structuralist Approach

Richard Hornby

PARAGON HOUSE PUBLISHERS

NEW YORK

First U.S. paperback edition, 1987.

Published by
PARAGON HOUSE PUBLISHERS
2 Hammarskjöld Plaza
New York, New York 10017

Library of Congress Cataloging-in-Publication Data

Hornby, Richard, 1938—
    Script into performance.

    Reprint. Originally published: Austin:
University of Texas Press, c1977.
        Bibliography: p.
        Includes index.
        1. Theater. 2. Drama—Explication.
3. Structuralism. I. Title.
[PN2039.H66 1987]   792'.01'5   86-30292
ISBN 0-913729-59-0 (pbk.)

TO MY STUDENTS

Contents

Preface

Terminology is always a nagging problem. It ought to be fairly easy for everyone to get together and agree on what certain key words mean in an intellectual discussion of drama. In fact, even words like *drama* itself have meanings that vary. Thus, there is a need, at the outset, for some definitions:

1. *Drama* and *theatre*. I use the word *drama* to mean playscripts, considered individually or collectively, and *theatre* to mean performance or anything that goes into the making of performance—including playscripts. There is a trend toward this usage in North America, but it is not yet universal; I teach in a department of drama, but the majority of its courses are really in theatre. It is also worth noting that the Greek word from which *drama* is derived means "deed"—that is, performance—so that, linguistically at least, my terminology is incorrect.

2. *Playscript* and *play*. There is similarly a growing tendency to use *playscript* to mean the written drama, and *play* to mean drama in performance. I have not gone along with this trend for two reasons. First, it would mean changing some standard terms in theatrical history; "Well-Made Play" becomes the awkward "Well-Made Playscript," for example. But, second, there are times when an ambiguous meaning is desirable. I often find myself writing sentences like "Gordon Craig once suggested that Shakespeare wrote his ———— by taking well-known stories and asking members of his company to improvise them." Is the missing word to be *playscripts* or *plays*? One's first impulse is to think of Shakespeare in his study, writing *scripts*; but, then, Craig was really implying here that Shakespeare created *plays*, in an improvisational manner; but, then again, assuming Shakespeare actually followed this method, he must at some point along the way have turned the plays into the *playscripts* that we now have and read. I have therefore used the word *playscript* (or, for

variety, *script*, *playtext*, or *text*) when I wanted to stress the written work, and *performance* or *production* when I wanted to denote the work on the stage; *play* thus stands as the more general term for either the text, or the text in performance, or both.

3. *Criticism.* I use this word to mean the analysis, interpretation, or judgment of drama, or any combination of the three. It is popularly applied to the third meaning alone, but that, in my opinion, is poor usage.

4. *Structure.* This is defined in the main body of the text. I would ask the reader to keep in mind that my concept of Structure and Structuralism is different both from traditional notions of dramatic structure and from the concepts of many contemporary Structuralists. I am more concerned with Structuralism as a broad trend in modern thought than as the specific formulations of celebrated (and usually French) writers.

5. *Wholistic.* For some reason, the more common spelling of this word is "holistic." Nevertheless, I much prefer *wholistic*—which Webster's Third (unabridged) recognizes as an acceptable alternative —because it looks less technical and also because its meaning is more immediately apparent: determined by interconnected *wholes*, which are irreducible to the sum of their parts.

6. *Function.* There are many ways of describing this mathematical concept. I use the word in the same way that Kenneth Burke uses the word *ratio*: "A ratio is a formula indicating a transition from one term to another. Such a relation necessarily possesses the ambiguities of the potential, in that the second term is a medium different from the first."[1] I have preferred the word *function* because, in mathematics, that more truly describes a *transformation*. A ratio is really a *comparison*, not a "transition," as Burke puts it. A ratio is also always invertible, while a function is not, and I was interested in describing situations in drama where a function's inverse is either something invalid or else nonexistent.

There were annoying practical difficulties in using mathematical notation in the particular instances that I was concerned with. One usually likes to take letter variables from the initials of the things they stand for (e.g., "Let M = the set of all males, F = the set of all females"), but in practice I found that words like *playscript*, *philosophy*, and *performance* all begin with the same letter! The reader is therefore advised to note carefully the letters I *did* use, which are not always those one would expect.

Some will be repelled by a mathematical approach, which may seem out of place in a book on theatre. Nevertheless, there are certain advantages to it. The deeper we look into the problems of art, the more our ordinary language breaks down. Words like Burke's *ambiguities* in the quotation above suggest that we are already at the borders of common sense. We find ourselves again and again coming up against paradoxes: a script has contradictory meanings; an interpretation exists both in the playscript and in the interpreter's head, but not in either separately; a playscript both is and is not literature; a performance both is and is not the same as the playscript. The temptation is always to oversimplify, so that many dramatic theorists will damn the torpedoes and steam straight ahead to a theory that concentrates on only one side of a problem, while rejecting or ignoring the other. Mathematical notation is also a simplification, but it enables us almost blandly to incorporate many more difficulties than the straightforward approach through ordinary language. Science at the beginning of the twentieth century was in the same predicament; the traditional theories, based on visual models, were quite straightforward and sensible but unfortunately did not fit the facts. For better or worse, science chose the mathematical approach, deciding that, whatever the values of simplicity, truth was a higher virtue. The mathematical models given here are unbearably crude when compared with those of modern science, but the goal is the same—to find a mode of description for problems that will not yield to common sense.

Script into Performance

ntemporary
Theatre

0-913729-59-0

Paragon

roversial today than the produc-
re should be a problem at all is
heatrical production everywhere
'erformance techniques changed
l in traditional ways that were
such as the Japanese Noh theatre
gestures and vocal expressions
could remain fixed for centuries. But, actually, most theatres were
never particularly concerned with producing great works of the past.
In England and America, certainly, revivals of former successes,
whether ancient or modern, were rare and were usually for some specialized purpose, such as providing a vehicle for a star actor or a study
aid for an intellectual coterie. The theatre public's basic demand was
to see new material, rather than a new treatment of something written
for another time.

Today this has all changed. If in the past theatres mostly did new
playscripts using traditional methods of performance, our theatres
mostly do traditional playscripts using radically new methods. On
the one hand, the regional theatres in North America (once the great
hope for native playwriting) restrict themselves almost exclusively to
standard works, and even Broadway (where revivals used to mean
disaster) tends more and more to regard the classic as the safe invest-
ment. But, on the other hand, the classics are almost never produced

in straightforward ways. Creative energy has to go somewhere, it seems, and it goes most often today into the "concept" production, the "updated" play, the "rearranged" text. *Hamlet* is set in Spanish Harlem, *Oedipus Tyrannus* performed in the nude, *Phaedra* turned into a rock opera; playwrights born hundreds or thousands of years ago are shown to have suddenly become "our contemporaries," concerned with Communism, or anti-Semitism, or the energy crisis. Even modern playscripts are not exempt from alterations, although the copyright laws make a difference—when a German director wanted to present *A Streetcar Named Desire* as a kind of 1930's proletarian novel, with a decadent Blanche DuBois seducing an innocent (and black!) Stanley Kowalski, Tennessee Williams was able to get a restraining order from a law court.

These are extreme examples, of course, and it is easy to make fun of them. But doing so does not answer the more serious underlying questions: Just what *is* the proper relation of text to performance? Is a playscript a work of literature, or a "scenario," or both, or neither? Does it demand absolute fidelity, like a musical score, or is it only a starting point, like a film script? After all, altering or updating playscripts is not new. A closer examination of the traditional theatre reveals that respect for classic texts never ran very deep. If producers felt no obsessive compulsion to make changes, neither did they feel much compulsion to copy exactly. Our text of *Macbeth*, from the First Folio, appears to be a cut-down version, and it contains several obvious interpolations; while this is not quite the same thing as a nude, country-western version set on the moon, a purist might still maintain that the play should never be performed at all until the original text is discovered. For all the conservatism of the traditional theatre, there was probably never a production that did not make *some* alterations to the playtext, however slight. Furthermore, people always recognized that two productions of the same text could vary greatly, and actors knew that even the same production varies a lot from night to night. Whatever a performance is, it is literally a living thing, and a playscript is not. So just how *should* a playscript be treated when it is performed?

I believe that these questions can be answered, at least partially, and a good deal of confusion in today's theatre cleared up, by taking a Structuralist approach to playscript interpretation. Structuralism is a radical way of thinking that has had significant achievements in the interpretation of literature, as well as other art forms and even the social sciences, but has had very little influence on what is officially known as "dramatic" criticism, and almost none at all on the practical theatre. This is unfortunate because Structuralism (and let the capital S show that I am definitely not talking about traditional concepts of dramatic structure) could resolve many problems in today's theatre, particularly in the performance of classical playscripts. It is frustrating to see a playtext that has been given an exciting new interpretation by a Structuralist critic—not just a new interpretation, but a new *way* of interpreting—receive only unimaginative traditional productions or bizarre updated ones. A Structuralist approach would not only help prevent some of the zany extremes in production that are becoming all too common (even a high school senior play is likely these days to be altered and updated); it could also actually inspire significant, exciting, new productions. Structuralism can clarify just what a playscript *is*, and may go a long way toward clarifying the relationship of text to performance, if that problem can ever be resolved completely. And, finally, a new approach to classical playscript interpretation might push excessive creativity in production back where it belongs, namely, to the writing and performance of *new* scripts.

Nevertheless, Structuralism faces many obstacles before it can be accepted in the North American theatre. It is no accident that it has had so little impact thus far. Despite the fact that we seem to be going through a period of wild experimentation, theatre remains, as it has always been, the most conservative of the arts. It is expensive and risky and requires the co-operation of a large number of people. Many things that seem radical and new are actually the result of long-term trends: the rise of the director, to the point where he is now often a creator rather than interpreter, began in the last century, as did improvisation as a serious acting technique. The Dadaist experiments in the 1920's; the Expressionists and Surrealists of the same period; the theories of Stanislavski, Artaud, and Brecht (all long dead); even the long-time attempts of university theatre departments to achieve recognition as a discipline separate from literature—all lie behind the most far-out performances of today. Change does not come quickly. Nevertheless, I believe that the changes I am calling for are not all that drastic, that (as I shall attempt to show) aspects of Structuralism can be found in many of the theatre theorists whose work is now influential. All that is needed is a change in emphasis, drawing on different aspects of the great theorists from those commonly used, and downplaying certain other aspects, to synthesize a new approach.

Yet there are other problems than mere conservatism. There seems to be a vague know-nothingism at work in our theatre which is suspicious of all theories, no matter how interesting or useful. Not only do directors and actors want increasingly to be creative, but they also tend to think of the creative as being the opposite of intellectual. Being convinced that inspiration comes only from pure sensation, and never cognition, they fear that any theorizing, other than the most crude and blatant, will somehow be artistically stifling. There is of course no basis for such fear; the great artists throughout history have all been seriously concerned with theory as well as practice. Each feeds on the other—artistic theory cannot advance without drawing on examples of specific works, but neither can artistic creation rise above the hack level without a certain amount of theoretical consideration. One feels that if the anti-intellectual artists of today had their way, Michelangelo would have spent all his time at Lorenzo de' Medici's Academy chipping stone instead of talking to the philosophers, and Shakespeare would have learned not only "small Latin and less Greek," but precious little English either.

In the same vein, the very idea of a playscript is often under attack today as being too intellectual, too "literary." Improvised or collectively evolved performances are put forth as a more creative, purer form of theatre than one based on a text, as if playscript interpretation and creativity were opposites. If Structuralism as an analytical method is to find acceptance in our theatre, the anti-intellectual prejudices of many performers must first be challenged, because it is hard to sell a new kind of playscript interpretation to people who look only inward for their inspiration or who are even suspicious of scripts to begin with.

Not all the blame should be placed on performers, however. A great deal of the fault for the anti-intellectualism in theatre performance can be placed on members of my own profession, the university teachers. In North American universities and colleges, dramatic literature is almost universally taught by the historical survey method; the student memorizes a series of names and titles, each attached to some external trend like Romanticism or Naturalism or Theatre of the Absurd. Close reading of playtexts is left for upper-level, specialized courses that potential actors, directors, and designers rarely take. Given this, it is no wonder that performers get in the habit of thinking externally and superficially about scripts; nor is it any wonder that they often come to think of the study of dramatic literature as a dry, pedantic specialty, no urgent concern of theirs, which may even stifle creativity. Given the way the subject has been presented to them, it probably *is* stifling. The situation is so bad that in most theatre departments there is a complete split between the teachers of theory and criticism and the teachers of practical courses. Far more than the traditional departmental feud, based on personalities, the clash reflects, and in turn reinforces, the split between theory and practice in the theatre at large. Typically, a department will produce a season of plays for the public, as part of the training for its students as actors and technicians; but the dramatic literature and theory courses offered by the same department will not deal with the playscripts involved or generally function in any way as if the department productions even existed. On the other hand, the directors and performers will make no attempt to use the skills of the dramatic literature and theory people in interpreting the scripts being performed. Since neither side makes any attempt to adapt to the other's needs, it is again no wonder that performers get the idea that playscript interpretation is something that has nothing to do with performance.

A similar problem has grown up in theatre scholarship. In the past, there were several North American journals that dealt with both playscript interpretation and performance: *The Drama Review, Drama at Calgary, Performance.* They either have changed this dual emphasis or have stopped publication, as have several other magazines that dealt with script interpretation alone. The discouraging thing is that no one seems to have noticed any loss. The hardest part in filling someone's need is convincing him that he has that need in the first place.

Still, there are signs that the pendulum is swinging back. Artists almost never march in lockstep, thank goodness, and I have noticed that recently many theatre artists, particularly younger ones, are becoming impatient with what they see as frozen, mindless attitudes. Theatre reviewers, and audiences as well, are becoming bored with wildness for its own sake, with "experiments" that have become merely repetitious, in fact forming a new tradition as rigid as the old. In recent years, also, books have been appearing, by writers like J. L. Styan, Bert O. States, Jackson Barry, and Roger Gross, which take a generally Structuralist approach to drama rather than the once-over-lightly historical survey approach of most earlier writers on the subject. It remains, of course, to see whether theatre people will actually read them. (In the past, they always seemed to choose John Gassner instead of, say, Francis Fergusson.) There has been a vicious circle in the past, or rather a downward spiral: ignoring playscript interpretation leading to bad attitudes toward dramatic literature and criticism, and the bad teaching of it, both leading in turn to a *habit* of ignoring interpretation, or even a prejudice against it. I can only hope that these recent writers will not be ignored, and the circle will be broken. Modern theatre performers have long since learned that artistic creation need not follow traditional techniques and rules. They must similarly learn that artistic *interpretation* need not follow them either.

I recall a situation a few years ago, when I was appearing on a convention panel that included a noted director and a distinguished literary critic. The two were very much at odds with each other, the critic strongly disapproving of some Shakespearean productions that had recently appeared at the director's theatre. The discussion was all so negative that I tried to pose a question from a more positive viewpoint: did the director ever make use of literary criticism, had he ever found it valuable in developing a production concept, for example? The director grimaced and replied in an offended tone that, of course, he "did his homework." Judging by his own description of his productions, I wondered whether he actually did it very often, but that was not the point. His use of the word *homework*, pronounced with distaste, showed that he thought of playscript interpretation as an unpleasant task to be got out of the way as quickly as possible before the fun of creation could begin. The critic on the panel was unwittingly reinforcing this attitude by putting his case in completely negative terms, acting like a schoolmarm slapping a student's hand for saying "ain't." There is a lot more to playscript interpretation than the mere correcting of mistakes (valuable as that may be). Neither the director nor the critic was treating interpretation as a genuinely artistic process, one that is potentially illuminating, inspiring, useful, and—even—fun.

Contemporary American Theatre

Anyone who has been exposed to genuine playscript interpretation, which is neither shallow nor pedantic, knows that it can be a fascinating kind of exploration, often turning up startling new insights, in a process not at all opposed to creation itself. I was trying to get the director on the panel to see interpretation in this positive, *active* way. His automatically defensive, negative response showed how deep the problem lies.

The purpose of this book is to develop approaches to the production of classical playscripts that will be valid, imaginative, and powerful; to rescue performers from the desert they have wandered into and restore them to paths that are not old ruts but important new trails. But it would be both naïve and arrogant to think that a book can do this by itself; nor can one consider himself a Structuralist who considers only surface phenomena like theories put forth in print. What must be changed are the underlying attitudes, the habits of thinking about playscript production. No single approach or method can, by itself, affect performers who automatically think of interpretation as "homework"; obviously, a whole *style* of thinking must be changed. For that, I can only hope that this book will be one small shove in the right direction.

2

Structuralism

It is hard to define precisely an idea that is as broad as Structuralism. It is far more an attitude than any rigid doctrine; in categorizing Structuralists, for example, one often finds oneself lumping together scholars who are in bitter opposition, or even including people who specifically do not want to be called Structuralists while excluding others who do. Briefly, the Structuralist approach sees a work of art— a play, a poem, a painting, a film—as an interrelated process rather than a thing or a collection of disconnected things. The method is not limited to art, however, and has been applied to language, religion, and social organizations, having ultimate implications for all human creations. In each case, Structuralism finds the essence of a work in the relation between parts rather than in the parts themselves; these relations form patterns or "structures" that define what the work truly *is*.

Defined in this way, Structuralism shows the clear influence of modern science. The table on which I am now writing, for example, appears to be a solid "thing." Nevertheless, a physicist would insist that this is only an appearance, that the table is actually composed of multitudes of tiny molecules, in a constant state of motion, bound to each other by various electromagnetic forces. Nor are the molecules themselves solid objects, but, rather, they are composed of even smaller particles—atoms—bound by still other forces. So far, so good; a nineteenth-century scientist would feel, with relief, that at last he had reached the "thing" level and could comfortably think of atoms as tiny billiard balls bouncing around in space. But a modern scientist would reject such a visual model entirely and maintain that atoms themselves are made up of still smaller subatomic particles, bound by still other forces again. The fact that over two hundred different kinds of subatomic particles have been discovered, and that some are known to be combinations of others, suggests that there may be another level yet to be discovered of subsubatomic particles, bound by more new forces. One begins to suspect that there may even be no end to this process, that ultimately there are no "things" at all in the universe, but only relationships. The subatomic particles themselves often do not act like things (although they are often depicted in popular magazines as neat little spheres). Sometimes they exhibit the properties of particles, and other times of waves. It is impossible to determine both their momentum and their position simultaneously. They move from one point to another without passing through the intervening space. Ultimately, it is impossible to construct visual models of them—that is to say, models which relate them to our own familiar world of things; one can only construct mathematical models, equations which will predict their behavior. Although these equations may seem strange and inhuman, to the physicist they express the true essence of matter. Matter is seen as a process rather than an object or collection of objects, and it is described in a "language" that is structural rather than propositional. A propositional language isolates parts of a system and ascribes qualities to them; a structural language, such as a set of equations, relates the parts of a system to each other. Ask a physicist "What is matter?" and he will not be able to answer you, but he *will* be able to relate matter to other phenomena with mathematical precision, through such equations as Einstein's famous $e = mc^2$, which demonstrates a constant relation between matter and energy. In similar fashion, a Structuralist critic of literature will not try to isolate and define an element of the work he is examining, such as its philosophical theme, but will instead relate a theme to a character, or a character to another character, or a setting to an action that takes place in it. Like a physicist with respect to matter, the Structuralist critic sees the work not as a collection of isolated things, but rather as a web of relationships.

Historically, however, there is no *direct* connection between modern physics and Structuralism as a method of analyzing a work of art. Perhaps the earliest example of the combination of science and Structuralist criticism is found in psychology, in the work of Freud. I am not thinking so much of the specific theories of Freud, which often have led sophomoric critics to make fatuous propositional statements about works of art (here a mother fixation, there a phallic symbol), but rather of his notion of the mind as having an unconscious component, more important than the conscious, which expresses itself through patterns of conscious thought and behavior. In treating a patient, the psychoanalyst rejects the conscious mind except insofar as it exhibits patterns from the unconscious; he attempts to explore this unconscious mind in order to determine the patient's true psychic problems, as opposed to the neurotic symptoms on the surface, which are mere reflections of something much deeper.

Notice the similarity between the Freudian technique and the explorations of the physicist in the previous example. In each case there is the notion of a hidden world, perceptible only by indirect means, that is nonetheless more real than what is palpably on the surface. There is in modern science something of a throwback to the occult, to all those ancient wizards, astrologers, and mystics who tried to deduce the secrets of the universe from the entrails of animals, the movements of the heavens, or the allegories of scripture. Starting in the seventeenth century, science specifically rejected such occult analysis in favor of simple, direct observation and common sense (or "right reason"). While the common-sense approach had some spectacular successes, by the late nineteenth century it was seen to have serious inadequacies. The phenomenon of radioactivity, the invariability of the speed of light—and the hysterical symptoms of neurotic mental patients—seemed to defy surface analysis of the kind that had become traditional. As a result, science took a "turn to the right" in favor once again of indirect, speculative, deep study. Today, the scientist is a bit of a wizard again.

For this reason, modern science is always somewhat controversial. Modern physics is fairly widely accepted because of the mass of evidence supporting its theories and perhaps also because of the very remoteness of the world it describes, but psychoanalysis remains controversial because the supporting evidence is more difficult to assess and because it seems closer to home, imposing on our very conception of ourselves as conscious, rational creatures. Behaviorism, for example, is a psychology that rejects the existence of an unconscious mind (and sometimes seems to challenge the existence of any sort of mind at all), describing behavior in simple terms of stimulus and response, which is to say, cause and effect in the visible, everyday world. Behavioral therapy thus treats symptoms directly; instead of regarding neurotic behavior as the mere reflection of a hidden mysterious unconscious, it sees the behavior itself as the important thing, which can be changed directly through conditioning. A child molester, for example, will simply be trained not to want little girls or boys, perhaps by viewing pictures of them while simultaneously receiving electric shocks. In taking a simple, straightforward, common-sense approach to a problem, Behaviorism thus returns to the seventeenth century, to the Enlightenment tradition in science. Its methods are simple, understandable by the common man without any special training, unconcerned with any mysterious complexities or unseen relationships, requiring no arcane jargon—all the goals of the early philosophers of science, such as Bacon. Behavorism is very much of this world, rather than a hidden world, and it sees this world as one of simple, discrete elements having only direct, linear relationships with each other.

A "this world" approach will always have an important appeal and will generally be less controversial than a "hidden world" approach. Structuralism takes a "hidden world" approach to artistic analysis and has always been controversial, just as psychoanalysis has been. And a "hidden world" approach to criticism does lend itself to abuses—to wild, unsupported, purely personal interpretations (commonly known in literary criticism as "reading in"); to secret, in-group codes (like the "spot the phallic symbol" game that undergraduates like to play); and, subtlest of all, to reification, substituting some "interpretation" for the direct experience of the work being studied, instead of using the interpretation only in order to enhance that experience. But a "this world" approach has its own possible abuses as well—accepting without question the prejudices, the standard attitudes, which "this world" always has in abundance; developing an insensitivity to nuance, to the *particulars* of the thing being studied, because it seems too familiar and obvious; reifying not with personal or arcane interpretations but rather with shallow, pedestrian ones. Ultimately, "this world" is not the world itself but only one view of it, just as, ultimately, the "hidden world" cannot be *completely* hidden. It is always possible to demand evidence for a literary interpretation, and even if that evidence is indirect, as with modern physics, if it is abundant and supports the interpretation better than any other, then that interpretation must be considered the best one, no matter how odd or nonsensical it may seem at first.

Freud himself did a certain amount of artistic analysis, including one essay ("The Theme of the Three Caskets," dealing with *The Merchant of Venice*) that qualifies as literary criticism. In his work, as in that of the best later Freudian critics like Ernst Kris or Norman Holland, there are no intellectual games of "symbol spotting." There is instead an attempt to determine how the work functions—how it is put together, why it moves us in spite of apparent flaws, what is really happening in it. Interpretations are supported by direct evidence from the text. In Kris's essay "Prince Hal's Conflict,"[1] for example, which deals with Shakespeare's *Henry IV*, Part 1, there are eleven direct quotations from the playtext, plus dozens of examples cited indirectly, to support an interpretation of the relation between Hal and Hotspur (which is an interesting problem, since they are never on stage together until their duel at the end). We are given a kind of map to help us explore the play better, to understand how it is actually constructed, which is certainly a useful aid to anyone wanting to produce it. A traditional, commonsensical, "this world" critic might simply reject the Hotspur plot as an unfortunate excrescence detracting from the fun of Falstaff. (The play has often been performed with the Hotspur plot trimmed drastically.) He might go on to discuss Falstaff in isolation, using a propositional language to describe his wit, his cowardice, his sensuality. Kris, on the other hand, while not insensitive to the vigor of Falstaff's characterization, sees that characterization not in isolation but rather in relation to others in the text:

> The position of the Prince between Falstaff and the King is almost as explicitly stated; he has two fathers, as the King has two sons. When he enacts with Falstaff his forthcoming interview with his father, the theme is brought into the open. . . . Henry Percy stands between a weak father, Northumberland, who is prevented by illness from participating in the decisive battle, and a scheming uncle, Worcester, who plans the rebellion. . . .

The triangular relationships are not only similar to each other, since they all contain variations of the theme of good and bad fathers and sons, but within each triangle the parallel figures are closely interconnected; thus the two Harrys, whom Henry IV compares, form a unit; Hotspur's rebellion represents also Prince Hal's unconscious parricidal impulses. Hotspur is the Prince's double.[2]

This passage is remarkable for its absence of psychoanalytic jargon; although Kris's essay does contain a necessary amount of it, in the end he is talking about the playtext, rather than Hal's Oedipus complex or Falstaff's libidinous impulses. Rather than being a propositional language, his is clearly a Structuralist one, which treats the characters as part of an overall, interconnected process. Falstaff exists not just as a character in himself but to define the character of the King, and vice-versa; both the King and Falstaff exist to define the character of Hal. Similarly, in a real sense Hotspur is part of Hal's characterization, and Hal of Hotspur's, even though they are hardly ever on stage together. There is a pattern underlying the text that gives it coherence, despite the apparent fragmentation of the surface, in the same way that a neurotic patient's behavior has an unconscious logic despite its apparent chaos.

In his exposure of a framework within the playscript, Kris can be considered a member of the movement known as the New Criticism, which is the earliest example of Structuralism in literary analysis. Although the movement is hardly new any longer—it began in the 1920's and was essentially over by the late 1950's—the name remains, because it stresses the fact that the New Critics were in rebellion against the then prevailing style of nineteenth-century criticism. (The term is thus probably derived from similar anti-Victorian phrases like "the New Drama" or "the New Woman.") One way of describing their conflict is that it existed between what were called "extrinsic" and "intrinsic" criticisms. Traditional criticism, the New Critics believed, had become primarily concerned with things outside the work ostensibly being examined—its historical background, including the life of the author; genre, leading to excessive generalizing at the expense of the particular; philosophy, especially ethics, reflecting that nineteenth-century tendency to make moral lessons out of everything;

character, taken out of the context of the work and analyzed like that of a real person. The New Criticism was instead to be *intrinsic*, examining the work in isolation and in considerable detail, with the only goal being, as T. S. Eliot put it, "to point out what the reader might otherwise have missed" (with the implication, however, that even an educated and intelligent reader might miss a great deal). It is clear, then, that Kris's essay is an example of intrinsic criticism, while that of another Freudian critic who, say, decided that Hotspur's problems were caused by a mother fixation complicated by early toilet training would be obviously extrinsic; the question is less a matter of one's philosophical starting point than of where one ends up.

The New Critical movement began in England in the twenties with the writings of critics T. S. Eliot, I. A. Richards, and William Empson and continued in the thirties with the group associated with the critical review *Scrutiny*—F. R. Leavis (its editor), G. Wilson Knight, and L. C. Knights. All were concerned with lyric poetry, with the later group focusing particularly on Shakespeare. They were in revolt against the kind of criticism typified by the famous critic A. C. Bradley, whose major work, *Shakespearean Tragedy*, appearing in 1904, was a culmination of the nineteenth-century critical tradition. Although Bradley's criticism is a lot less extrinsic than is commonly believed (the question "How many children had Lady Macbeth?" is often ascribed to him but is actually a parody invented by Leavis), he did insist that the action of a Shakespeare tragedy is rooted in character—specifically, the character of its hero—and he did proceed to analyze character in an ethical rather than dramatic way. In contrast to this, the New Critics insisted on analyzing Shakespeare's plays, as G. Wilson Knight put it, "spatially," that is, all at once, with character seen as only one element among many interrelated elements. All details were thus in a sense equal, so that a minor character like Fortinbras might be shown to have as much artistic importance as the more noticeable Laertes (and have subtle connections with him), and a particular turn of phrase or choice of imagery in a character's speech might be as important as his "moral dilemma."

It is interesting to consider the similarity of the Bradleyan approach and the nineteenth-century method of producing Shakespeare's plays —the star system, with a great actor magnificently declaiming the role of one of Shakespeare's heroes but supported by a desultory cast (or series of casts, since the stars usually toured the various repertory companies), in front of standardized scenery, often using a cut-down text. Everything was subordinated to the principal role in performance, just as Bradley tended to subordinate all the elements of the text to a discussion of the principal role in his criticism. The New Critical approach, then, paralleled the reforms in production of the early twentieth century—the ensemble instead of the star system ("There are no small parts," insisted Stanislavski), specially designed scenery contributing to the atmosphere of the particular play, and restored texts. Modern theatre production, like the New Criticism, tended to consider the play as a whole, rather than as the vehicle for a single lead role or, at most, two or three such roles.

But if there was a theatrical influence on the New Criticism, the influence in the opposite direction has been slight. The New Criticism had no direct influence on the English stage until the 1960's (after the New Criticism was itself practically finished as a movement) and has never had much influence at all on the North American stage. For example, despite the affinity of aims between the New Criticism and the modern theatre, the most common method used by North American actors to analyze character is still that of Bradley, despite the fact that nowadays even freshman English classes are taught not to lift character from its textual surroundings. The writing of elaborate character biographies, the improvisation of scenes from a character's early life (even when the text provides contradictory details about that life, as in the case of Lady Macbeth's children), or just plain sitting around and chatting about a character's supposed attributes ("I see Ophelia as bitchy, but not *too* bitchy, if you know what I mean") are all practically standard practices in our theatre. On the other hand, for directors and actors to discuss character in the poetic, interrelated way of the New Critics is almost unheard of. The ensemble system has come to mean, in the minds of most theatre people, that "every actor's performance is a gem," but few recognize the need to organize those gems into a coherent mosaic. Having read the New Critics (including the Kris essay), I once suggested to an actor playing Hotspur—"the Prince's double"—that he look carefully at the Prince Hal scenes and the actor playing the role; they could suggest possibilities for parallel makeup, costuming, vocal intonations, movements, gestures. The actor found this to be an extraordinary suggestion, although he had found nothing strange earlier in theorizing about Hotspur's mother, whom Shakespeare neglects to mention.

Nevertheless, there are solid reasons for the failure of the New Critics to influence our theatre. The fault is not all on one side; the New Critics often chose to analyze Shakespeare in exceedingly undramatic ways, making no distinction between lyric and dramatic poetry. Their reaction to Bradley was so extreme that they often appear to be denying character altogether as an artistic device, even in an integrated sense, and their principal interpretive technique—the analysis of poetic imagery—can be pushed to such extremes of refinement as to become an affectation. The American New Critic Cleanth Brooks, for example, published an essay on a single short passage from *Macbeth*:

> a naked new-born babe,
> Striding the blast, or heaven's cherubim, hors'd
> Upon the sightless couriers of the air . . . (I.vii.21–23)

Brooks maintained that this complicated and confusing image informs the entire playscript, containing in kernel form the whole underlying structure.[3] While he makes an interesting and often ingenious argument, it is hard to grant so much weight in a *dramatic* work to a single passage of such opacity, which requires about five seconds to recite, in a scene that depends for much of its effect on a banquet going on simultaneously in the next room. In a lyric poem, it would not be necessary to consider real time and space in this way—one can read a poem at leisure, lingering over a passage for hours if necessary, and the only setting is that which is specifically described in words. Brooks was committing an error similar to Bradley's in considering an element of a playscript out of context; surely the chief effect of this passage is the feeling of confusion and urgency it evokes while Macbeth is considering the murder. Brooks does not consider this, explicating nakedness and clothing, weakness and power, children and revenge in terms of similar images elsewhere in the script rather than in terms of the immediate temporal context. For all of G. Wilson Knight's insistence on looking at a Shakespeare playscript "spatially," the component of time—both clock time and psychological time, in the sense here of an overall feeling of urgency, with time running out—cannot be ignored.

Rather, time itself must be treated spatially, as in a musical score, because in a work that is written to be performed it is a major artistic element. While the method of imagery analysis contains important implications for the stage designer, who can translate verbal images into visual ones, it is simply too static to be adequate by itself for the actor or director.[4]

Brooks's choice of such an extremely complex passage is typical of the New Criticism as practiced in the United States. The movement caught on here in the thirties with such writers as Brooks, John Crowe Ransom, Allen Tate, R. P. Blackmur, and Robert Penn Warren (all of whom appeared in a book by Ransom, published in 1941, which was entitled *The New Criticism*, which popularized the name), as well as others like Yvor Winters and Kenneth Burke. Influenced by Empson's book, *Seven Types of Ambiguity* (1930), and attempting to restore dignity and importance to literature in an increasingly pragmatic, technological society, the American New Critics laid particular stress on complexity in a literary work. Literature was shown to be difficult, serious, and deep, a form of thought different from science but no less important. Thus, where a scientific treatise would be straightforward and linear in its reasoning, a poem would be complex; where it would be logical, a poem would be ambiguous; where its meaning would be on the surface, a poem's meaning would be subtle and deep. Poetry was thus not a simple-minded or sugar-coated form of expression, as the technocrats would have it, but rather a serious kind of discourse that could express ideas and feelings that would be impossible to express scientifically.

The key terms for poetic analysis, which were decidedly antiscientific, were *ambiguity* and *complexity*. These and related terms, such as *resonance, irony, tone*, and *tension* were applied with considerable success to lyric poetry but were found to be less spectacular with other forms of literature. With respect to drama, Cleanth Brooks and Robert B. Heilman produced a book, *Understanding Drama* (1945), which must now be considered a failure. Like A. C. Bradley, Brooks and Heilman were influenced by the theatre practices of their day, which in their case were those of Naturalism. This led them to make statements that now seem merely quaint: "The dramatist is much more limited than the novelist in the number of characters he can use"[5] and "the dramatist does not have the practically complete freedom in the use of place that the cinema and the novel do"[6] are typical examples. Had Brooks and Heilman been more experienced in theatre as a performing art—or had they been writing fifteen years later with the experience of the open stage, Brecht, Artaud, the Theatre of the Absurd, and so on—they might have produced a much better book. But they did not, and this failure more than anything else has led to the belief, widely heard around English departments, that "the New Criticism doesn't work for drama." This is an unfortunate attitude, which has contributed to the resistance of the theatre to Structuralist principles in interpreting playscripts. Of course the New Criticism does not work for drama if one treats a playscript as if it were a lyric poem, or otherwise ignores the attributes unique to drama as a form. But critics with theatrical experience, such as Francis Fergusson or Eric Bentley, have had considerable success with Structuralist techniques. Fergusson, for example, can be considered part of the New Critical movement, but rather than analyzing images in a static way, or searching for supersubtle complexities to explicate, he comes to drama with the terminology of an actor—Stanislavski's concept of the "objective," which Fergusson relates to Aristotle's concept of "action." The result has been a number of excellent critical essays on various playscripts that might well be useful as maps for performances, although, again, they have unfortunately had little influence on the practical theatre.

One should therefore not dismiss the New Criticism entirely. The English critics had considerable success with Shakespeare; their approach is at last beginning to bear fruit in the English theatre, particularly through the performances of the Royal Shakespeare Company. There is still great theatrical potential in the interpretations of Leavis, Knight, Knights, and so on—especially, again, in the area of visual elements. Furthermore, the failures of the New Criticism with drama do not contradict the importance of ambiguity and complexity. As operative principles these could have a salutary effect on our theatre. The main objection to "concept" productions, for example, is not so much that depicting King Lear as a Mafia boss or Phaedra as a Bronx housewife is historically inaccurate (the schoolmarm complaint), but rather that such an approach is crude and reductive. Such productions find a modern equivalent for a single aspect of the playscript—Lear's power struggle or Phaedra's marital jealousy—and ignore all the rest, the multiple levels of meaning, the contradictions, the quirks, the resonances that occur when particular characters operate in a unique world. It is not necessarily bad to turn something old into something new, but it is disgusting to turn something subtle and complex into something simple-minded and dull.

Nor can ambiguity, as a basic structural principle common to all artistic writing (as opposed to expository writing, where it is simply a flaw), be ignored in theatrical performance. There is a deplorable tendency today for stage directors to look upon ambiguities in a text as something to be cleared up in performance: we are shown that Hamlet delays because of an Oedipus complex, that Alceste's social maladjustment is the result of sexual impotence, that Chekhov's three sisters do not go to Moscow, because they are secret lesbians. Directors must learn that difficulties like Hamlet's dawdling, or Alceste's obsessions, or the three sisters' inertia are actually part of the playscript's structure and should similarly be part of performance. *A playscript is not a problem to be solved*; it is rather something to be fully realized in performance, which means *problems included*. It is widely accepted that a painting is improved when it is done "warts and all," not just for the sake of accuracy, but because such paintings are more interesting, more varied, more challenging. "Warts and all" should be the motto of those producing classical playscripts. The New Critics' sensitivity to detail and their habit of accepting and analyzing apparent quirks and "mistakes" instead of merely rejecting them are attributes worth cultivating by theatre artists.

The end of the New Criticism came in the nineteen-fifties and can perhaps be specifically marked by the appearance in 1957 of Northrop Frye's *Anatomy of Criticism*, which once again took up the question of genre, which for the New Critics had been an "extrinsic" consideration. A generation of critics had grown up who were uneasy about the limitations of the New Criticism already noted: the virtual exclusion of character as a literary technique, the obsession with imagery, and the necessity always to be subtle and revelatory could become a new kind of artificiality, especially as the method filtered down to second- and third-rate writers. This was the time when *Structuralism* as a term began to be used; it even became common to see Structuralism as in direct opposition to the New Criticism. This belief is still widely held today, but it is mistaken. Structuralism as a movement owes a great deal to the New Critics; it merely extends the earlier techniques to large collections of works rather than focusing on individual ones. Frye spread his net wider than did the New Critics; by examining literature as a whole, rather than analyzing specific works in detail, he has been able to disclose archetypes of plot and character—standard patterns and types that recur throughout literary history. This is a far different approach to genre from the prescriptive methods of, say, the neoclassical critics of the sixteenth and seventeenth centuries who derived the Three Unities from logical principles (and a cursory reading of Aristotle and Horace) and only then proceeded to look at literature itself, making judgments on it as to what constituted "true" tragedy. Frye specifically eschews judgment, which he sees as mere "taste." He sees the critic's job as one of wide reading, leading to the discernment of repeating patterns, which are then categorized and discussed; the movement is from the particular to the general rather than the other way around.

Nevertheless, Frye's emphasis is on the big picture, rather than the analysis of particular examples, and because of this I do not see much of his work as applicable to theatrical performance (except perhaps for the theatre company wishing to present a series of related plays). Nor do I believe that judgment, the question of artistic value, can be dismissed as easily as he thinks. But Frye is certainly helpful in emphasizing that value judgments are the results of one's study and not the starting point for it. While neoclassicism may be dead, prescriptive criticism is still with us, and, whatever its merits in an abstract sense, judgment before the fact is harmful in the practical theatre. I recently attended a celebrated playwriting conference at which a writer was castigated for not following the "rules of farce" (whatever they are); rather than helping the unfortunate playwright, the critics were actually stifling him, letting abstract considerations prevent them from analyzing what was actually happening in the particular play. Furthermore, much of the inanity that arises in contemporary productions of the classics is the result of premature value judgment. The director starts with the idea that a playtext is bad or old-fashioned and proceeds to improve or update it, exactly like those neoclassical producers who thought Shakespeare was ever so much better after one removed his vulgarities and improbabilities. Or, again, a director will have learned from his university drama survey courses that plays fall into neat categories that imply a particular style of playing.

(Molière wrote farces. Farce is "a dramatic piece intended to excite laughter and depending less on plot and character than on exaggerated, improbable situations, the humor arising from gross incongruities, coarse wit, or horseplay."[7] Therefore, it would be a great idea to have Alceste's pants fall down at key moments in *The Misanthrope.*) Frye, in showing what *true* genre criticism can be, perhaps could prevent such misapplications of the concept of genre. Genre is an abstraction made after the fact and should thus not be turned back on the creative process itself.

The nineteen-fifties also saw the spread of Structuralism to other countries, and to other fields of thought, with the French New Criticism, Structural Anthropology, Structural Linguistics. The French New Critics deserve mention here because their work demonstrates one more important principle that is applicable to theatre performance. The French critical tradition is anything but "extrinsic." The traditional method, known as *"explication de texte,"* involves the painstaking analysis, line by line and even word by word, of the meaning of a literary work. It is rather like footnoting carried to an extreme. Imagery can be studied exhaustively, and ambiguities explicated, but in piecemeal fashion. French New Critics like Roland Barthes attempt to get away from such minutiae and construct a view that will deal with the work as a whole, seeing it as a *system* rather than a mere collection of details. For example, a standard French edition of Racine's *Phaedra* offers the following comments on Phaedra's death speech (lines 1622–1644): "She confesses without repenting because she does not feel herself responsible: the culpable ones are the gods and her nurse (lines 1625–1626); she was herself only the victim of this double incarnation of destiny."[8] Barthes's view of the play is not only much larger than this, it actually contradicts the impression obtained from reading Phaedra's speech in isolation: "Phaedra's objective guilt (the adultery, the incest) is in sum a sham construction, destined to normalize the pain of the secret, to transform conveniently the form into content. . . . All of Phaedra's effort consists of *fulfilling* her fault, which is to say, to absolve God."[9] I do not wish to comment on which of these two views is correct, but only to point out that the second is broader; it cannot be proven by any *single* textual citation. The first quotation considers Phaedra's confession in isolation and takes it at face value: because she blames others for her woes, she must consider herself a blameless victim. Barthes's view of her attitude, in the context of the entire playscript, is much deeper: Phaedra is blameless but actually *wishes* herself guilty and performs evil acts in order to fulfill her guilt.

Barthes is aiming at what he calls a "system of unities and of functions"[10] and in so doing starts to look like an *extrinsic* critic. Indeed, the traditional French critic Raymond Picard has attacked the New Critical movement in his country on precisely those grounds, in his book *Nouvelle Critique ou Nouvelle Imposture* (1965). In a complete reversal of the English or American experience, Picard the traditionalist maintains that Barthes the New Critic substitutes a personal vision of the work for the direct experience of close reading. Actually, Barthes and his colleagues are just as capable of close reading as anyone else, but this conflict does point out an essential of the Structuralist approach. Structuralism is not content with detailed analysis, important as that is; Structuralism is ultimately wholistic. Since its view of reality is not atomistic but interconnected, it must attempt to construct a vision of a literary work that informs all of its details. Paradoxically, the method is both close and distant, both detailed and general. This has definite implications in the theatre in dealing with the production concept. Most "concept" productions today do not exhibit this doubleness; the relation between the general and the particular is limited and tenuous at best. But, on the other hand, in traditional productions the relation was often tenuous as well; where we now usually find productions that are strong on overall concept but weak on the execution of details, we formerly had productions that were often too piecemeal in their approach, with great care given to the execution of a historically accurate costume or a beautifully delivered speech but little sense of an overall system.

To sum up the results so far, one can say that a Structuralist method of interpretation is one that
1. Reveals something hidden
2. Is intrinsic
3. Incorporates complexity and ambiguity
4. Suspends judgment
5. Is wholistic

These are, if you like, "first principles" of Structuralism, although it can be seen that they are less axioms than guidelines. They imply a view of drama—and of all literature, and indeed of all art—as something difficult, serious, and important. They also imply that the interpretation of drama is something important as well, an active exploration of a text rather than simple explanation or airy philosophizing. The principles are of course my own formulation for my own purposes, rather than an abstract description of the nature of Structuralism; many will disagree with my particular emphases. Nevertheless, they are worth keeping in mind, even if one disagrees with them, because they form the basis for this entire book. I shall expand here on each:

1. *Reveals something hidden.* The Structuralist linguist Noam Chomsky has distinguished between what he calls "surface structure" and "deep structure"; the former is exposed by the traditional grammar of nouns, verbs, adjectives, and so on, while the latter can only be discerned through the use of the "transformational grammar" that is the goal of his research. The distinction is useful for the interpretation of playscripts. There are traditional categories of dramatic structure, mostly derived in the long run from Aristotle, that are found in the introductory textbooks used in university survey courses. They are described in terms like rising action, falling action, climax, beats, acts, scenes, French scenes, reversal, recognition, denouement. It will be clear that these fit almost none of the aspects of Structuralism listed above; they are instead elements of "surface structure." They have never been much use to performers, and they do not particularly point out important things that a reader or audience member "might otherwise have missed." These concepts can become subsumed into a Structuralist scheme—some Structuralists start by breaking up a play into French scenes, for example—but they only become so when they reveal something beyond themselves, some hidden pattern of genuine significance.

Hidden is perhaps a dangerous word, since Structuralism always carries the risk of falling into the merely arcane or personal. *Hidden* should be defined simply as "not immediately obvious" and is in fact a quality that is always changing. As a result of the widespread acceptance of the theories of Freud, for example, the sexual symbolism in the following passage from Strindberg's *Miss Julie* seems all too obvious: "In my dream I'm lying under a great tree in a dark wood. I want to get up, up to the top of it, and look out over the bright landscape where the sun is shining and rob that high nest of its golden eggs. And I climb and climb, but the trunk is so thick and smooth and it's so far to the first branch."[11] Ninety years ago when the play was first performed, a sexual interpretation of this passage might have seemed forced and even perverse; now all the business about the tree and the eggs and the "thick and smooth" trunk seems so obvious that it is hardly worth discussing. (This shows that criticism is not a passive reflection of "the truth" about a play but that it is active, that it is supposed to do something for you.)

Of course, Structuralism is not aiming for something that is literally, totally hidden. To the physicist, subatomic particles are not totally hidden, either; it is just that their perception requires specialized, indirect methods. A Structuralist interpretation of a playtext must be manifested, in some major way, in the surface of the text, or else it is merely phony, a kind of modern witchcraft. The true process is something like the method used to test for colorblindness: the subject is shown a series of mosaiclike designs containing patterns visible only to those whose color perception is normal. The patterns are obviously "there," and there is nothing mysterious about them. To the colorblind person, however, they are hidden because he lacks the physical ability to see certain colors. If he could be cured of his affliction, the patterns would immediately leap into view. In the same way, the critic "cures" a reader's inability to perceive fundamental patterns in a text. Luckily, the inability to perceive a playscript interpretation is not really a disease; correction requires only basic intelligence plus a certain openness to the critic's ideas. This, in fact, is one test of a genuine interpretation: can it be demonstrated to a neutral person, that is, one with moderate intelligence and no particular prejudices about the text? Hamlet goes through the process with Polonius:

> *Hamlet.* Do you see yonder cloud that's almost
>   in shape of a camel?
> *Polonius.* By th' mass and 'tis, like a camel indeed.
> *Hamlet.* Methinks it is like a weasel.
> *Polonius.* It is backed like a weasel.
> *Hamlet.* Or like a whale.
> *Polonius.* Very like a whale. (III.ii.361–367)

In accepting interpretation after interpretation without question, Polonius clearly shows that he is *not* neutral, that he is more interested in humoring Hamlet than in sharing his vision. The proper response would have been to ask questions about it: "Which way is the camel headed? Where is the hump? Does it have four legs?" and so on. If a critic can give intelligent answers to similar questions about his view of a playscript, one can conclude that his is a valid interpretation. Indeed, the reader should be able to carry on the critic's interpretation on his own. Polonius might have said (if his conversation had been genuine, with Hamlet providing helpful answers to questions), "Oh, *I* see. Why, there's the tail. And there's the head. It looks like he's eating something."

Thus, the Structuralist does not seek hidden interpretations out of a love of the arcane. It is just that he sees a text as a complex thing having many possible interpretations, like a complicated mosaic. The standard, obvious views will always be limited or prejudiced; he attempts to get at something more profound. If he is successful, this more profound view is of course *no longer hidden*; it may even, with time, become blatantly obvious, requiring other critics to try new approaches.

2. *Is intrinsic.* This concept again demonstrates the scientific influence on Structuralism. An important concept in science is that of the *system*; the scientist must define a clear boundary around what he is examining, or his experiments will be meaningless. A chemist's test tube is a good example. Not only is it a simple container, but it also acts as a device for isolating chemicals from the rest of the world while a reaction is taking place; obviously, if contaminants were allowed to enter the system, the experimental results would be ruined. The concept can be extended to the social sciences—the sociologist and the well-defined ethnic group or the anthropologist and the isolated primitive village choose their objects of study precisely because they can be considered as closed systems. The sociologist who decided to study people in general, rather than a clearly defined group, would have little success.

While criticism is not entirely a science, it is clear that the critic stands a much greater chance of success if he knows what he is talking about, in both senses of that phrase. Nineteenth-century English criticism, for example, was often unclear as to whether it was talking about a work of literature or about biography, history, philosophy, or morality. The early New Critics were successful precisely because they knew what they were talking about—the individual work. While their particular system was later attacked as too limiting, subsequent critics have been careful to define their area of attention—all of Racine's dramas, for example, or all of Ibsen's, or, like Northrop Frye, all of literature. The stage director, I have suggested, should limit himself to analyzing the particular playtext (or perhaps a series of playtexts if he is involved with staging a Shakespeare festival, for example) and suspend value judgments, historical considerations, discussions of genre, philosophical speculations, and the like.

It will be argued that this is impossible. The arguments against the New Critics were that, first of all, artists are influenced by their historical milieu and create as part of a tradition. Many works depend for their effect at least in part upon their audience's knowledge of other works. A good deal of Shaw's playwriting technique lies in his parodying nineteenth-century theatrical conventions, for example. How could one analyze *Arms and the Man* without considering the Well-Made Play? Second, argued the opponents, the notion of "intrinsic" criticism is an illusion. The literary analyst is not a blank tablet; he has an education, a culture, a view of life. Jacques Barzun puts the case shrewdly: "The close reader and all other text analysts make use of etymology, which is a branch of history. Semantics and connotation, like the things and ideas to which words refer, are but fragments of history; and so is the famous 'logic' and structure of the work, since much or all of it derives from tradition. As for the meanings and symbols and echoes below the surface, we know it takes an 'educated' reader to find them, and his education is only more history distilled."[12] These are powerful arguments for a return to a more traditional criticism; in fact it seems we never left it. The New Critics were more traditional than they realized, since it appears that the extrinsic is inescapable. One recent theatre text attempts to get out of the dilemma by suggesting a compromise—playscripts contain "two kinds of meaning,"[13] the extrinsic *and* the intrinsic, and the good director or performer must take into account *both*.

Nevertheless, I stand by my original belief, which is that valid, effective playscript interpretation for performance must be intrinsic. Actually, all the problems with this concept, as well as the attempt at compromise, arise out of a categorical error: the equating of the critic's interpretation of a playscript with the playscript itself. "Intrinsic" and "extrinsic" refer not to a playscript's meaning, but *to the act of interpretation*. Playscript interpretation is not the script itself or the mere passive reflection of it; it is a kind of action. This action is either intrinsic or extrinsic depending upon where it ends up. If one is left with a statement about the work itself, the critic has been intrinsic; if one is left with a statement about history, or the author's life, or the nature of man, or whatnot, the critic has been extrinsic. It is thus perhaps necessary to modify my former insistence on suspending judgment, history, genre, and so on; these things need not, and in fact cannot, be suspended entirely, but they must be subsumed by the critical act, made means to its end, which is a construction of a vision of the work-in-itself.

Of course, Structuralist critics start with some viewpoint. It may be a formal, clearly stated one like Ernst Kris's Freudianism or an informal, implicit one like Cleanth Brooks's etymology. It is how the philosophical position is used, with respect to the text, that matters. Recalling Roland Barthes's terminology, one can represent the relation of a philosophical system to a playtext mathematically (but not too rigorously!) by a *function*, which for intrinsic interpretation would look something like this:

$$I(S) \longrightarrow T$$

I represents the act of interpretation, which is a function of a philosophical system *S*, which can be explicit or implicit, *into* the playtext *T*.[14] A function is a kind of transformation, in which every element in the first set connects with a single element in the second set. (The reverse is not necessarily true.) A valid interpretation of a text is thus not identical to the philosophical system that is its starting point, but is instead a projection of one into the text. Extrinsic analysis, by contrast, can be expressed like this:

$$E(T) \longrightarrow S$$

E represents a different function or transformation this time, but T and S can be the same text and philosophy. In this case it is the play-text that is projected into the philosophical system, becoming in a sense incorporated by it.

Note that the words *intrinsic* and *extrinsic* refer to the functions, and not to either the text or the philosophical position. Potentially, all types of criticism can be used intrinsically—even historical or biographical approaches—just as all types can be used extrinsically, even imagistic analysis. As L. C. Knights put it in one of his later essays: "It is the presence of the universal in the particular that compels the use of such generalizing terms as 'themes' or 'motifs.' Of course, like other critical terms, they can be used mechanically or ineptly, can harden into counters pushed about in a critical game. But as simple pointers their function is to indicate the *direction* of interest that a play compels when we try to meet it with the whole of ourselves."[15]

A function is a simple mathematical concept, but one with powerful implications. I shall be using it again in later chapters. While mathematical notation may seem a bit out of place in a book on drama, its use at times has advantages over ordinary language. In this case the functional configuration can express simply and clearly what would otherwise seem confusing or paradoxical. Our everyday language can hold traps for us, particularly in the case of relations between two sets of things that are talked about as single things. Consider, for example, the word *wife*; it appears to refer to an individual thing, but after a little reflection one realizes that it actually refers to a relationship. There has never been, and there never can be, a wife without one or more husbands. A Platonist might try to talk about "pure wifehood"— uncontaminated by any husbands—but that would really be nonsense. Wifehood is not a quality residing in a woman alone, but rather in her *relation to her husband*. Preserving the same notation as before, we can represent the relationship functionally:

$$W(F) \longrightarrow M$$

Here F stands for the set of all married females and M the set of all married males (living or dead, in each case), and W is the "wife" function. (For it to be strictly a function we must assume that no woman can have more than one husband.) Our word *wife* really refers to this function as a whole, and not to the set of females by themselves. Like the functional relationship between philosophical system and text, the "wife" function is not a single thing but a *pairing*, considered as a unit and denoted by a single word.

Consider then the problem in critical interpretation: where does the interpretation itself reside? Is it just *there*, in the playtext like Columbus's America, waiting to be discovered? Or does it exist instead in the critic's own head, making critical analysis a subjective, imaginary process like the creation of art itself? The functional notation used earlier depicts the fact that it lies in both. *It is impossible to talk or think seriously about a playscript interpretation without simultaneously considering both the text and the critic's viewpoint.* It is for this reason that playscript interpretation is both imaginative and analytical, both art and science.

Most difficulties with interpretation arise from attempting to oversimplify, to identify it solely with a text or solely with a position. On the one hand, some critics, and many stage directors, will insist that they have no philosophical viewpoint at all, that they just look at the script and talk about, or produce, what is "there." What they really mean is that they interpret it from a set of personal prejudices and unconscious conditionings. Directors "know," for example, that Shaw's playscripts were written simply to broadcast his ideas, and thus their productions are all oratory and "wit"; they ignore the deeper, poetic values because their very approach to the script precludes them, even though they do not think of themselves as having *any* approach. But, on the other hand, there are directors and critics who believe that they have suddenly become profound after they have stumbled upon some new philosophical approach to drama analysis—Eric Berne's game theory is currently very fashionable—when actually the choice of philosophical system is less important than what one does with it. And what directors and critics of this sort all too often do with it is to present the theory at the expense of the work, obscuring the script with an extrinsic interpretation that turns *Mother Courage* into a series of examples of Transactional Analysis or *King Lear* into a tribal village.

I cannot stress too much that Structuralist interpretation is not a matter of taking a particular position or identifying with a particular author. The dry pedant who teaches the traditional drama survey course has, as an alter ego, the wide-eyed theorist who thinks he has the final solution to all problems in drama through his application of some bold, new method. He may even call his method "Structuralism" and dignify it with the name of an actual Structuralist like Roland Barthes or Claude Lévi-Strauss, but he will apply the techniques of his hero as rigidly and extrinsically as the pedant does with his "historical trends." Structuralist interpretation involves far more than the mere application of a fixed set of procedures, no matter whose they are. Structuralism is far more *style* than fixed method. It is never a single thing, but rather a way of making connections, or "functions," between different things.

3. *Incorporates complexity and ambiguity.* The two terms are of course related, *complexity* implying multiple meanings and *ambiguity* implying *contradictory* meanings. Both are important concepts because they go to the heart of how a play *means* something, as opposed to how a scientific treatise or newspaper article (i.e., writings in expository prose) means something.

The theatre is, in the broadest sense, a communications medium. It is important, however, to distinguish between logical and aesthetic communication. Communications theories that treat theatre as merely passing along meaning, as does a telephone line, are distortions. Theatre communicates meaning in a far different way. The trouble is that we have become so conditioned by our technological society that we have come to believe that direct, logical meaning is the only kind that is important, or even the only kind that exists. Actually, logical thinking is the exception in human beings and can only be learned with difficulty and applied with a certain amount of pain; our natural way of thinking is not linear but *associative*. That is, for example, as I drive past a drug store I think, not of the definition of a drug store, but rather of the fact that I need to buy some tooth paste. All day long we are making complex, multiple associations: I see my house and think immediately of mortgage payments, my dinner, and the fact that the lawn needs mowing. As you read this book, you do not merely follow its logical line of argument but are constantly thinking of examples, arguments, qualifications, objections, and theories of your own.

The meaning of a work of art is of this indirect, associative, complex kind. This is not the same thing as saying that it is mysterious, occult, wild, or incomprehensible. Art is not meaningless, it just expresses meaning in a different way from logic. Both kinds of meaning are important. A society that is given over entirely to associative thinking will always be passive and stagnant, since any course of action will immediately suggest multiple associations that militate against it—the gods will be angered, that's not the way our ancestors did it, it might mean a lot of hard work, and anyway it's time to eat. Primitive societies, which are always very artistic but which have no science at all, tend to operate like that. But a society given over too much to logical thinking, as ours tends to be, has the opposite problem, a tendency to hyperactivity. The Vietnam War, the ecology crisis, and the energy crisis can all be seen as failures resulting from a lack of associative thinking, from looking at life as a series of problems to be solved in direct, linear ways without considering side effects or questioning assumptions.

The tendency in our society to overemphasize linear thinking has naturally had its effect on the theatre. Indeed, many of the problems in playscript interpretation that I have been discussing can be summed up as an attempt to squeeze a linear meaning out of a script that is decidedly *un*linear. This is always done with considerable planning and effort (today's directors are nothing if not energetic), because a linear meaning is always the most difficult kind to achieve. Anyone involved in writing expository prose understands all too well how hard it is to be clear, direct, and unambiguous. The irony is that, in creating a work of art, clarity and unambiguity are specious goals! Art is *supposed* to evoke multiple meanings. I recall a class in which I was completing what was (I thought) a subtle and deep interpretation of a playscript, when a student remarked, "That's very interesting, but how do you present seven levels of meaning on the stage?" My answer was, "How do you *not* present seven levels, or ten or a hundred? It is presenting a single meaning that would be difficult." And it would be not only difficult, but also wrong. Theatre people should accept the fact that their work will always arouse multiple associations, that theatre is not a matter of simple, direct, conscious communication, a "telephone line" between actors and audience, but at once something more complicated and more easy, more playful.

Note that I am not taking a solipsistic point of view, that meaning does not exist in the playscript or on the stage but solely in the head of the observer. That a literary work has many meanings does not imply that it has all possible meanings, that one can make whatever one likes with it. As with a critic's interpretation, the meaning of a work of art is a kind of function, which cannot be understood except as a pairing. I have sometimes preferred the terminology that a work of art "signifies" something, rather than "means" something, to suggest that the observer *finds* meaning in the work, rather than having it simply handed over to him without his participation. For example, this chair that I am sitting on has all kinds of significations: its simple design and lack of ornamentation signify a pragmatic or technological attitude toward life; its undisguised steel and unstained wood imply a materialism in the literal sense, that is, a belief that materials themselves can be decorative without being made to look like something else; the neat, obvious rectangles that make up its design reflect a love of mathematics. Now, one cannot say that anyone put these "meanings" there, in an attempt to communicate directly with me; I had to find them, and the people who made the chair would probably be surprised to hear them. But the meanings are not hallucinations, either; I am able to support my interpretations by pointing to parts of the chair itself and to communicate the interpretations to others, as I am communicating them to you now. Meaning is a transaction, or function, between myself and the chair.

The meaning of a work of art, then, is not linear and not isolatable in either work or observer. Works of art themselves (including plays) and the artistic response are complex processes rather than simple "things." To the notion of complexity must be added that of ambiguity. Scientific reasoning makes use of a principle known in logic as "the law of the excluded middle." That is, a statement is either true or false but not both and not something else. A sum of figures is either correct or incorrect, a triangle is equilateral or it is not, a theorem in geometry can be either proved or disproved. The fact is, however, that, with respect to the meaning of a work of art, the law of the excluded middle does not hold. (For that matter, science and even mathematics have often had to reject it.) Art assumes that life is more complex and contradictory (and more interesting) than science does, and it reflects life with ambiguous meanings. Problems of ethics, of one's place in the universe, of the purpose of life and the significance of death, are never in a good work of art painted in black and white, but always in intermediate shades.

In the theatre it is a cliché that "drama is conflict." It must therefore follow that if this conflict is to be genuine, and not the mere knocking down of a straw man, there must be something to be said for both
sides. The conflict need not be in opposing characters but may instead
occur within the same character, or within the play as a whole. Is
Macbeth good or evil? Is Hamlet justified in delaying, or damnable?
Is *Waiting for Godot* a play of despair or of hope? Most would agree
that the answer in each case is not one or the other but both. In fact,
because of the slippery nature of the human mind, its tendency always
to make unforeseen associations, plays that attempt to be unambiguous
—solemn attacks on bigotry or militarism or sexual repression—often
backfire, and one comes away more sympathetic toward the object of
attack than opposed to it. In the medieval moralities, the "Vice" character came to dominate the entire play. One came away from the satire
Macbird actually liking Lyndon Johnson, which was something his
public relations staff could never have effected. Such plays are ambiguous in spite of themselves.

Thus, the principle of ambiguity is fairly well established. Even
John Gassner, who was far from being a Structuralist, realized toward
the end of his life the importance of ambiguity as an aesthetic necessity, writing that "it is of paramount importance in the practice of
playwriting and play production as well as dramatic criticism."[16] The
reason is that whenever drama is unambiguous it becomes trivial.
After all, how can a play ever logically "prove" anything? It is something fictitious, made-up, loaded. Even in "the Theatre of Fact," where
the script is drawn exclusively from real-life documents, the facts
can be chosen and colored to prove any point one wants, and thus, in
the end, prove nothing. A good playscript is not a pamphlet, and a
good performance is not a sermon. This is not to say that there is anything wrong with pamphlets or sermons, but that they are different
things having different purposes from works of art. Those who would
turn the stage into a pulpit would be better off to use a real one.

4. *Suspends judgment.* There is nothing wrong with value judgment as such. There are many in the arts these days who would try to
do away with the notion of artistic value entirely (reflecting their fear
of criticism), but in fact this is impossible. For some years I had the
students in my dramatic criticism class perform an experiment: they

were to write down, surreptitiously, everything they heard in their daily lives about drama or theatre. (Formal situations, such as classes, rehearsals, or lectures, were to be excluded.) This exercise produced a number of interesting results: first, the sheer volume of conversation they recorded shows that we are surrounded by a sea of criticism of which formal or professional criticism is only a tiny part. Second, by far the most common kind of criticism that people engage in is judgmental. But third and most interesting of all is the fact that the very people who were known to be most vocal in their opposition to value judgment were found to be making such judgments all the time themselves, often in the most brutal (and unsupported) form.

There is thus no escaping judgment. On the other hand, knowledge of this fact should make one careful to *suspend* judgment when the situation demands. The director (or actor or designer) in analyzing a script for production will often feel that it is not very good, that it has flaws of one kind or another. This is a perfectly normal human reaction of which no one should feel ashamed. But, recalling that the flaws are not entities isolated in the script, but rather exist as transactions between himself and the script, the director should alter his relationship to them. If he wants to achieve the best possible production he should analyze the script *as if* it were perfect. Only then will he be likely to find any dynamic structures beneath its surface, because structures must take into account the *entire* script rather than just those parts one finds immediately attractive. In fact, often when one starts with the assumption that a bad script is good, one learns in the end that it really was good all along, that it was just a matter of seeing it in a different way.

The whole history of art shows that value is not a matter of fixed standards against which works are judged. Standards are constantly changing, not because they are a matter of mere "taste" as Northrop Frye would have it, but rather because value is an example of what the dramatic theorist Roger Gross has called a "heuristic" problem,[17] which is one requiring constant adaptation and improvisation. That is, *finding standards is always part of the problem*, rather than simply *applying* standards that are unchanging. Value in art is the kind of function mathematicians call "recursive"—that is, one which generates new terms on the basis of former terms. It is thus literally impossible to make valid judgments of value before the creation of the work to be judged. This limitation of course puts the director of a play in a peculiar position. In interpreting the playscript for production, he has the script, which is in a sense a finished work, but he is working on a performance, which is not. It is therefore possible to make value judgments of the script that may be, from the director's point of view, perfectly valid, but making them will be disruptive to the creative process of preparing the performance. He must remember, therefore, that the standards for his judgments are not fixed, that they will probably be changed by the time the play opens, that, indeed, his production will become part of the process by which the particular playscript is judged.

All this is not to say that value is totally relative and judgment totally subjective. The fact that artistic value is a dynamic process or "heuristic problem" should not plunge us into that kind of despair. Many problems in life have neither clear goals nor clear means of attaining those goals, but it is the second-rate mind that shuns them. In fact, such problems usually turn out to be the ones that are really interesting. If artistic judgment really were a matter of applying abstract standards like mathematical formulae, art would be dull and judgment trivial.

5. *Is wholistic.* "Wholistic" means here that one treats a work as essentially already unified. Unity as an aesthetic concept appears to be a problem with modern drama. In the neoclassic period, it was fairly clear what was meant by it—namely, homogeneity and plausibility. From these underlying concepts were derived the famous "Three Unities" of time, place, and action, each designed to make a play smooth, rational, and uniform. Other principles, like that of "decorum" (fitting a character's style of speech and behavior to his social status), were extensions of the same desire for unity. These principles made it easy to judge that Shakespeare's playscripts, for example, were badly disunified, which led late-seventeenth-century writers like Davenant, Dryden, and Tate to try to homogenize them.

Modern drama, on the other hand, delights in variety, incongruity, and even the bizarre. Furthermore, modern critics, in looking at Shakespeare, no longer see the subplots, the irregularities, the changes in locale and leaps in time, or even the improbabilities, as things to be deplored or rewritten. The New Critics, recalling Coleridge's idea of "organic" form, have found relationships among the apparently chaotic elements which arrange Shakespeare's plays into kinds of unities the neoclassicists never conceived of. (Indeed, this kind of interpretation has become standard; the relation of plot to subplot, for example, that great neoclassical bugbear, has become a critical pushover.) All this has led to an examination of the very concept of unity. Some would reject it entirely; others would qualify it as "thematic unity," "unity of effect," or "symbolic unity," to explain why, for example, the drunken porter scene in *Macbeth* is so satisfying to the audience in spite of—or even *because* of—its incongruity.

Such abstract discussions of the nature of artistic unity may be interesting, but they obscure an important point, which is that, for a Structuralist, *unity is never at issue*. Although the New Critics had spectacular successes in proving that a work was unified, their very success was the result of their starting from the assumption of unity. Unity, for a Structuralist critic, is something taken for granted. This is of course both a great strength and a great weakness. On the one hand, it leads to impressive results when relationships are discovered in a work that have hitherto gone unnoticed, or when apparent "mistakes" are shown to be not only justified but also essential. But, on the other hand, a fact that has been overlooked is that this kind of criticism cannot really determine when a work is *not* unified. The neoclassical critic had no trouble telling why a work was bad (because it did not follow the rules) but could not really say why a work was good, since many playscripts that followed the rules perfectly were still obviously unsatisfying; the Structuralist critic is often profound in explaining why a play is good (by explicating its "thematic unity") but cannot show that a play is bad. Any reason he could give might be overruled tomorrow by someone more perceptive. The neoclassicist was always suspicious, the Structuralist always gullible, because the Structuralist can never be sure that there are not relations, organic forms, thematic unity, and so on that he has simply overlooked.

Pushed to an extreme, then, the Structuralist approach implies that all playscripts are unified—not in the older sense of uniformity, but rather in the sense of being interconnected. Structuralism shows an affinity with Gestalt psychology, which has demonstrated that we perceive in integrated wholes, drawn from a mosaic of sense impressions. The Rorschach test, for example, shows that the human mind is capable of perceiving unity even in random blobs of ink. Unity, like the related concepts of interpretation, meaning, and value, is a kind of function, a transaction between the brain and the world. Unities are everywhere, if we only seek them.

The director preparing a playscript for performance, then, should *expect* to find unities. The Structuralist approach does not seek to find whether unity exists—it assumes that it does and seeks to find *how* a particular unity is manifested. Nor does it see unity as a kind of ideal, to be attained only with great difficulty through "improvements." There is always unity; the difficulty is rather to find it and then to realize the same unity on stage.

3

Current Performance
Theories

The concepts developed in the last chapter—intrinsic analysis, hidden patterns, complexity and ambiguity, suspension of judgment, and wholistic treatment—have implications for the criticism and practice of all the arts. In this chapter I shall examine them in relation to theatrical performance, with regard to four theorists who seem to me to be most influential today—Stanislavski, Brecht, Artaud, and Schechner. While Richard Schechner is not as well known as the others, his work has certainly been influential on certain kinds of contemporary performers, and his writing has the advantage of being more articulate and organized than that of other advocates of the "New Theatre," many of whom cannot really be called theorists at all, but only enthusiasts.

These four writers were and are theatre practitioners as well as theorists. This immediately distinguishes them from Aristotle (and his descendants), who had no theatre experience and who was almost entirely concerned with the written script. For this reason I am calling them *performance* theorists; unlike Aristotle, they are more concerned with plays than with play*scripts*. In fact, the interesting thing they have in common is that, perhaps in overreaction to the Aristotelian tradition, they all express in one form or another a lack of understanding of or outright hostility toward literature. A study of their work will enable us to understand better the relation of script to performance, and the place of literature in the theatre. It is noteworthy that, for all their antiliterary bias, none of these theorists has been able to escape from the script in actual practice.

Stanislavski. Stanislavski's great contribution is in the theory of acting. I do not want to get involved in disputes about the "real" Stanislavski as opposed to the supposedly debased versions of his theories in America and elsewhere. Any really great thinker will have disciples who will not merely follow him blindly but will adapt his ideas to the particular problems they are facing. Stanislavski himself always insisted that his was no rigid system and not only encouraged continued experimentation by his followers but also practiced it himself. In this he can already be considered a Structuralist in his realization that art is never a matter of rigid, prescriptive rules, but rather a kind of organism that always grows and adapts.

Acting is the least understood of the arts. This is the reason for its low prestige—if the arts are ranked in order of their intellectual respectability, it will be seen that those on top are the ones with an abstract theory capable of being learned and discussed *even by those who cannot practice the art itself.* Painting became respectable, for example, with the discovery of perspective in the Renaissance; even someone who could not paint at all could learn the theories of perspective, recognize it in a painting, and judge its execution. Stanislavski's contribution was not so much a new system (as perspective was in painting), but rather that he provided a nomenclature, a way of talking about acting in the abstract, with the result that it is now possible to understand and appreciate it better than ever before.

Before Stanislavski, acting was taught entirely by the apprentice system. A young actor in a theatre company, often the son or daughter of one of the older members, would gradually learn his art under the direct, day-to-day supervision of his elders while actually rehearsing or performing. Such a method has a lot to be said for it, but, since it has little need for theory, it will not develop one beyond the most simple and rudimentary. By Stanislavski's time, the system of the permanent repertory company was breaking down; today, it is not uncommon for a young actor to find himself with a completely new cast, none of whom he knows, for every play he is in. Even in Europe, where repertory companies are more stable than here, there is a high turnover of members, and actors are always going off to make films or television shows on the side. In such a situation, it becomes necessary to learn acting in a classroom, or even from a textbook. Since one cannot always have one's teacher at one's side, theory becomes essential. Stanislavski, foreseeing this, in the last two decades of his life attempted to codify the ideas that had been in operation at the Moscow Art Theatre, in a series of books (actually one long, unfinished work in Russian) that have been translated as *An Actor Prepares, Building a Character,* and *Creating a Role.* These books are extraordinary. Although their boy-scout style is often displeasing (one finds it blamed variously on the translator, Stanislavski himself, or the reader for being prejudiced), they provide a number of operative terms which make it possible for the first time to talk theoretically about the art of acting. The result in Russia and Europe has been a considerable growth of respect for acting as an art (as opposed to adulation for stars), as well as better acting itself, and far better audience sensitivity to what the actor is doing. In North America the commercial theatre has largely obscured Stanislavski's achievement. Since the system can easily take a person of mediocre ability and make him a star, or conversely can ignore someone of genuine talent and training, the prejudice remains that acting is a fairly easy, low-level activity, on the fringes of art, that practically anyone could do if he put his mind to it. Such an attitude is not only false; it is also damaging to an understanding of the theatre as a whole—including even the understanding of playscripts.

The key terms that I wish to examine can be taken directly from Stanislavski's chapter titles: "Units and Objectives," "The Super-Objective," "Relaxation of Muscles," "Communion," "Adaptation," "Emotion Memory." (Although their use is so widespread among good actors as to be almost standard, one will search long and hard before finding any of them in an American newspaper review or hearing them discussed by audience members.) The idea of the objective, it is widely agreed, is central to Stanislavski's method. Francis Fergusson has related it to Aristotle's concept of "action" (*praxis*), which does not imply physical activity but rather "the whole working out of a motive to its end in success or failure."[1] In Stanislavski's approach, the objective (sometimes also called, as in Aristotle, the "action" and sometimes the "spine") is always a wish or desire, expressed in the form "I want to . . ." followed by an active verb. The actor programs his role as a series of these desires: "I want to prove Claudius's guilt," "I want to stage a play," "I want to get revenge on Rosencrantz and Guildenstern," and so on. These desires are not necessarily hidden or deep, but neither are they necessarily what the character says he wants or believes he wants. There is thus a connection with the Structuralist notion of the hidden pattern that is not completely hidden, that is directly manifested through relationships in the work. Note that, because this kind of action is hidden, the *surface* action, the physical activity, need not necessarily be very busy. This explains why a performance of a static role from Corneille or Racine can be so much more exciting than a television character's fist fights, car chases, and shoot outs. In the former case the excitement comes not from the character's beautiful words (as if words could ever be beautiful in the abstract, like music), but rather from the strong sense of the character being driven from within; in the latter case we often sense that all the frenetic activity is a hollow shell, that it is not the expression of any strong inner objective but instead an attempt to cover up the lack of one, with a collection of disconnected gimmicks.

The use of the objective is a powerful acting technique that can have the effect of drawing a performance together, focusing the actor's attention, making him unselfconscious and energetic. The inexperienced actor's typical error is to look upon his role in piecemeal fashion, wondering how to say a particular line, what word to emphasize in a sentence (as the old joke goes, "*Hark*, I hear the cannons roar," "Hark, *I* hear the cannons roar," etc.), what postures to assume, which hand to gesture with. The Stanislavski method looks upon such things as merely the outward expressions of the underlying objective; when the proper objective is determined, solutions to most such problems fall into place automatically. The basic unit of acting, then, is definitely not the individual speech, as is widely believed, but rather an underlying pattern, defined by the objective, which might take up many speeches or, conversely, only a small part of one; furthermore, the objective subsumes both the speeches *and* the accompanying physical activity. The method is thus wholistic: a performance becomes *one thing*, rather than a set of isolated speeches, or speech with movement added as an afterthought. Nor are the individual objectives a piecemeal collection; for Stanislavski they are subsumed for each role by an overall "super-objective" that connects them together. Thus, for Macbeth the super-objective might be "to obtain absolute authority"; this would manifest itself in the individual objectives, such as the desire to kill Duncan, to destroy Banquo and his issue, and, finally, to accept death at the hand of Macduff rather than submit to defeat.

Thus, the Stanislavskian idea of the playtext, at least as far as the individual role is concerned, is wholistic. It looks upon the script not as a piece of beautiful literature to which performance is only an embellishment (which sensitive souls might do without, as T. S. Eliot once said he would prefer), but rather as a program for performance. But neither is the method here antiliterary, since the script is the very source of the essential objectives that the actor must uncover and portray. It is neither biased for words and against physical activity (like, say, the French neoclassicists) nor against words and for physical activity (like, say, Artaud). It assumes that words and physical activity are co-equal, the expression of the same impulse. The Stanislavskian actor need never worry about how to "suit the action to the word, the word to the action," because he regards the two as essentially unified from the beginning; it is only our conventions of writing that make them appear to be separate in the script. The concept of the objective, then, is Stanislavski's greatest contribution to acting theory. It also satisfies almost completely the Structuralist criteria outlined in the last chapter. That is, the objective expresses a hidden pattern; as a method it is intrinsic, since it draws on the script rather than something outside it; it can incorporate complexity and ambiguity, since unlike other acting systems it deals easily with situations where the character says something different from what he means; it suspends judgment, since it requires no "typing" of a character or ethical comments on his behavior but instead tries objectively to ascertain his particular desires; and it is wholistic, since it views all aspects of performance as interconnected.

The idea of "communion" (more often called "relating" and sometimes "concentration") is another important concept in the same vein. It means that the actor performs in a state of heightened awareness, that he is sensitive at all times to what is actually happening around him. The idea of "adaptation" is associated with this; the actor is always adapting to changing circumstances, to the particulars of the actual performance. The results are the most spectacular when something goes wrong on stage. I recall a performance in which an actor in a Greek comedy literally had the set collapse around him. "These damned earthquakes!" he shouted, and went on with the play. The beginning actor lives in terror of something occurring in performance even slightly different from what was planned in rehearsal; the actor trained in communion and adaptation recognizes that performances will vary from night to night and learns even to enjoy it. For him, nothing can ever go wrong—there are only new circumstances to be dealt with. But there is more to these concepts than merely learning to deal with disaster. Through them, the actor comes to think of his performance not as an isolated "role" but as part of an interconnected process. It is popularly believed, for example, that when a good actor plays a scene with someone weaker, the weaker actor will make him look good by comparison. Nothing could be further from the truth. The weak actor will always drag down the stronger, because he is actually *part of the other actor's performance*. In the same way, the sets, the lighting, the costumes, the props, and all the other characters are part of an actor's performance—even when the actor is not on stage. This has always been obvious to an audience—if Desdemona is played as a bitch, for example, it certainly affects our attitude toward Othello—but Stanislavski was the first to make actors think this way. Moreover, communion is not just a matter of being aware of another actor's overall characterization, but of being aware, moment by moment, of nuance—a slight change in inflection, a tiny gesture, the glint of the lights on a prop, a wisp of smoke curling into the air. Such awareness often makes the difference between an electrifying performance and a merely adequate one. Audiences can sense when a performance is not quite right; although the actors may be energetic, their characterizations well conceived, and their voices and movements beautifully polished, the stage seems dead. The reason is that the actors are not "communing" with each other and their surroundings, causing slight lapses in timing, reactions that are either a bit too big or a bit too small, line readings that are somewhat rapid and blurred, emotions that do not quite reach their peaks. Stanislavski called this kind of acting "mechanical" and proposed communion as a way of dealing with it. It might actually be considered an adaptation of Structuralist principles to a living work of art, stressing its interconnected, wholistic nature.

Similarly important to Stanislavski was "relaxation," by which he specifically meant the relaxation of muscles, rather than acting coolly and casually. Recognizing that acting is not simple, conscious behavior, like adding up a column of figures, Stanislavski insisted that the body must be relaxed at all times—all the more so in big emotional scenes—to allow it to be both expressive and expressing. That is, it not only expresses what the actor has already conceived in his brain, but also has a kind of unconscious creative energy of its own. A common case occurs when an actor first puts on his costume; if he is relaxed and "communing" with it, he often finds himself moving and gesturing *automatically* in new and characteristic ways. Relaxation of muscles, then, is really an extension of the "communion" principle to the actor's own body. Indeed, one might say that, for the Stanislavskian actor, mind and body are not separate just as words and physical activity are not separate. The body is actually an extension of the actor's imagination. Far from being "internal" acting, as it is often called, the Stanislavski approach rejects the duality between inside and outside, seeing mind and body as a single integrated process. "Wholistic acting" might well be a better name for it.

Nevertheless, there are aspects of Stanislavski's teaching that are definitely not Structuralist, not wholistic. "Emotion memory" is one of them. This is the aspect of Stanislavski's approach that has received the most notice from the public in North America, the one that has created the popular image of the "Method" actor, as a kind of autohypnotic. The public relations media have delighted in promoting this image, in the same way that they like to publicize an actor's taking drugs, because it enhances the notion of the actor as an exotic personality. Whether it has much to do with acting as an art is questionable. The emotion memory technique is definitely not central to Stanislavski's system (that place belongs to the objective), nor does it involve, as is commonly believed, the direct recalling and reliving of an emotion. It is instead a sort of Pavlovian technique (Stanislavski knew Pavlov and admired his work) in which the actor recalls the background events *surrounding* an emotional experience earlier in his life, which then trigger an emotional response in the present. An actor playing King Lear, for example, in order to get the proper emotional reaction to Cordelia's death, might use a death in his own family, but he would not try to recall the death itself but rather such things as the weather at the time, the clothes he was wearing, the smells in the air, the pattern on the wallpaper. These would set off an emotional response in the same way that Pavlov's bell stimulated the dog to salivate. Because the technique can produce striking results (guaranteed to liven up an acting class, for example), it is always in danger of being overused, as it clearly was by American actors in the 1950's. The problem of course is that with respect to a performance it is extrinsic. Applied with Stanislavski's own rule of thumb—that the test of any technique is how well it works for the particular actor in the particular play—emotion memory can at times be useful. But, unlike the other Stanislavskian techniques discussed so far, it does not draw upon the performance itself or the playtext but upon something totally external to them. It may even be destructive to other techniques like communion, since it takes the actor's attention off his immediate surroundings and into a private world of his own. Actors who are addicted to emotion memory often appear on stage to be in a dazed trance, oblivious to what is actually happening around them. The result is as "mechanical" as the performance of the most old fashioned, bellowing, ham actor, because in both cases the performance is not part of the continuous process that exists in a good production.

The other area of weakness in the Stanislavski approach arises from Stanislavski's own poor understanding of dramatic literature. Stanislavski actually recognized his own deficiencies in this area, but, instead of trying to learn more about literary interpretation, he tried to solve his problem by dividing responsibilities between himself and his co-founder of the Moscow Art Theatre, Vladimir Nemirovich-Danchenko. Stanislavski was to have the final say in performance matters, while his partner was to have it in all questions of literature. Of course the scheme did not work, and the two men fought constantly, because the performance and literary aspects of play production cannot ultimately be separated.

Stanislavski's literary lapses were appalling. He did not like Chekhov's *The Seagull*—which practically made the reputation of the Moscow Art Theatre by itself and which still stands today as its emblem—and was only persuaded to produce it after much argument with Nemirovich-Danchenko. Against Chekhov's objections, he insisted on treating *The Three Sisters* as a gloomy tragedy and *The Cherry Orchard* as a slice of life, complete with live animals on stage. He prepared for his production of *Othello* by visiting Venice, to soak up color and bring back real props—even though Shakespeare never had to go there himself, and though most of the play takes place on Cyprus. All his life he was terrified of symbolism, always insisting that he did not understand it. His own literary preferences included the worst kind of kitsch. Gorchakov's book on Stanislavski's directing contains descriptions of a sexy French farce, an old-fashioned melodrama, a historical romance—and nothing by Tolstoy, Gorki, Chekhov, Ibsen, Strindberg, Hauptmann, or any of the other great playwrights of Stanislavski's lifetime.

This literary insensitivity, of course, has had detrimental effects on performance practice. I mentioned that Stanislavski's method is wholistic *for the individual performer*. Unfortunately, he tended to think of the play itself as merely a collection of individual character portraits, interrelated to be sure, but interrelated as humans are in real life rather than as part of a unified construct provided by the playscript. His own greatest role, for example, was that of Dr. Stockmann in Ibsen's *An Enemy of the People*, yet he was dissatisfied with the production as a whole and always admitted that the Moscow Art Theatre had never succeeded with Ibsen. The reason in this case was actually that he glorified the part, making Stockmann into a noble hero (the audience even stormed the stage to shake his hand during one performance), instead of seeing that the playtext, with subtle irony, undercuts Stockmann repeatedly. Stanislavski blamed his recurrent failures with Ibsen on a supposed inability to understand the Scandinavian soul, but the problem was really his own inability to interpret a playscript.

Stanislavski realized fairly early that individual scene-by-scene objectives were not enough for a good performance, which is why he conceived of the "super-objective," to connect the individual objectives into a coherent whole. But, although he occasionally hinted in his writings that there might be such a thing as a super-objective for *an entire play*, he never pursued this idea, as, for example, Francis Fergusson later did. Nor did he ever adapt the principle of communion to the close reading of the playtext. Although he always castigated actors who acted "in general," presenting broad stereotypes instead of varied, detailed performances, he himself read *playscripts* "in general," stereotyping them as mournful tragedies or expressions of the

Scandinavian soul or exotic travelogues. Therefore, while Stanislavski's theory is potentially sound with regard to playscript analysis and interpretation, Stanislavski's personal weaknesses and biases led him to many lapses in practice.

Thus, although Stanislavski was always dedicated to the idea of the performance *ensemble*, a system in which there are no stars and all actors see themselves as part of a group, in practice his method has led, as Robert Brustein once pointed out, to an extension of the star system in North America. It is common to blame this effect on the commercialized nature of our theatre, but that is only part of the story. There is an inherent contradiction in a theatre company composed of actors dedicated only to each other, on a personal basis, and not to the unifying, driving vision of a playwright. If an actor thinks his main job is to create a full-length character portrait (especially if he delves into emotion memory) rather than a piece in the mosaic of the total performance, why aside from personal loyalties should he not pack up his portrait and sell it to the highest bidder? What *artistic* principle does he have to help him resist commercial temptation? It is hard to practice group art if one conceives of his role as existing in isolation.

All this is not to deny the greatness of Stanislavski's achievement. But that very greatness should not blind us to his weaknesses. The popular image of the mumbling, scratching Method actor is *not* a distortion of the "true" Stanislavski. It is an unfortunate but perfectly logical extension of certain contradictions in Stanislavski's approach, which can lead certain actors to think of themselves as *independent* artists. Stanislavski enhanced the art of the actor, but it was often at the expense of the art of the playwright, which means, in the end, at the expense of the art of the theatre itself. We still suffer from this conflict.

Brecht. If Stanislavski is strong in theory but runs into contradictions in practice, the opposite might be said of Brecht. Contradiction is at the heart of Brecht's theory, but, because, unlike Stanislavski, he was aware of the contradiction, he was actually able to build an aesthetic upon it. The basic problem for Brecht, which obsessed him all his life, was whether there should be "Theatre for Pleasure or

Theatre for Instruction," as the title of one of his essays puts it. While he was never able completely to resolve the dilemma theoretically, his plays themselves resolved it in practice.

The duality between pleasure and instruction in art is at least as old as the ancient Romans, for Horace speaks of "profit or delight" or, again, "pleasure and some useful precepts"[2] as the dual aims of literature. It recurs again and again in the history of literary criticism, variously expressed as "delight and teaching," "pleasure and instruction," and so on. For Brecht, these seemed contradictory goals. In his mind, as in most of ours, instruction implied something displeasurable. One thinks of all the ghastly moralistic stories children used to have to read, of the moral-uplift literature of the nineteenth century, or— more relevant in Brecht's case—of agitprop theatre and the Soviet "tractor plays." Actually, there is no reason why pleasure and instruction must be incompatible; it is perhaps an indictment of modern education that they seem to be, since the contradiction never bothered earlier writers. (It is interesting to note that our word *school* is derived from the Greek word for leisure, a meaning now unfortunately lost.) Nevertheless, for Brecht there was a contradiction, and he based his theatre upon it. On the one hand, he wanted to teach his audiences the harsh truths about the modern world, rather than lull them with pleasant stories in the manner of the bourgeois theatre, which he called "a branch of the opium trade." But, on the other hand, he was afraid of driving the audience from the theatre by becoming dry and moralistic. The solution was to create a theatre of what he called "alienation."[3] He would have *both* pleasure and instruction, each working against the other. He could write a scene, for example, that would be very entertaining in the traditional sense, but then destroy the audience's reverie with slides, posters, films, songs, slogans, and all the other paraphernalia of agitprop. Brecht's theatre, then, is one of essential ambiguity.

This ambiguity is the very thing that makes Brecht's theatre great, for, as we have seen, ambiguity is a structural principle in good art. Ambiguity was respectable for Brecht because, as a Marxist, he was dedicated to the Hegelian "dialectical" form of thinking, which makes a virtue of contradiction. For Hegel and Marx, the truth is never to be found in a single viewpoint, but always in a combination of opposites. Thus Hegel, in analyzing Sophocles' *Antigone*, declared that it is a great playscript because neither of the two antagonists, Antigone or Creon, is in the wrong; there is not a conflict of good against evil but of good against good. Neither good is by itself total, however; truth is to be found in the combination of the two goods, even though they are in opposition. Brecht's theatre is similarly dialectical, a combination of opposites, but the opposition often does not reside in the playscript by itself. It resides instead in performance—in a conflict of playscript and performance, in fact. This is why the true playscript for a Brechtian production is not found in the text, but rather in the "model book," a meticulous pictorial record of a presentation, which must be considered in addition to the words. The printed text is only the *inner* script, which must be contradicted in performance rather than staged directly.

For Brechtian theatre to be any good, it must embody this conflict. Many experimental groups loudly proclaim that they are producing Brechtian "Epic" theatre, when they are actually putting on agitprop. The result backfires, as agitprop always does. The only ones who are ever convinced are those who were already committed to the play's point of view, while those who need convincing end up more repelled than ever. The Living Theatre's *Paradise Now* was a perfect example; a combination of shouted slogans about oppression in America and a group fondling session, it was great fun for the 1960's flower children but only led to a more repressive attitude among the bourgeoisie, by confirming their worst fears. On the other hand, establishment theatres often give us only the poetic, romantic side of Brecht—and Brecht was literally a poet and very much a romantic—ending up with sentimental kitsch, plays about honorable thieves or courageous mothers or noble scientists. This is why Brecht is so extraordinarily popular in our repertory theatres. But the exciting thing about Brecht's theatre is the battle between the sentimental and the didactic. Without both, there is nothing.

The same can be said of Brechtian acting. Brecht became prominent in North America in the nineteen-fifties, at a time when there was considerable conflict between internal and external approaches to acting, the so-called Method and Technique schools. The tendency was therefore to identify Stanislavski with the former and Brecht with the latter. Actually, neither fits into these neat categories. Stanislavski's technique of the objective transcends such dualities entirely, while the principle of communion can be considered an *external* technique, since it forces the actor's attention away from himself and onto his surroundings. Emotion memory is internal for the actor but external to the play. Similarly, Brecht's theory of acting incorporates both extremes. Brechtian acting is not, as is popularly believed, cold-blooded, mechanical, noncommittal acting of the kind usually seen in amateur productions. Instead, the Brechtian actor tries to balance his inner feelings with rational control. To achieve this, Brecht would employ such methods as having the actor, during rehearsal, read his speeches in the third person, or transposed into the past tense, or with the stage directions spoken aloud. Brecht was concerned not with destroying emotion but rather with destroying *empathy* between actor and character or actor and audience. He was convinced that empathy was the cause of noninstructive, escapist performances like those of actors in the commercial, bourgeois theatre, and he employed alienation effects specifically to destroy such empathy. He called his kind of theatre "anti-Aristotelian" because he was convinced that Aristotle had stressed empathy in his theories. (Actually, Aristotle has little to say on the subject, and Brecht's own examples on empathy are drawn from Horace, not Aristotle. The term was thus an unfortunate choice, which has led to misinterpretations.) But there is nothing in the anti-Aristotelian approach that implies a lack of emotion itself, as Brecht himself stressed: "The rejection of empathy is not the result of a rejection of the emotions, nor does it lead to such. The crude aesthetic thesis that emotions can only be stimulated by means of empathy is wrong. None the less a non-aristotelian dramaturgy has to apply a cautious criticism to the emotions which it aims at and incorporates."[4]

Thus, what Brecht wanted was not an "external" form of acting, but rather *a dialectical relationship between internal and external,* just as he built performance as a whole on a dialectical relationship. The actor could feel emotions, but they were to be different from those felt by the character, just as the audience's emotions were to be different from the character's as well. In the dramatic theatre, he said, "I weep when they weep, I laugh when they laugh"; while in his own Epic theatre, "I laugh when they weep, I weep when they laugh." There is nothing in this that is incompatible with Stanislavski, who even insisted that when preparing a role the actor should "leave feeling and spiritual content alone"[5] and quoted Salvini with approval when that actor said, "An actor lives, weeps, and laughs on the stage, and all the while he is watching his own tears and smiles."[6] Brecht's alienated acting, then, can be easily reconciled with the major parts of Stanislavski's theory, such as the concepts of the objective and communion. We also find in both theorists a belief in the acting ensemble, a hatred of exaggeration, a stress on relaxation. In fact, the one area where there appears to be definite incompatibility is in Stanislavski's technique of emotion memory, which, as we have seen, is also the very area that sets up incompatibilities *within Stanislavski's own system.* Aside from the element of emotion memory, the performance theories of both can be called Structuralist, seeing performance as a complex process incorporating ambiguity.

But what of Brecht's attitude toward the playscript? As with Stanislavski (as well as Artaud and Schechner), this is an area of difficulty, though perhaps less of one than with the earlier theorist because Brecht was not only a better literary scholar than Stanislavski, but also himself a playwright. The problem with Brecht is that he altered texts for performance—not only classical playscripts, but even his own. He often wrote several versions of the same work, because of his changing attitudes toward the subject matter, as with *Galileo* (the first version celebrates Galileo's recantation as a shrewd kind of heroics, while the second, written after the invention of the atomic bomb, depicts it as a sellout of science to the interests of money and power), or even because of advice from actors, as with *He Who Says Yes* (the children performing the piece objected to its negative ending, in which an injured boy has himself killed to save the party with which he is traveling, leading Brecht to write a second version, called *He Who Says No*, in which the boy refuses to die, inventing a better way to save them all). Yet there is a significant difference between Brecht's approach to a text and those of most playscript jugglers today. It has to do with the fact that we speak of Brecht's *Antigone* or Brecht's *Edward II*, and not merely Brecht's *production* of Sophocles' playscript or Brecht's *version* of Marlowe's. That is, Brecht changed classical texts for the same reason that he changed his own, not to find a modern form for an old content but rather to create an entirely new work. The alterations in *Galileo* or *He Who Says Yes* were not mere "updatings" but thorough reworkings, profoundly changing the scripts' significance; similarly, his revision of *Antigone* changed the balanced struggle between Antigone and Creon in the classical version into a whole new conflict against unreasonable authority (which is to say, ultimately, fascism). There is nothing wrong with making a new playscript out of an old playscript. In fact, the history of playwriting shows that it is almost the norm; more playscripts are rewrites of older playscripts (or other forms of literature) than are completely original constructions. We do not fault Shakespeare for being "untrue" to Holinshed or Fiorentino or the author of the ur-*Hamlet*. Brecht's productions really had brand-new playscripts, even though they were based on old ones, with new focus, new meanings, new purpose.

Unfortunately, many theatre companies today have not made this subtle but important distinction. There is the belief that any play from the classical repertory, or even new plays, can be livened up with a touch of the Epic theatre. But the Epic approach is not a mere *style*, to be added on in decorative fashion after the fact. The Epic theatre is wholistic, incorporating both style and content in a unified (though contradictory) whole. Nor can one make piecemeal alterations in the text, to point up a contemporary parallel or to add a cute little personal message. The world of art will tolerate no such half-way methods. A playscript must be either completely reworked, into a new whole, or it must be left alone.

Brecht never altered a text just to be novel, in order to dazzle the audience with his cleverness, but always with a profound purpose. His own concept of just what a playscript *is* was quite sound. The model books show that he certainly did not want anyone tampering with *his* work after his death! That is, they show that he conceived of a playscript not as something to be treated casually but rather as the source of precise, governing ideas for production. (And, of course, once one conceives of a playscript in this way it makes no difference whether it is in the form of words, pictures, or some kind of coded notation.) Furthermore, his concept of the "*gestus*" shows that, like Stanislavski, he did not think of the physical aspects of production as mere added accessories. "*Gestus*," as John Willett explains, "means both gist and gesture";[7] it is the way in which physical action can *embody meaning*. As Brecht wrote:

Each single incident has its basic gest [Willett's translation for *gestus*]: *Richard Gloster courts his victim's widow. The child's*

*true mother is found by means of a chalk circle. God has a bet
with the Devil for Dr. Faustus's soul. Woyzeck buys a cheap
knife in order to do his wife in,* etc. The grouping of the characters on the stage and the movements of the groups must be
such that the necessary beauty is attained above all by the
elegance with which the material conveying that gest is set out
and laid bare to the understanding of the audience.[8]

Performance for Brecht was wholistic—not text plus production but
text *in* production. Both words and action can convey meaning; both
are rooted in the script. But this aspect of Brecht's work is unfortunately the least understood, and the least practiced, by his North American followers, who have confused Brecht's *playwriting* techniques
with his theories of *performance.*

Artaud. Unlike both Stanislavski and Brecht, Artaud never had
much opportunity to test his theories in actual performance. As a result, they tend to be far more extravagant and unqualified than those
of the other theorists and often cannot be taken too literally. In order
for Artaud's ideas to be understood, they must often be seen against
the context of the French theatre tradition, as well as the personal
problems of Artaud himself.

Artaud often wrote in elaborate metaphors which can make him
seem more abstruse than he actually is. Such is the case with the famous essay "The Theatre and the Plague" (1933), which forms the
opening chapter of his book *The Theatre and Its Double.* Here theatre
is compared to a lengthily described plague, a conceit that is all the
more confusing because the description itself, while based on an actual
outbreak of plague in Marseilles, has no scientific basis whatsover.
This plague causes wild signs and symptoms in its victims, such as
blisters, fever, a blackened and swollen tongue, and discharges through
all the body's orifices, yet it is caused by no detectable microbe. The
corpse, when opened, shows no lesions. The main effects appear to be
social rather than medical: "The obedient and virtuous son kills his
father; the chaste man performs sodomy upon his neighbors. The
lecher becomes pure. The miser throws his gold in handfuls out the
window. The warrior hero sets fire to the city he once risked his life to
save. The dandy decks himself out in his finest clothes and promenades

before the charnel houses."[9] Artaud had been a surrealist in his youth (though he broke with the movement when its members turned Communist), and the influence of surrealism is obvious here. Actually, all that is being described in this outlandish manner is the quality that theatre has of depicting all kinds of terrible acts and moving us deeply, yet of course doing us no physical damage. As Aristotle was the first to note, the theatre, like all the other arts, has remarkable powers of transformation, changing objects and events that in real life would be disgusting into sources of beauty and pleasure. A Macbeth in real life would be a loathsome horror, a Hitler or a Stalin, yet on stage he evokes not only our understanding but also our admiration. "Compared with the murderer's fury which exhausts itself, that of the tragic actor remains enclosed within a perfect circle,"[10] Artaud writes.

What, then, is the purpose of theatre? The answer for Artaud is actually quite simple and traditional: "By means of the plague, a gigantic abscess, as much moral as social, has been collectively drained; and . . . like the plague, the theatre has been created to drain abscesses collectively."[11] This is nothing more than a return to Aristotle's concept of *catharsis*, the idea that theatre is a kind of social safety valve providing for the release of dangerous emotions that might otherwise be released in actual life. Catharsis was a controversial idea in Aristotle's time and remains so today. Censors, both official and unofficial, maintain that works of art which they do not like, far from acting as a safety valve, actually stimulate the kind of behavior they depict. There is no simple answer to these charges. Racine's *Phaedra* is about a sexually obsessed woman, yet its effect is, if anything, anti-erotic; a pornographic movie, by contrast, has arousal as its very purpose. *King Lear* is full of violence, yet arouses only pity and fear, while a television serial can make violence seem like a pleasant kind of sport. Obviously, catharsis is more a matter of the *treatment* of the emotional subject matter than of the subject matter itself.

For Artaud, the proper treatment could exist only in a highly stylized, ritualistic form of theatre like that of Balinese dancers. On the one hand, he despised the stale theatres of the *boulevard* or the over-refined neoclassical style of the Comédie-Française. But, on the other hand, he definitely did not want a Grand Guignol kind of theatre either, which would try to stimulate the audience directly, through realistic illusions of blood and violence. In his "theatre of cruelty," there must be violence, but it must remain "closed within a perfect circle," by being presented in a stylized manner. Thus, for Artaud as for Brecht, what is required is a *relation* between content and form, rather than a specific form or content by itself. And, as with Brecht's, Artaud's theories have often been debased when put into practice by those who would provide one aspect without the other. Treating Artaud in a non-Structuralist way is the cause of a good deal of the vulgarity in our theatre, the nudity and crudity for the sake of immediate shock, the physical assaults upon the audience, the orgiastic chaos. It is worth pointing out that Artaud himself never, in theory or practice, called for audience participation, collective improvisation, or cheap vulgarity; his was always to be a theatre of discipline and style.

But, on the other hand, Artaud cannot be let off completely for the excesses committed in his name. For one thing, his metaphorical way of writing easily lends itself to misinterpretation; anyone reading "The Theatre and the Plague" superficially might well believe that Artaud wanted to see actual murder, sodomy, arson, and exhibitionism on the stage. Furthermore, his attitude toward playscripts has created serious difficulties. Artaud despised literature in the theatre, for example, calling for "no more masterpieces" and even wanting a kind of dance theatre, a theatre without verbal language. Seen against the French theatrical tradition, which since the seventeenth century has overglamorized the spoken word and tended to reject all physical action, this might make some sense, if not taken too literally. But seen in the context of the English-speaking stage, which has never looked upon theatre as mere recitation, it is disastrous. Actually, Artaud's own productions never did away with verbal language entirely, and in stressing the artistic importance of the *mise-en-scène* (what we call the "blocking and business," the physical movements controlled by the director) he had a corrective effect on the traditional Comédie-Française style of playing. But on the English stage, which lacks the French traditions of style and restraint, the result is far less helpful; pushing for more vigor can lead to chaos.

Like Brecht's theory of the *gestus*, Artaud's theory of the *mise-en-scène* is valuable because it stresses that on stage the physical actions carry meaning in themselves, rather than just being a decorative addition to the meaning found in the words. But in rejecting words entirely (at least in theory) Artaud overlooked the reverse possibility, that words themselves can become a kind of action. Brecht realized this and extended the idea of the *gestus* to words, and even to music. But like so many stage directors today, Artaud saw verbal language as having only its logical, denotative function. He therefore wanted to turn it into "incantations" devoid of direct meaning or to abolish its use entirely. But words in literature have always done far more than carry direct messages. As the New Critics showed, they have an aesthetic or associative function, in which multiple and ambiguous connotations are always carried along with the principal meaning; and, as Stanislavski and Francis Fergusson showed, they can also have a dramatic or rhetorical function—to convince, deceive, flatter, command, subdue. The politician haranguing a crowd, the man seducing a woman, and the salesman pushing a product are not just communicating meanings, they are using words actively in pursuit of a specific goal. Language is action for them, and it is just this kind of language that dramatists use for their characters.

Artaud was ignorant of both the aesthetic and the rhetorical functions of verbal language. His prejudice against words, moreover, turned him, like Brecht, into a text changer, but one with a very different purpose. He believed the *mise-en-scène* to be a kind of language, which is well and good, but rather than seeing it as a language that extends and reinforces the verbal language in the playscript, or comments on it in a dialectical relationship, he insisted that it should *replace* the verbal language. Believing that verbal language had become repressive, and thus no longer able to produce a cathartic effect, Artaud wanted not so much to abolish masterpieces entirely but to rework them, translating the words into a physical language through the *mise-en-scène*, "materializing these old conflicts and above all giving them *immediacy*; i.e., these themes will be born directly into the theatre and materialized in movements, expressions, and gestures before trickling away in words."[12] Instead of imagining a theatre in which words and actions are one, a unity, he merely turned the French tradition on its head, loving physical action at the expense of words where the seventeenth-century academicians had loved words at the expense of physical action. Furthermore, his concept of the language of physical action turns out to be not that of a unique, continuous, "presentational form," as Susanne Langer would call it, signifying meaning only in overall configuration, but rather of "a language of signs, gestures and attitudes having an ideographic value."[13] This physical form of communication, while supposedly capable of evoking ideas in a mystical realm unattainable through words, thus turns out to be *structured* exactly like verbal language into a discrete vocabulary; it communicates not aesthetically but as crude sign language. The value of physical language is actually that it communicates in an entirely different *way* from verbal language. If one restricts physical language to ideographs, there is no reason to prefer it to the verbal; Artaud sounds like those people who maintain, vaguely, that French is more "precise" than English or that German is more "poetic" than French.

If this were not bad enough, the worst thing about Artaud's theory of the playscript is that he sees the text as the reflection of hidden ideas which can be expressed equally well in verbal or physical language: "Beneath the poetry of the texts, there is the actual poetry, without form and without text," he writes.[14] This sounds like a Structuralist idea, with its evocation of a hidden world of meaning, but that impression is deceptive. Structuralism does not separate meaning from its expression the way Artaud does. It is this separation that leads Artaud to think of different languages as merely *carrying* meaning rather than *embodying* it. Meaning for him is not hidden *in* the text, like the pattern in a complex mosaic or the molecular structure in a chemical compound; rather, it exists for him in a completely separate world, a Platonic heaven of ideas that is *apart* from both text and performance. In a word, his theory is extrinsic.

The extrinsic nature of his theory has led to ridiculous effects in performance—not so much in his own, for he produced very little, as in those of his followers. A notorious example is in the "collage" productions of Shakespeare by Charles Marowitz, one of the co-founders of the British Theatre of Cruelty. In one of his manifestoes Artaud had called for the production of "works from the Elizabethan theatre stripped of their text and retaining only the accouterments of period, situations, characters, and action."[15] The assumption is, of course, that elements like character and action have an independent existence and can meaningfully be treated in isolation, rather like those popular nineteenth-century critics who used to pose questions like "What would happen if Ophelia were to meet Desdemona?" Luckily for Artaud, he was prevented from realizing such fatuous productions in his lifetime, but, unluckily for us, Marowitz has been able to stage a number of them. "Is it possible, today, to sit through the play as Shake-speare wrote it and still respond to its story and structure?" he asks. The answer is of course no. One must redo the script because "a society no longer thinks the way its author did at the time of writing." One must juggle language and narrative, respecting "the director's right to reinterpret a classical work according to his own lights," yet "still maintain contact with what is essential in *Hamlet*."[16] Notice the as-sumptions here: despite his use of the word *structure*, Marowitz is ob-viously thinking only in terms of surface structure, the sequence of acts, scenes, events. "What is essential in *Hamlet*" is for him not a structure but a static *thing* that can be stripped from the text. For a Structuralist, on the other hand, the essence of *Hamlet* is a pattern, an organization. One can no more strip it from the text than one can strip a picture from its forms and colors, or a melody from its musical notes. Or, to use a famous example of Gilbert Ryle's, Marowitz is like a visi-tor to Oxford who is shown all the colleges, libraries, playing fields, offices, museums, and so on and then asks to see the university itself, as if it were a separate entity, distinct from the parts, instead of the overall organization *of* the parts. And if one were to alter those parts, of course he would automatically alter the organization. The structure of a playscript is a function of the playscript, a dependent variable. Unlike Tom Stoppard, for example, whose *Rosencrantz and Guilden-stern Are Dead* is a new playscript based on *Hamlet*, Marowitz be-lieves he is only giving us an updated "version" of Shakespeare's work, but the point is that a new version is *always* a new work—and in Marowitz's case not even a very interesting one.

Elsewhere Marowitz speaks of Hamlet, the character, rather than the whole play:

> I despise Hamlet.
> He is a slob,
> A talker, an analyser, a rationalizer,
> Like the parlour liberal or the paralysed intellectual, he can
> describe every fact of a problem, yet never pull his finger out.
>
> . . . .
>
> You may think he's a sensitive, well-spoken fellow, but, frankly,
> he gives me a pain in the ass.[17]

What is this but a return to nineteenth-century character criticism of Shakespeare in its most extreme form, a kind of parody of Bradley? Marowitz here talks about Hamlet the character as if he were a real, living person, independent of text or performance, whom one can discuss in isolation and even chastise. He might be talking about Eric Sevareid on the CBS News. Fifty years of Shakespeare criticism have passed Marowitz by; today even high school students are taught that character is something embedded in a text, that it is a high-level generalization taken from a web of interrelationships, not an isolatable thing but a process. But Marowitz? Well, frankly, Hamlet gives him a pain in the ass.

Marowitz is an extreme case, but he exemplifies an inherent danger in Artaud's theory. While one can applaud Artaud for giving artistic dignity to the *mise-en-scène*, and even admire some of his productions (real or conceived), one must condemn his attempt to separate meaning from its expression. Instead of envisioning an integrated process, he saw meaning as separate from playscript, playscript separate from performance, and, even, in the case of one of his followers, character as separate from text *or* performance.

Schechner. With Richard Schechner, I do not intend to discuss his practices so much as his theories. His directing is interesting primarily for his use of an "environmental" style, a return to medieval methods of staging in which the entire performance space (which need not be a traditional auditorium) is potentially the stage—in which, in fact, there is no distinction made between the audience's space and the performers' space, and sometimes none made between the theatre building and the outside world. But an important aspect of the Structuralist approach is that it is independent of particular genres; as Northrop Frye has shown, genre is a matter of relationships among different works rather than within individual ones. Environmental staging (or proscenium staging, arena, thrust, etc.) is, we might say, an element of surface structure rather than deep structure. Schechner's basic theories of the script-performance relationship are applicable to any kind of stage (just as they are applicable to any kind of script).

Schechner is thus far the only theatre practitioner-theorist who is consciously Structuralist in his approach. The theories of Stanislavski,

Brecht, and Artaud have Structuralist aspects, but only Schechner has a direct Structuralist influence. In an important essay, entitled "Approaches," he develops his theory of the playtext in relation to performance, citing many Structuralists by name but adapting primarily the methods of the French Structuralist anthropologist Claude Lévi-Strauss. Schechner rejects thematic, or what he calls (drawing on Susan Sontag) "interpretive" criticism as "a way of imposing form and extracting a meaning."[18] In other words, he rejects as useless for performance criticism that is extrinsic. Instead, he insists that "the modern theatre critic . . . takes as his major job the examination of a play's structure." The method of examination is defined simply, as the analysis of "the actions stated or implied in the text, and the relationships among the characters."[19] From this the Structuralist critic develops a kind of map of the text, which is not meant to substitute for the text itself but rather to aid performers in preparing a production.

All this is excellent advice, so much so that it is unfortunate this aspect of Schechner's work has had so little impact. Schechner's own dramatic criticism is very good in this regard also, analyzing particular playscripts in line with his own criteria and developing interpretations that could be quite useful to other theatre practitioners. But he has, alas, published very little dramatic criticism, and his followers tend to fasten on the more flamboyant elements in his work, such as nudity and text alteration—both of which occur less often in his productions than is popularly believed.

Another important element in his theory is his stress on the two-way relationship between Structuralist criticism and performance: "The structural critic who cannot carry his research through a production will not be able to write meaningfully about theatre. And a director who does not understand structure will be scarcely able to shape an artwork."[20] Structuralist criticism is not, for Schechner, a fixed and final *thing* but rather an unending process. Given this, why should a critic not learn from a production, just as a director can learn from a critic? Furthermore, putting the connection this way stresses the great similarity between the work of the Structuralist critic and that of the director—each must explore the work in detail (the director, in fact, has little choice in the matter); each finds relations among these details (why one scene follows another, how a character's words or actions relate to previous and future events, how a particular bit of action relates to its surroundings, and so on); each must see these relationships composed into a wholistic vision. The similarity of their work suggests the possibility of a close and fruitful collaboration, which in turn points up the importance, in any theatre devoted to the production of classical plays, of the position of *Dramaturg*. The *Dramaturg* is simply a literary advisor to the director; the position was founded by Lessing in eighteenth-century Germany and is now very common in European repertory companies but only rarely found in North America. Often, in fact, when the position does exist in one of our theatres, the *Dramaturg* does not work in this collaborative way; the name is just given as a glorified title to the play reader or the person who writes program notes. Schechner points out that not only would the true, collaborative *Dramaturg* improve theatrical performance, but also theatrical performance could improve dramatic criticism through a *Dramaturg* who would "carry his research through a production," rather than merely in his study like most critics. In that way, everyone could learn about a playscript from a production, and not just the performers involved and the audiences who saw them. This kind of analysis, which might be called "dramaturgical criticism," at present scarcely exists, with the result that discoveries made in a production about a playtext are usually lost forever.

Thus far, Schechner's theory seems intrinsic, nonjudgmental, process oriented, wholistic. But, like the others discussed in this chapter, he too has his lapses. For one thing, he has the same prejudice against literature found in Stanislavski and Artaud. He tends to use "literature" and "literary" as code words to mean anything he does not like in the theatre. He writes, for example, "Literary criticism works too easily on the verbal surface of scenes, accepting as 'fact' only what the text can verify."[21] Whose literary criticism, one wonders? That of A. C. Bradley? G. Wilson Knight? Francis Fergusson? Richard Schechner himself? One of the surest signs of prejudice in a writer is a failure to recognize distinctions in the group he is attacking, and for Schechner here it appears that all literary critics look alike. And as for accepting only what the text can verify, wasn't that what the Structuralist critic was *supposed* to do, analyzing only "the actions stated or implied in the text, and the relationships among the characters"? These mysteries are cleared up only when one realizes that

Schechner does not really mean literary at all but is instead using the word as an automatic pejorative; substitute the word *bad* and his intended meaning becomes clear.

Of course, Schechner's sloganeering only increases the prejudice already existing in the theatre against literature: the idea that theatrical performance has nothing whatsover to do with literature, that playscripts have only a shadowy existence except in performance, that the methods used for analyzing literary works are incompatible with those for a play, and so on. With Schechner, the prejudice cuts even deeper. He treats the playtext as just one out of many performance elements, including performers, space, audience, and so on. Instead of the text being seen as the generating idea of the performance, it is merely a single aspect of no special importance. (The next step, which thank goodness Schechner does not take, is to see it as having actually *less* importance than the other elements.) This can lead to text alterations, but, as I have noted, that is really not so important in Schechner's method. What is important is that his attitude toward literature leads him to see the playscript itself as a vague, amorphous thing, of interest only for the working out of its structural principles. That is, like Artaud, whose influence on him is strong, Schechner tends to see the essence of a text as something separate from its specifics. This leads him to say, for example, that there is no "best" structure of a playscript, but rather that "there are many structures."[22] But of course there is only one structure of a playscript (unless it is rewritten). Schechner is confusing structure itself with descriptions of that structure, that is, the specific critical interpretations, which are of course always incomplete. In the analogy given before of the molecular structure of an object, the molecular, atomic, and subatomic relationships are not really different structures, but rather different ways of looking at one (difficult and complex) structure. An object does not change when we look at it through an electron microscope instead of an optical one; we are merely looking at it in a different way. Nor does the director choose, supermarket style, among a number of possible structures in a playscript and then decide which one to produce. He produces the entire structure, which is to say, the entire playscript. Structuralist analysis exists only to help him understand and produce that playscript, not to turn the playscript into a "structure." Schechner tends to fall into a trap of his own description, interposing an interpretation between the playscript and the audience, when he treats structure as a thing (or, in the quotation above, a selection of things) more real than the text, rather than as an abstraction taken *from* the text.

Schechner sees a similarity between the concept of myth, as developed by Lévi-Strauss (and it is typical of Schechner's bias that he would come to Structuralism via anthropology rather than literary criticism), and a playtext: "The problem of performance is homologous to that of myth. We have the original text; it is not immutable; it can lead to contradictory performances."[23] But the problem is not homologous. For one thing, playscripts are written by playwrights; no single person writes myths. Only *versions* of a myth exist—there is no "original text." A myth is only manifested as an abstraction drawn after the fact from all the versions, while the playscript has an obvious, solid manifestation on the printed page. What happens with myth is that someone one day invents a story of, say, Oedipus (or perhaps a real man of that name existed, and his story is told). Other storytellers take up the story, each changing it for his own purpose, until there are a large number of versions evolving over a long period of time. Then a Structuralist anthropologist, like Lévi-Strauss, comes along and abstracts what is common to all the versions—the oracle, the Sphinx, killing the father, marrying the mother, discovery—and decides that there is something significant in all this, that these details are an unconscious code that tells something important about the society to whom the myth belongs. Perhaps his decoding is apt and perhaps it is not, but even if correct that does not imply that each individual version is a working out of a pre-existing myth. The myth does not even exist until someone looks at all the Oedipus stories at once, after they have been told. With playscripts, the situation is the reverse. Like the storyteller, the stage director can look back and draw upon many different versions (i.e., productions), but he also must draw upon something the storyteller *does not have*, which is the playtext. It is fixed. Even if it allows for considerable latitude in performance, it still presupposes certain specifics. If the specifics are changed, the playscript and performance will both be changed. One can then consider that he is doing a different version of a myth (if, as often happens, the playtext is drawn itself from other works), but he is not doing a different version *of that playscript.*

The cause of Schechner's problem here is that, again, he wants to make structure something apart, separate from specifics, which is the "true" playscript in the same sense that the anthropologist's decoding represents the "true" myth. The implication is that directors or performers need only concern themselves with performing this vague, general, yet "true" script, while rearranging the surface structure to suit contemporary taste or their own predilections. I suppose this is better than saying that the text can be rearranged willy-nilly. But it is a wrong attitude nonetheless.

All four theorists in this chapter can be considered in some sense Structuralists, but there exist with each problems in dealing with the playscript, which with some go as far as demonstrating an outright bias against dramatic literature. It is not hard to understand the reason for this. All these theorists are reacting against a cultural tradition that includes a bias against theatre as an art form, rating it far lower than nonperformed literature. Aristotle, for example, put "spectacle" as last on his list of acceptable playwriting techniques and insisted that a good play could make its effect without a performance at all, through reading alone; he too was fighting a bias against theatre, although he chose the opposite tactic from his modern counterparts in making it appear respectable. Actors throughout the Middle Ages were considered to be vagabonds and could not be buried in hallowed ground. French academicians accepted theatre only when it was static and oratorical. Theatre in Elizabethan times (one of the art form's two greatest periods!) was considered a debased and trivial pastime, which is the reason the playtexts of the period present such editorial problems today, and why none of the theatre buildings survive at all. In our century, theatre has had a difficult struggle in getting accepted as a university discipline. George Pierce Baker had to leave Harvard in the 1920's to form his drama school at Yale, a change which still causes difficulties since so many North American institutions model themselves on Harvard. Yet one should not let the struggle against all this opposition lead to an overreaction. It is not necessary to prove that theatre is something unique, totally independent of literature, superspecial, in order to gain respectability for it. For one thing, the battle has largely been won. We no longer treat actors like vagabonds, but rather like royalty. Repertory theatres are subsidized by governments

and private foundations. Universities everywhere are establishing theatre departments—even Harvard has a modest program—to the point
where now an instructor with theatre credentials is far more likely to
find a university post than is a literature professor. There are other art
forms, such as poetry, that are in far greater danger of disappearance
today than theatre. Actually, the most oppressed person in the theatre
today is the playwright—the live one cannot get his playscripts produced, and the dead one has his playscripts regularly mangled.

4

What Aristotle Might Have Said

If Stanislavski, Brecht, Artaud, and Schechner are representative of contemporary performance theory, Aristotle still dominates dramatic theory, that is, the theory of playscripts considered as literature. Whitehead once said that all of philosophy could be considered as 2,400 years of footnotes to Plato; all of dramatic theory can be similarly considered as a set of footnotes to Aristotle. Although he was only interested in describing a small and fairly fixed body of work, the dramatic literature of one city over a period of less than two centuries, he has since had enormous influence on all western drama. No one can be around the theatre very long without hearing him cited in some context or other; he is the one theorist that all performers are likely to have read, or at least heard about, and the one that no modern theorist can ignore.

Actually, the work on which all this reputation rests, the *Poetics*, turns out to be a strange piece of writing when one looks into it. The book is clearly incomplete, since Aristotle says, "Of the poetry which imitates in hexameter verse, and of Comedy, we will speak hereafter" (vi.1),[1] but he never gets around to it. There are gaps in the text, poorly made or nonexistent transitions, and even contradictions, as when he says in Book XIII that the best tragedies end unhappily, and in the very next book that the best ones are those in which unhappiness is averted. In contrast to Aristotle's other works, the *Poetics* seems very badly written, which has led some to conclude that what we have is actually only a set of lecture notes. The erratic quality of the writing has not hindered the influence of these "notes," however. Just the opposite—it has made it easy for subsequent writers to fill in the gaps for themselves, to take the attitude that "what Aristotle really meant to say was . . ." followed by the writer's own pet theory. The neoclassicists looked at the *Poetics* and inferred the Three Unities; Brecht looked at it (or did he only look at Horace?) and inferred empathy, which he detested; Francis Fergusson looked at it and inferred Stanislavski's theory of action. Everyone has his own Aristotle, including me, as will be seen shortly.

Aristotle was in many ways a Structuralist. Although he was certainly interested in problems of genre—he provides a formal definition of Tragedy, for example—his method was like that propounded by Northrop Frye, isolating the corpus of tragic plays and drawing inferences from them, rather than starting with logical first principles. This is not surprising, since his whole philosophic method presupposed that universals are generated by particulars, in opposition to Plato who maintained the reverse. Genre for Aristotle was not a question of logical deduction, but rather, as with his scientific studies, a question of observation, categorization, and, finally, inference of general principles. With Tragedy, this meant examining all existing playscripts, categorizing them as to type (for example, those with "simple" plots versus those with "complex" plots), and finally making a philosophical generalization, such as "a perfect tragedy should . . . be arranged not on the simple but on the complex plan" (xiii.2). The problem with many subsequent theorists is that they reversed this process, taking Aristotle in an idealistic, Platonic way. The neoclassicists, for example, started with the assumption that the theatre should imitate life as closely as possible, proceeded to the Three Unities as restrictions that would prevent the audience's credulity from being unduly strained, and only then went to Aristotle to find corroborating passages. But many such passages, such as "Tragedy endeavors, as far as possible, to confine itself to a single revolution of the sun" (v.4), were really neutral observations of fact rather than rules. If Aristotle had been living, like the neoclassicists, in the seventeenth century, he would have been drawing upon a very different body of dramatic literature and would have drawn different principles from it.

The general tendency in dramatic theory, however, has been to look only at Aristotle's results, and not at his basic method, thus "turning Aristotle on his head." In the last few decades, Aristotelian scholarship—most notably Gerald F. Else's extensive study[2]—has gone a long way toward establishing just what Aristotle actually did say, and mean, in the *Poetics*. But this scholarship has not yet had much influence on those who teach drama in the universities, or on theatre practitioners. Tennessee Williams, for example, writes in his recent memoirs that *Cat on a Hot Tin Roof* is his favorite among his plays because, among other things, that play "adheres to the valuable edict of Aristotle that a tragedy must have unity of time and place and magnitude of theme."[3] But, for Aristotle, this was hardly an "edict." Aristotle's actual statement on time, quoted above, is simply an observation about tragedies as he knew them, in the context of a comparison to the Epic poem. His statement on "magnitude" is similarly an observation rather than a judgment, and he does not mention unity of place at all!

For Aristotle, Tragedy was not an *ideal*, as it has become for us. If it were, it would have made no sense for him to talk of a "perfect" tragedy, since ideals are already perfect. Aristotle's definition of Tragedy is quite neutral: "Tragedy, then, is an imitation of an action that is serious, complete, and of a certain magnitude; in language embellished with each kind of artistic ornament, the several kinds being found in separate parts of the play; in the form of action, not narrative; through pity and fear effecting the proper purgation of these emotions" (vi.2). It has become common to talk of "Aristotle's definition of Tragedy" as if it included the elements of reversal, recognition, and tragic incident discussed later in the *Poetics*, but those are actually what Aristotle considered to be aspects of the *best* tragedies. His real definition is nothing more than what is above. Some modern theorists define Tragedy so narrowly that one comes to feel that *nothing* is a tragedy, except Sophocles' *Oedipus Tyrannus*, and possibly not even that. Books with titles like "The Death of Tragedy" harangue playwrights, or modern society in general, for not producing "true" tragedies that reach the Greek ideal. But Aristotle himself was never so restrictive in his approach to the subject. His definition is quite broad, encompassing a wide number of plays, *both good and bad*; the definition is not stated in the form of a judgment, but only an observation.

Genre is thus for Aristotle a high-level generalization, drawn from a fixed set of playscripts that have already been written. Like the related concept "Style,"[4] genre is simply that which is common to all members of the group. Thus, when one applies the concept of Style or genre to an individual script, one becomes automatically extrinsic, since the individual playscript's Style or genre only exists in relation to other playscripts. Like the anthropologist's concept of myth, concepts of genre or Style are constructs, made after the fact, and, as with myth, the process is not really reversible. In other words, the definition of a genre or Style is a *function*, in which genre or Style is the dependent variable, and *the function has no inverse*. It is a transformation from a group of scripts into a particular abstraction and will not work the other way around. Directors who start by asking genre questions about a script (Is this a tragedy? comedy? melodrama? tragical-comical-historical-pastoral?), or playwrights who set out to create a playscript of a certain genre (like T. S. Eliot trying to write solemnly correct Greekish tragedies), inevitably produce banal results, because the concept of genre or style automatically implies the ordinary, the average, the stereotyped. Hack works fit categories of genre far better than great ones. (In teaching the theories of Northrop Frye, for instance, I have always found that TV dramas or comic strips make the best examples.) In fact, when dealing with something first rate, one usually finds that the most interesting aspects, with respect to genre, occur where the work does not fit. *Hamlet* considered as a tragedy is bizarre, and as a revenge play, inept; *The Merchant of Venice* is tragic and comic simultaneously; *A Doll House* is interesting only insofar as it is *not* a women's liberation piece.

Thus, while genre can be treated in a Structuralist way, it is a dangerous concept when applied to the interpretation of individual works, or when applied at all to the creative process. Aristotle himself avoided both traps, because genre was not really an artistic problem for the Greeks. Tragedy was just the kind of play one saw at the end of March, and Comedy the kind one saw at the end of January. Aristotle's purpose in providing definitions for them was scientific, not aesthetic. No one proceeded to write a play from a definition, any more than anyone started from a fixed myth. Only in modern times have we seen genre as something *generative*, which the word *genre* (a modern term that Aristotle never uses) actually means. In studying Aristotle, and having at our command thousands of playscripts that he could never have dreamed of, we should become more concerned with his manner of analysis than the specific categories that he generated. We could note, first of all, his method of isolation of Tragedy—treating it as an independent form, rather than just a debased kind of Epic. Second, we could note his constant citation of specific examples (there is hardly a book in the *Poetics* without one), rather than appeals to logic, in making his points. Third, we could note his sensitivity to complexity—his insistence that good tragedies should be "arranged not on the simple but on the complex plan" (xiii.2), with reversals of fortune, characters who are both good and bad, and, most paradoxical of all, "probable impossibilities" (xxiv.10). Clearly, Aristotle did not view Tragedy as something stately and monotonous, like all too many modern productions, but rather as something flexible and alive. Finally, we could note his concept of artistic unity: "In the case of animate bodies and organisms a certain magnitude is necessary, and a magnitude which may be easily embraced in one view; so in the plot, a certain length is necessary, and a length which can be easily embraced by the memory [vii.5]. . . . The plot, being an imitation of an action, must imitate one action and that a whole, the structural union of the parts being such that, if any one of them is displaced or removed, the whole will be disjointed and disturbed" (viii.4).

Unity is a kind of function or transaction between the work and the viewer. It is not a matter of bland homogeneity, but of having a structure that is "easily embraced." Kenneth Burke has made a similar observation: "In an exhibit of photographic murals (*Road to Victory*) at the Museum of Modern Art, there was an aerial photograph of two launches, proceeding side by side on a tranquil sea. Their wakes crossed and recrossed each other in almost an infinity of lines. Yet despite the intricateness of this tracery, the picture gave an impression of great simplicity, because one could quickly perceive the generating principle of its design."[5] For both Burke and Aristotle, a good work of art contains both unity *and* complexity. This apparent contradiction is resolved by the idea of the one whole action, or "generating principle," underlying the work. There is complexity on the surface but unity beneath it. This is clearly a Structuralist idea, as are the other examples I have cited; all are aspects of Aristotle that have received too little attention.

The aspect that has received the most attention is Aristotle's analytical tendency, his habit of always breaking things up into parts. A noteworthy example is his separation of the playtext from perform-ance. It has become so common now to read playscripts as independent works, separate from performance, that we take it for granted. Yet Aristotle's assertion that Tragedy "reveals its power by mere reading" (xxvi.3) must have been a startling idea at the time. After all, origin-ally *all* literature was meant to be performed, either as a play or, more commonly, by singing or recitation. (Aristotle's mention of reading, in fact, probably refers to public recitation, which was the standard form of "publication" in the ancient world, rather than silent reading to oneself, which is the norm for us.) Writing was a fairly recent in-vention, and illiteracy common; in such circumstances, writing tends to be considered in the way we look at Morse code, as a means of storing or transmitting "real" language rather than as a language in itself. We should remember, too, that it was standard practice for playwrights to direct their own plays and, originally, even to play the leading role. By isolating playscripts, Aristotle was taking a major step forward in dramatic theory—for his time.

His reason for this isolation is made clear in the *Poetics*: It was to answer those who, like Plato, had censured the drama as an inferior form because it required spectacle for its effect. "We are told," says Aristotle, "that Epic poetry is addressed to a cultivated audience, who do not need gesture; Tragedy, to an inferior public" (xxvi.2). Here we see how ancient is the prejudice against theatre. Aristotle answers it in part by saying that much of the censure is really attached to *bad* performers—flute players who twist and turn as if they were playing quoits, actors who gesture so extravagantly they are called "apes"— rather than to the idea of performance in general. But his other strate-gies in defending the art of Tragedy were to prove unfortunate in the long run. By stressing the possibility of reading, and also by placing "spectacle" as the last and least of his six elements of Tragedy, Aris-totle made possible the split between dramatic criticism and theatrical performance that still exists today. His comments on spectacle, in par-ticular, sound as bad as the prejudices of the Platonists: "Those who employ spectacular means to create a sense not of the terrible but only the monstrous, are strangers to the purpose of Tragedy" (xiv.2), he writes. Aristotle was probably not as antispectacle as he seems; there is plenty of indirect evidence in the *Poetics* (including the fact of its having been written at all) to show that Aristotle was an outright theatre buff, who must have enjoyed spectacle, in the fullest sense, a great deal. But in defending what was a minority position among intellectuals of his day, he had to find some common ground, a compromise position that would not be rejected out of hand by the Platonists. (It is rather like the way Abraham Lincoln had to assure voters that he did not believe in the equality of the races; taken out of context, his statements seem like vile prejudice, but they were probably necessary for the candidate of an antislavery party to get a hearing at all in certain areas.) Thus, just as many modern performance theorists are antiliterary snobs, so Aristotle, despite an obvious love of the theatre, sometimes sounds like an antiperformance snob.

Aristotle's strategy of separating text from performance, while certainly advancing the art of dramatic criticism, was therefore an approach that played into the hands of those who believed that performance is somehow morally inferior to literature. With neither Plato nor Aristotle seeming to value performance *per se*, performance theory languished for millennia. So deeply ingrained now is the separation of text and performance, and the idea that the two can be given a moral ranking, that, when writers of our own time took up, at long last, the problem of performance, they tended to accept the traditional division and merely to invert the traditional preference. (I shall return to this problem of the relation of text and performance in the next chapter.) Aristotle was quite right in seeing that, in a sense, a playscript is a finished work, but to go as far as he did, and consider scripts as totally independent of performance, even a hypothetical one, caused considerable damage.

Here then is the problem with Aristotle in the *Poetics*—his tendency to analyze, to break into parts, is not balanced by a tendency to *synthesize*, to see the parts in relation to the whole again. He does not follow through on a key sentence in his definition of unity: "a whole, the structural union of the parts being such that, if any one of them is displaced or removed, the whole will be disjointed and disturbed" (viii.4). (This again may not be his fault, since the *Poetics* is an unfinished work.) Instead of exploring how this "structural union" comes about, so that, for example, spectacle can become a valid and *necessary* part of Tragedy, Aristotle tends to *rank* elements, which only underlines their separation. He separates text from performance.

He separates Tragedy into six parts—the three internal ones, namely plot, character, and thought, and the three external ones, namely diction, song, and spectacle. He separates plot into further parts, such as reversal, recognition, and denouement. It is all very simple and symmetrical. H. D. F. Kitto has written of the "bogus clarity" of the Greek language that led thinkers to make all kinds of neat distinctions in logic that were not necessarily reflected in reality. The *Poetics* is often an excellent example of this process. It has left us a legacy of piecemeal rather than wholistic dramatic criticism, so that even theorists who may slice up the pie differently from Aristotle still end up with isolated chunks. One modern writer speaks of the "auditory, visual, and kinetic" elements of theatre, another of "composition, picturization, and movement"; composition, it turns out, is further broken down into elements like stability, sequence, and balance, while balance can be symmetrical, asymmetrical, or "aesthetic." These elements are not considered as parts of an integrated whole, but rather as independent things that one is almost expected to reach out and touch. It is as if music theory had never got beyond naming the notes, or painting theory the color wheel. Analysis without synthesis is sterile and purposeless; if that were all there were to dramatic theory, performers would be quite right to be suspicious of it. What good would it do to tell an actor that he had to perform a denouement, or a designer to provide a touch of aesthetic balance? Unless such elements are seen contextually, in relation to the whole significance of the unique script, the proper response to having them pointed out is a shrug. So what?

Consider Aristotle's categories: spectacle, for instance, whether done properly or exaggerated, Aristotle sees as something that is merely *added* to the text. But what about situations like those so common in Shakespeare, where a character paints a scene with words? In *King Lear*, Edgar's description of the cliffs and beach at Dover (IV.vi. 11–24) is as spectacular as anything a designer could create. In the audience's imagination, the description is an important part of the spectacle, even though they do not see it. In fact, they must not see it, because the description is all a sham put on for blind Gloucester's benefit; the contrast between the verbal picture and the visual picture forms the true spectacle of the scene. Spectacle is thus not something always isolatable. Susanne Langer has written of architecture:

"The place which a house occupies on the face of the earth—that is to say, its location in actual space—remains the same place if the house burns up or is wrecked and removed. But the place created by the architect is an illusion, begotten by the visible expression of a feeling, sometimes called an 'atmosphere.' This kind of place disappears if the house is destroyed, or changes radically if the building undergoes any violent alteration."[6] Here is the key to the true meaning of spectacle. It is what Langer calls "virtual space," that is, the imaginary world in which the action of the play takes place. Individual design elements like composition, sequence, or balance are swallowed up by functions, transformed into this imaginary space, and these functions are the true concern of the designer rather than a grab bag of separate elements. Actually, the imaginary, atmospheric space is a function of the stage itself (i.e., the real space being used), plus the creations of the designer, plus the language in the script, plus the performances of the actors. By talking softly and moving about furtively, actors can make a room seem looming and ominous; if they change and talk forcefully and move about confidently, the atmosphere will become more relaxed and friendly, even without a single set or lighting change. Our response to a setting depends strongly on the nature of the characters who inhabit it. Ibsen often exploits this effect, by introducing new characters or changed characters who alter the audience's attitude toward the setting: Nora's "doll house" seems warm and cozy at the beginning of the play but in the final scene becomes petty and stifling; Hilda Wangel enters Halvard Solness's plain, practical workshop and transforms it through the force of her presence into a mystical world of elves and trolls and "harps in the air." While it is common for textbooks to talk of design as being divisible into this or that group of elements, or the stage setting itself as having the three usages of decoration, establishing locale, or creating an illusion of reality, in actuality all such purposes or aspects are superseded by the idea of the creation of an imaginary world. Aristotle's approach cannot make allowance for the imaginary world, because that is a synthetic rather than analytical concept; "virtual space" cannot be broken down into, say, six kinds of compositions or three kinds of balance without destroying its very essence, which is an *interrelation* among elements rather than a collection of isolated parts.

Consider also "thought": while Aristotle does treat this rhetorically, rather than as just the handing over of ideas from playwright to audience, the very fact of its isolation has led subsequent theorists to conceive of thought in the latter way. In fact, this is the source of much of the prejudice in the theatre against literary criticism; it is commonly believed that criticism consists primarily of expounding the "meaning" of a play—that is, criticism is confused with philosophizing. Michel St.-Denis writes of a production of *Hamlet*: "At the end my French friend asked me, 'Do you think they [the audience] understand?' 'What,' I replied. 'The meaning of the play, the philosophy.' 'Oh,' I went on, 'certainly not. They have listened to the story which has unfolded in front of them as if it were a chronicle, in keeping with their traditions. They are fascinated by poetry, by sound, by rhythm.' "[7] Like Aristotle, St.-Denis is ranking the elements of Tragedy, although in a different order; he implies that poetry, sound, and rhythm have primary importance, while meaning is just a minor element that the average theatregoer might as well ignore. A reviewer once said that Bernard Shaw gave his audiences sugar-coated pills; the audience ate the sugar and spat out the rest. But of course meaning is not something that can be simply discarded. It is part and parcel of poetry, sound, and rhythm—it is impossible to respond to them without responding to meaning as well. Just try listening to a performance in a strange language and see how much there is to "poetry" in the abstract! And just what is this "philosophy" of *Hamlet* that St.-Denis and his friend talk about so casually? A moral lesson on obeying one's father? An existential treatise on meaninglessness of life? Polonius's epigrams? All are certainly meanings to be found in the playscript, but all are profoundly affected by their context. Polonius's little sermon to Laertes, for example, actually contains a lot of sound advice; only in the context of the corruption at court, and Polonius's own intriguing, does it seem phony. Something is rotten in the state of Denmark, and, alas, it is goodness. Even the "To be or not to be" speech is not a direct expression of a philosophy, because the *real* question at that moment is "to kill or not to kill Claudius," and Hamlet is avoiding it. A play simply does not have an extractable meaning the way a scientific treatise does; a play can only be understood as an interconnected whole. Aristotle's rhetorical approach points in this direction, but it does not take care of situations where, for example, a character unwittingly says what he does not mean, and, more important, it does not take care of situations where the play as a whole says something different from what is said by any single character. *Hamlet,* in the end, does not mean any of the individual meanings found in it. All the characters (even Polonius) are struggling to find meaning in the play, and the philosophical speeches they toss out are nothing more than incomplete attempts to that end. The total meaning is not to be found in the attempts themselves, but rather has something to do with the very fact of attempting, both the inevitability and the futility of it.

Or, consider "character": nineteenth-century criticism shows us the danger of considering character out of context. In Book XV, Aristotle does the same kind of thing: character must be good (but not too good, he implied earlier), show propriety, be true to life, be consistent. But even accepting that these are valuable attributes in characterization, where do they arise? Not just in the character's own speeches and actions, as Aristotle states: "Any speech or action that manifests moral purpose of any kind will be expressive of character: the character will be good if the purpose is good" (xv.1). For is not Othello's purpose good, or Brand's, or the Inquisitor's in Shaw's *St. Joan?* And is it not, again, context that shows their goodness to be, actually, evil? Alfred Harbage has written of Iago's character: "We begin to realize that his 'character' is being determined not simply by what he does but by the 'character' of the one to whom he does it. Then our eyes shift to Desdemona, and we discern a special kind of consistency. If what he does to Othello is inadequately motivated, what he does to Desdemona is not motivated at all. From her he has suffered not even fancied wrongs. But although she trusts him so fully that she turns to him for help, he destroys her without mercy. *Our conception of the 'character' of Iago derives in large measure from our perception of relationships.*"[8] Iago's purpose in *Othello* is, by his own light, good, justified by the wrongs he has suffered; but, when we examine the working out of that purpose with respect to the other characters, we see that it is actually evil. Harbage is here putting character back into context, and he notes what Aristotle did not—that it too, like spectacle and thought, is always a matter of an interrelationship with a larger whole.

Finally, consider "plot": For Aristotle, this was the most important of the elements of Tragedy, and perhaps of all drama. At first, Aristotle defines plot as "the arrangement of the incidents" (vi.6). So far, so good; this is a simple, neutral definition, like his definition of Tragedy itself, that is applicable to *all* playscripts rather than just an ideal few. It is also Structuralist in stressing a pattern made by the parts rather than the parts individually, an "arrangement" of incidents rather than incidents of a particular type. Unfortunately, this is the definition no one ever remembers, because Aristotle goes on to talk about, not an arrangement, but rather the incidents themselves, such as reversals or recognitions. Recognition is defined as "a change from ignorance to knowledge" (xi.2), and five different kinds are listed—recognition by signs, by revelations, by memory, by reasoning, and by "natural means." This is the part everyone remembers, so that university undergraduates can usually get good grades by pointing out that Macbeth's recognition of Macduff's being not "of woman born" involves both types two and four, but not the best type, which Aristotle with his penchant for ranking considers to be number five.

Thus, we have come to think of plot as a readily recognizable *thing* that can be pointed to, rather than as a variable. Modern playwrights like Bernard Shaw or August Strindberg even went so far as to insist that they wrote plays *without* plots, something that under Aristotle's basic definition ("the arrangement of the incidents") is impossible. What they meant was not that the incidents in their playscripts had no organization, since *some* arrangement always exists, but instead that their scripts lacked the particular kinds of incidents that had become standard—the hidden secrets dramatically revealed, the prop gimmicks where everything turns on what happens to a piece of paper or a glass of water, the obligatory confrontation scene between hero and villain. (Actually, such incidents often did turn up in their plays in slightly altered form, but that is another story.) The idea of plot had become so debased in the nineteenth century that people could think of it only in terms of formula. This is probably further than Aristotle ever intended to go, yet an exclusively analytical approach will always generate formulae. It would be possible to take the latter part of the *Poetics* and use it, as Francis Fergusson has described it, like a "cookbook" for writing a playscript. And, as with all formula approaches to art, one could easily write a bad playscript that followed the recipe perfectly, or a good one that broke every rule.

What is needed is to return to Aristotle's basic definition of plot, the arrangement of the incidents, which is not a formula but a description of a process, fitting all playscripts and not just those having certain kinds of incidents. Though deceptively simple, this definition could be highly significant. If the arrangement of incidents is more important than incidents themselves, for example, that logically leads to that other important but overlooked phrase in the *Poetics* quoted earlier, that "the structural union of the parts [is] such that, if any one of them is displaced or removed, the whole will be disjointed and disturbed" (viii.4). Here is the fundamental objection to text alteration—that when one rearranges, alters, updates, adapts, or cuts a playscript he is changing not only surface details, but also a "structural union" that is unique. If the essence of a playscript is an arrangement. then obviously to rearrange is to destroy. I said earlier that I had my own Aristotle, and here he is. Unfortunately, he does not develop the "arrangement" idea beyond what occurs in Book VIII.

In the great tradition of Aristotelian commentators, I shall consider how he might have developed it. First, since it is a neutral definition, what is wanted are *terms for analysis*, rather than a *particular* analysis, which is the direction Aristotle takes. Furthermore, these terms must not imply individual things or "parts," but rather processes or "arrangements." In other words, we need terms not just for analysis but for synthesis as well. I suggest the following (and the ranking of them is *not* important):

1. Choice
2. Sequence
3. Progression
4. Duration
5. Rhythm
6. Tempo

These terms treat plot as a process occurring in space and time. Some are suggested by music, another temporal art form, and some by the unique qualities of the theatre. Since the terms are spatial and temporal, they may be of some use to the director or actor, while Aristotle's famous "parts" are really of use only to the critic. Each term requires some expansion:

1. *Choice.* The most obvious case occurs when the playscript is based on an existing myth, legend, novel, historical record, or another playscript. (By far the great majority of playscripts ever written are based on sources, rather than entirely invented by the playwright.) In this

case, it is easy to see the choices forced upon the writer by simply comparing script to source. The writer has first had to choose where to begin and where to end—the traditional "point of attack" and "conclusion" of a plot—since his source is usually more vast and lengthy than what he wants to create. It is also important which variants of a myth are drawn upon, which incidents in a story or historical record are included and which excluded, and so on. Indeed, we might distinguish between "story" and plot as anthropologists distinguish between myth and variant. Story is the raw material of the playwright and includes all the possibilities of a given subject, its characters, and its events. All versions of the Hamlet story include the father's call for revenge, Hamlet's feigning of madness, and his killing of the usurper-king. (It should be noted, however, that the situation might not be so simple—there may be *no* elements common to all variants, for as Wittgenstein once said, it may be that no one strand runs the full length of a thread.) But the father might call for revenge by crying "Hamlet, revenge!" like a fishwife, as we are told was the case in Shakespeare's immediate source, or he might speak through an oracle, or write a letter while he was dying, or merely be a figment of Hamlet's imagination, or any of dozens of other possibilities. Shakespeare had to choose among all these—a wide range of possibilities, but not an unlimited one. By examining Shakespeare's choice, the critic may be able to divine the meaning of this particular *Hamlet*. The use of a letter would have pushed the plot in the direction of simple naturalism, like a TV murder mystery, while using a dream or hallucination would have set up a psychoanalytic study of the central character. But the use of a ghost is odd, especially since it is used so little—where is the ghost at the end, for example? Shakespeare's choice has set up an ambiguous conflict in the play between the natural and the supernatural—a supernatural we cannot completely understand yet cannot dismiss as nonexistent either.

It might seem extrinsic to ask of a plot what there might have been otherwise. In fact it *would* be extrinsic if the critic stopped with the analytical part, merely cataloguing the possible choices for the call for revenge and noting which one Shakespeare actually took. What the analytical part must do is lead the critic further, force him to ask questions rather than just supply him with a pat set of answers. Ultimately, we must know not just "what are the choices?" but "what is the significance of this particular choice?" Otherwise, the critic is just spinning his wheels.

As long as it does not become an end in itself, it is often useful to consider what might have occurred instead of what actually does occur in a plot. Plays often depend for their effect on the audience's expectations. These expectations may be based on extrinsic knowledge (the ancient Greeks' intimate knowledge of Homer, for example, would have affected their response to any play based on the *Iliad* or *Odyssey*), but they may also be intrinsic to the script. In Sophocles' *Oedipus Tyrannus*, for example, it turns out that there is a discrepancy between Oedipus's remembrance of the killing of the man at the crossroads and the official story of the killing of Laius as it is known in Thebes. Oedipus says: "You said that he [the peasant who escaped from the incident] spoke of highway *robbers* who killed Laius. Now if he uses the same number, it was not I who killed him. One man cannot be the same as many. But if he speaks of a man traveling alone, then clearly the burden of guilt inclines toward me" (ll.842–846).[9] Oedipus demands that the peasant be sent for, to establish the truth, but when the man appears at line 925, *Oedipus never asks him about this discrepancy*. The powerful expectation that this was going to be a murder mystery whose resolution depended on evidence, in the fashion of an Agatha Christie play, is unfulfilled. Critics have attempted various explanations for this (including, alas, simple ineptitude on the part of Sophocles), but suffice it to say that it is very revealing of Oedipus's character. Again, in *Hamlet* the plot sets up numerous expectations— that Hamlet will seek quick and just revenge, that he will use a play to establish Claudius's guilt once and for all, that Polonius will observe Hamlet with a view to his cure, that Hamlet will be killed in England, and, finally, that Claudius will have Hamlet neatly dispatched in the fencing scene. In each case, something very different happens from what was expected. In a plot, what is not there may be as important as what is, just as rests are important in music.

But equally important, at least for the theatre, is the choice between putting scenes on or off the stage. Choice in the sense of "what is not there" exists for all literary forms, but choice in the sense of "seen or unseen" is an important question only for the stage. Film, with its great spatial flexibility, tends simply to show *all* important scenes. Indeed, when a play is turned into a film, the usual procedure is to "open it out" for the new medium, showing all the settings and events that were merely talked about in the play. In a novel or short story, it does not really matter very much whether the author describes some event directly, or indirectly through the mouth of a character who is talking at another time and place. The act of imagination is the same for the reader; he forms a new construct of time and space based on the new description, which is just what he has been doing all along anyway. When Marlowe, the narrator, spins a yarn in one of Conrad's novels which turns out to last for the whole book, we simply forget about him most of the time and forget entirely the place where he is supposed to be talking and the characters he is supposed to be talking to. On stage, by contrast, it would be a matter of great importance whether we continued to see Marlowe and just heard the story, or saw the story without his telling it, or somehow saw both the story enacted and Marlowe speaking simultaneously.

The analyst of drama must therefore note very carefully not only which incidents are included and which excluded in a plot, but also whether the included incidents are shown or merely alluded to. Chekhov is famous for putting major incidents offstage in his plays—the suicide at the end of *The Seagull*, the duel in *The Three Sisters*, the auction of the estate in *The Cherry Orchard*. In most cases they are the very scenes that a lesser dramatist would definitely place onstage. Chekhov really turns melodrama inside out, showing only a group of people chatting and drinking tea while the blood and thunder is taking place elsewhere. This led some critics to believe that his plays had no plots at all; actually, a Scribe or Sardou could have taken the same stories and, by reversing what was and was not shown, made them into standard melodramas. Chekhov's vision of life is one in which spectacular events do indeed occur, but so imbedded in trivia that we hardly notice them; he shows this primarily through the technique of choice.

2. *Sequence*. Naturally, the order in which incidents are shown is important. As an artistic variable, however, this has been of less importance to drama than to film, which has made great use of the flashback technique. Except for the Expressionists, playwrights have generally restricted themselves to chronological ordering. Even this, however, often allows for some alternatives. In *Macbeth*, for example, it is obvious that the killing of Duncan must occur before Macbeth

becomes king, and Macbeth must become king before anyone can depose him, if Shakespeare is to follow a chronological sequence. But there are numerous minor incidents in the playscript that could be rearranged without violating chronology: the first two scenes could be reversed, for example, so that the play began with the Bleeding Sergeant's description of Macbeth's valor, followed by the "When shall we three meet again" scene with the witches, which would then blend into their meeting with Macbeth and Banquo. Shakespeare's method is to bracket the description of Macbeth with the witches' two scenes; this casts a pall over what would otherwise be straightforwardly heroic. In other words, rearranging sequence actually rearranges meaning.

3. *Progression.* Stanislavski speaks of the action of a character, and Francis Fergusson of the action of an entire play, as moving toward some objective, "the working out of a motive to its end in success or failure." Similarly, Susanne Langer speaks of the essence of drama being a "virtual future," in which the future is always imminent in the present action being shown:

> Drama, though it implies past actions (the "situation"),
> moves not toward the present, as narrative does, but toward
> something beyond; it deals essentially with commitments and
> consequences. Persons, too, in drama are purely agents—
> whether consciously or blindly, makers of the future. This
> future, which is made before our eyes, gives importance to the
> very beginnings of dramatic acts, i.e. to the motives from which
> the acts arise, and the situations in which they develop; the
> making of it is the principle that unifies and organizes the con-
> tinuum of stage action. It has been said repeatedly that the
> theatre creates a perpetual present moment; but it is only a
> present filled with its own future that is really dramatic.[10]

Thus, progression is the way in which an incident foreshadows another incident or, conversely, the way in which a future incident reflects the earlier one. The first three scenes from *Macbeth* form a simple but effective progression leading up to Macbeth's actual entrance: the first scene suggests that he is doomed, the second that he is about to receive extraordinary honors. By the time he actually arrives on stage (one of the most demanding entrances an actor ever has to face!), the audience is in a state of heightened expectation and conflicting emotion. But progression need not involve contiguous scenes—the blind Teiresias in *Oedipus Tyrannus* foreshadows the blind Oedipus at the end of the play, after several intervening scenes. The important point is that incidents do not exist just for themselves but are always reflecting other incidents.

Bertolt Brecht insisted that in his, Epic, theatre the scenes did exist for themselves, rather than as part of a progression. Anyone who has tried rearranging scenes in one of his plays knows that he was wrong. Even he generally followed strict chronology in his plots and avoided flashbacks; but, more important, he set up sequences like the deaths of the three children in *Mother Courage* (first the clever one, then the stupid one, then the dumb one) that are clearly progressive in effect. Progression remains a powerful technique for the playwright—indeed, if we believe Stanislavski, Fergusson, and Langer, a *sine qua non* for drama.

4. *Duration.* By this I mean the length of an incident, in the sense of both real chronological time and psychological weighting. Duration can be considered a kind of *choice*—it is important not only which incidents are chosen, and which are placed on stage, but also how long or important an incident is made. Chekhov not only places major incidents offstage; he also keeps references to them very brief, unlike, for example, the classical and neoclassical playwrights who employed long-winded messengers. Racine stretched two dozen lines in the Aeneid into a five-act play, *Andromache.* Marlowe in *Dr. Faustus* gives great length and emotional weight to the first and last incidents in his plot, the selling of Faustus's soul and his damnation. The intervening scenes of Faustus's adventures over twenty years are treated briefly and perfunctorily. (If you have read the playscript, you probably cannot even remember them.) One can easily imagine a lesser playwright handling the story the other way around; the temptation for directors who stage the script is always to enhance the scenes of Faustus's adventures with magnificent scenery, gorgeous costumes, and ingenious stage effects. But even if not a single word in the script is changed, such an approach would change its nature drastically, making Faustus's damnation seem a cheap price to pay for a life of thrills

and excitement. The adventure scenes should be brief and tawdry. Simply through *duration*, Marlowe is making a statement about the vanity of earthly powers. To alter his emphasis is to alter the play at a very deep level.

5. *Rhythm.* As with progression, this term refers to relations among incidents but is more simply concerned with the direct relation between two that are contiguous. Susanne Langer has pointed out that rhythm need not imply regular recurrence: "The essence of rhythm is the preparation of a new event by the ending of a previous one. A person who moves rhythmically need not repeat a single motion exactly. His movements, however, must be complete gestures, so that one can sense a beginning, intent, and consummation, and see in the last of one the condition and indeed the rise of another. Rhythm is the setting-up of new tensions by the resolution of former ones."[11] With rhythm, then, we are concerned with the *transitions* between incidents. Common types of such transitions in drama are *augmentation*, *diminution*, *alternation*, and *tension/release*. I have already spoken of Shakespeare's use of alternation in *Macbeth*, where he alternates the witches' scenes with a scene describing Macbeth's heroics instead of running the witches' scenes together. But *Macbeth*, one of the most rhythmic plays ever written, provides excellent examples of all four types of transition.

Augmentation (commonly called "building" in theatre jargon) occurs through the first two scenes, setting up the encounter between the witches and Macbeth. The witches' first scene plunges us into the mysterious, violent world that dominates the first half of the play. The second scene builds from that into the exciting reports of the Bleeding Sergeant; here the tone of the verse is elevated from the witches' simple, rough speech to a high epic style through the use of such epic conventions as epithets, inverted syntax, and extravagant similes and metaphors like the one comparing Fortune to a "rebel's whore." There is a further augmentation as the Sergeant describes the second part of the battle, with hyperboles like "cannons overcharged with double cracks," and "doubly redoubled." The scene reaches a peak at the next incident, as Angus and Ross enter in haste to describe the final victory. There is then a slight release of tension in the final incident, in which Duncan announces that he will reward Macbeth for his valor by giving him the title of the conquered traitor, the Thane of Cawdor. The reintroduction of the witches in scene 3, however, starts the tension building again, up to the first major peak in the play, which is the hailing of Macbeth as a future king.

There is then a series of *diminutions* through to the end of scene 4. All seems well at this point—a victory won, peace restored, honors gained, a banquet in the offing. The entrance of Lady Macbeth, however, provides a strong contrast or *alternation*; indeed, if she can be seen as a kind of witch herself (she is first seen reading about them and then calls upon demons to possess her), we begin to see a kind of pattern of alternation, between the supernatural (and female) world of the witches and the natural (and male) world of Duncan's court. Lady Macbeth's opening speeches are powerful, evil, and terrifying. This peak is sustained for a fairly long time, but the scene ends with a diminution:

> *Macbeth.* We will speak further.
> *Lady Macbeth.*   Only look up clear.
>   To alter favor ever is to fear.
>   Leave all the rest to me.   (I.v.69–71)

This diminishing continues into the low point at the beginning of the next scene, as Duncan enters the castle:

> *King.* This castle hath a pleasant seat. The air
>   Nimbly and sweetly recommends itself
>   Unto our gentle senses.   (I.vi.1–3)

But augmentation begins again in scene 7, leading from the plotting to the second major peak in the play, which is the actual murder. This is almost immediately followed by the *release* into the drunken porter scene.

The traditional concept of "comic relief" is thus an example of a kind of *tension/release*. The idea of comic relief has fallen into disrepute generally, but, nevertheless, despite whatever other functions the drunken porter scene may have here (and critics have noted many important thematic and symbolic ones), a release from tension is still its major effect. This is not just a concession to the audience's weakness; the entire play has a pattern of waves, of action and reaction, sin and retribution, rising and falling. There are many other examples of tension/release in the play that are not comic at all, such as in the very last scene. The final major peak has just occurred with the killing of Macbeth; now the soldiers relax, discuss the battle, contemplate the future. There is nothing funny about it—there is even sadness in the description of Young Siward's death—yet the scene is a release that serves the same function as, and in fact is a parallel to, the scene of the drunken porter. The play actually moves in two waves of murder and retribution, each in a general series of augmentations with occasional alternations, and each ending in a scene of release.

In producing a play like *Macbeth*, the director (and the critic, if he wants to be of any help to the director) must be sensitive to its rhythmic patterns. Often one sees productions with reasonably good actors, carefully chosen sets and costumes, and a general smoothness and polish that are still terribly dull to watch because of a plodding sameness throughout. A common error is to play the low points far too intensely—I have seen productions of *Macbeth*, for example, that made the drunken porter into a zany clown, instead of the sodden fellow he actually is in the text. Much to the frustration of the actor and director, the scene did not get many laughs, because what is essential at that point is a release, rather than another augmentation. In theatre slang, one cannot "top" something as big as Duncan's murder; instead, one has to undercut it. Again, the chilling horror of Lady Macbeth's opening scene ("Unsex me here," etc.) will not be as effective as it should be if the previous scene, where Duncan is passing out honors, is played with stiff and gorgeous pomp instead of easy, jovial camaraderie. Yet the former is almost standard, no doubt reflecting the belief that Duncan is a king after all, and kings are always grand and formal. Or, again, the actress playing Lady Macbeth usually performs the sleepwalking scene as a histrionic *tour de force* (I can recall one great lady of the stage ringing the rafters with "The Thane of Fife had a wife. Where is she *no-o-o-o-w*!"), when what is required is diminution; Lady Macbeth goes out not with a bang but a whimper.

6. *Tempo.* Tempo is a function of the number of incidents occurring per unit of time. It should not be confused, in performance, with mere speed of playing time. Directors who work by the clock are gen-

What Aristotle Might Have Said

erally unsuccessful in pacing a performance; cutting minutes off running time by rushing the actors usually produces a blur, which only makes the performance drag more than ever. In other words, rushing creates a situation in which there appear to be fewer distinct incidents; thus the ratio of the number of incidents to the amount of time is decreased even though time is shortened. Bernard Shaw once wrote in this regard that, when people say that a scene is too slow, "the remedy in nine cases out of ten is for the actors to go slower and bring out the meaning better by contrasts of tone and speed."[12] It seems paradoxical that the audience's impression of speed can be increased by playing a scene slower, but the reason is that tempo is actually a function of *two* variables—both clock time *and* the number of incidents that occur—rather than of playing time alone.

For the same reason, tempo should not be confused, in a playscript, with length. *Macbeth* is a short playscript (2,113 lines versus 3,776 for *Hamlet*), but that is not why it seems fast in performance; it is rather because so many incidents tumble over one another in the short space of time. Actually, *Hamlet* is a fast-tempo playscript also, even when performed uncut, because it is so rich in incident. Furthermore, when it *is* cut for performance, out of regard for the audience's bedtime or whatever, it often seems slower, unless it is trimmed very carefully, speech by speech. To cut, say, the entire Fortinbras scene (IV.iv) will not make the play seem to be moving any faster, because, although time is reduced, so too an important incident is removed. (And it goes without saying that one is removing an important symbolic element from the play as well.)

Macbeth again provides an excellent example of the artistic use of tempo. Although the main body of the playscript is very fast, there is an exceedingly slow scene in IV.iii. It is the longest scene in the play (240 lines), but things pick up after the entrance of the Doctor at line 140. Until then, there have really been only two incidents, performed simultaneously: Macduff has convinced Malcolm to lead the rebellion against the tyrant Macbeth, while Malcolm has elaborately tested Macduff by pretending to be a scoundrel and observing Macduff's reaction. This gives a ratio of incident to line of 1:70; the scene in which Duncan is murdered (II.ii), by contrast, has 73 lines but contains three murders, the shriek of an owl, the voice that seemed to cry "sleep no more," the business with the daggers, the knocking, and the cover-up plan ("Get on your nightgown"). Even if the murders are considered as a single incident, that still gives a ratio six times as high as that in IV.iii. For this reason, directors are often tempted to trim the later scene, but there is a reason for its slowness. In the first part of the play, leading up to the murder, everything involves quick thinking, improvisation, boldness; the final part, leading up to the killing of Macbeth, involves instead care, caution, and thorough planning. It is interesting that both involve deception: Macbeth and his wife pretend to be good in order to do evil ("False face must hide what the false heart doth know" [I.vii.82]), while Malcolm pretends to be evil in order to do good. The slowness of retribution is not a flaw but rather a part of the play's effect: in the first part, our reaction is that things are out of hand, happening too fast, while in the final part we feel that they are moving too slowly, that Macbeth will never be deposed, that possibly there is no force for good operating in the universe. The "Stop! Stop!" feeling of the beginning is replaced by one of "Go! Go!" It is something that can only be felt in an actual performance, or at least an imagined one, but it is an important feeling that expresses a view of how the world works, of the nature of evil versus the nature of God's retribution. Both critic and director must be sensitive to Shakespeare's use of tempo in this playscript and not attempt to speed up the slow passage in performance any more than one would speed up a slow passage in a piece of music.

With all these terms—choice, sequence, progression, duration, rhythm, tempo—I have tried to avoid a suggestion of a rigid analytical system. They are neither abstract "categories" nor a how-to-do-it procedure for staging plays. Their order is unimportant, their meanings often overlap, and in many cases other terms could be substituted for them. Their purpose is to channel the intellect and imagination of the critic or director in confronting a playscript, to make them see spatial and temporal considerations as an integral part of it rather than a "spectacle" to be added on afterward. In other words, the terms are intended to make one consider a playscript as something to be performed. With both Aristotle and the modern performance theorists discussed in the last chapter, the tendency has been to treat the script as something only to be read. Because the Platonists had set the grounds for debate, Aristotle adopted a strategy that seems to view performance as hardly more than an accident, since for him reading alone is adequate for a tragedy to "reveal its power." The performance theorists (with the exception of Brecht) tend to view the *script* as an accident, a literary form that developed by chance out of the theatre, almost as an excrescence. They really would not disagree with Aristotle's view but would instead see it as irrelevant to their concerns. Let Aristotle and his followers read all the scripts they want to, but don't let them imagine that such reading has anything to do with the art of the theatre, would probably be their attitude. No one has really looked at a playscript as something *having spatial and temporal elements implicit in it*, to be projected into a performance.

5

Text & Performance

The relationship of playtext to performance, as a general problem, has hardly been examined. Both literary critics, from Aristotle onward, and performance theorists like those discussed in Chapter III tend to ignore the relationship or treat it only perfunctorily. Are script and performance essentially the *same* art form, which might be called the conservative view, or are they completely different, as in the more modern view? Or is there some third alternative possible? Before considering specific methods of analyzing playscripts for production, one should have a clear idea of just what the connection is between the two.

The conservative and modern views, limited as they are, might be called the "symphony" model and the "cinema" model. The symphony model is very popular among literary critics, particularly when they are expressing their exasperation with performances they have seen. Norman Holland, for example, writes: "I can count on the toes of one foot the productions of Shakespeare that have really been exciting and wonderful experiences in the theatre, and I suspect most Shakespeareans would, if pressed, admit no more. This is truly an astonishing situation—as though, to shift arts, there were not an orchestra in the country that could play a Beethoven symphony properly. And is that so farfetched an analogy? . . . Is producing a play so different a thing from performing a symphony?"[1] The symphony model views the playscript and the performance as essentially the same thing. One is the direct mirror of the other; while of course variations occur from production to production, because of different actors and settings, such variations are of minor significance. To use another analogy, they are of no more importance than the differences between two houses built from the same set of blueprints—there may be changes in colors, variations in trim, even minor alterations in construction because of site differences, but they are essentially the same house. As for the foremen and laborers (analogous to the director, designer, and actors), they are neutral and interchangeable—interesting only when they are incompetent! In this view, performance is in no way creative. Good productions of plays are the result, as with an orchestra, of a talented company, an intelligent and scholarly director, a good auditorium, an adequate budget, and perhaps something intangible like spirit or enthusiasm, but nothing more. Bad performances can result from the lack of any of these but, from the point of view of a Shakespeare scholar like Holland, more often seem to arise from simple stubbornness or stupidity. After all, everything one needs is written down in the playscript.

The cinema model is widely heard among proponents of the new theatre, who see performance as an independent art form, often requiring no script at all. Such practitioners prefer to use the word *scenario* for the script, stressing that, like a film scenario, the playscript is just one variable among many in the theatre, including performers, stage (or "space"), and designer. As in a film, the director is really the guiding force, not the playwright, and the script is likely to be changed at any time under the director's guidance, in the same way that an actor can change his performance or a designer his settings. Playwrights like Sam Shepard or Megan Terry, who write for such companies, work with the group in rehearsal, changing the scenario as the director or actors might require, often even taking their basic material from actors' improvisations. As for dead playwrights, well, the great ones were all men of the theatre, weren't they? If Shakespeare were writing for today, he would be happy to go through the same process as a Shepard or a Terry; since he is dead, the director can do his rewriting for him. The director is really doing the playwright a service, preventing his play from being performed as a stale "museum piece." In films, after all, some of the biggest disasters have occurred when the director has treated his source, such as a great play or novel, *too* reverentially; and some of the greatest films have occurred when the adaptation was extensive. And, if this is true of the film, how much more true it must be of the theatre, which is a *living* art form. The theatre's effect, so the argument goes, must always be immediate, sensuous, direct; the greatest sin it can commit is to be outdated.

The fact is that neither the symphony model nor the cinema model is adequate for describing the relationship of playtext to performance. A symphonic score, particularly as developed in the nineteenth century, implies an exact, one-to-one correspondence with performance. Human nature being what it is, two conductors can disagree on an interpretation, or a composer might not always be as clear about his intentions as the performers would like, but at least in theory everything in performance is *directly* controlled by the score. In other words, in theory there is only one way of playing the music, even though in practice musicians might differ as to what that way is. Anything in performance that does not come from the score *does not count* as a part of the artistic experience. The fact that one violinist is fat and another thin is supposed to be ignored by the audience—or it is to be neutralized, which is why musicians wear a standard costume of evening dress, or band players wear uniforms even when they are not in the military. As for the stage itself, only the acoustic properties are considered; otherwise it is kept as bare and neutral as possible, so that the audience can ignore it also. While it is fun to watch the musicians play their instruments and there is a certain element of excitement at being present at a live performance, these things too, strictly speaking, are not part of the music, which can just as well be listened to on the radio or from a record.

It is obvious that a theatrical performance of a playscript is drastically different from a symphonic performance in every one of these respects. Although in the nineteenth century playwrights, like composers, became more precise in specifying their intentions, in their case through more elaborate stage directions, playscripts are still far less exact than musical scores. Even Brecht in his model books could not achieve the precision that a composer can, and his were created *after* the fact of production. To create in advance a full "score" for *Hamlet*, for example, that would specify sizes, shapes, colors, inflections, tones of voice, word emphasis, rhythms, durations of pauses, placement of actors on stage, movements, tempos, and so on would require thousands of pages and would still be less precise than the score of Beethoven's Fifth Symphony. (It would also be so difficult and frustrating to perform that no one would touch it.) Furthermore, although there might be one best way for a particular company to perform a playtext at a particular time, in a particular theatre, and at a particular period in their development, there is obviously more than one way of performing it in general. Roger Gross has pointed out that a playscript has what he calls parameters and tolerances—that is, what must occur in performance, and what must not—but that within these margins there is a great deal of choice possible. The script of *Hamlet*, for example, does not say (at least directly) whether Hamlet's hair coloring is blond or dark or red. But, on the other hand, the actor's hair coloring will have an effect in performance. It is part of the artistic experience of the performance and not something to be ignored or neutralized. Furthermore, the stage itself is far from neutral in theatrical performance. It is altered for every production and often altered many times within the same production through set and light changes, because the setting too is part of the performance, and an important one at that. A change in setting, even with the same actors performing in exactly the same way, will profoundly affect the quality of a scene. This is why touring of play productions is always so difficult, while the touring of symphony orchestras is standard practice. With an orchestra, the difficulties in changing auditoriums are primarily technical—restoring balance, finding the proper overall volume, and so on. Changing the theatre for a production of a play has similar technical problems, plus additional ones of lighting and sight lines, but the main difficulties are not technical but aesthetic. I once directed a play that was set in a small basement room, where a kidnap victim was being held. The production worked very well in an intimate theatre with a small stage—so well, in fact, that the production was later moved to a much larger auditorium with an enormous stage. Adaptation of the set and blocking was fairly easy, but the whole feeling of confinement, so important to what was happening in the play, was lost on the large stage, and the sense of conspiracy diminished when the actors were forced to project to the back of a large auditorium instead of speaking in soft whispers. The result was a very different play—and, unfortunately, a much less successful one.

Finally, the audience is a major factor in play production. In some kinds of musical performance, such as rock concerts, audience involvement is important as well, but in general a symphony orchestra performs as if the audience were not present. Indeed, it often literally is not there, in the case of broadcasts or recording sessions. But in the theatre, even in a proscenium production of a Naturalistic play, the audience is very much a part of the overall work of art. Laughter, applause, and even silence (as opposed to shuffling and coughing) communicate to the performers and affect what they do. An insensitive audience can vulgarize a play, by forcing the actors to exaggerate the obvious effects and skip quickly over the more subtle elements, while an alert and responsive audience can draw out elements that the performers did not even know were there. The university at which I teach once put together a production of Ben Jonson's *Every Man in His Humour*. One of the least known of Jonson's works, it is loaded with Elizabethan slang and other obscurities, which were presented almost unchanged. It was simply too much, even for a university audience, but the play was later presented at the World Shakespeare Congress in Vancouver in 1971. The audience of Shakespeare scholars, who could understand the conventions and the jargon, enjoyed it immensely, but even more interesting was the fact that the actors also gave a much better performance than they had ever done. They were more relaxed, their timing was improved because they could count on laughs, they could play at a faster overall tempo, and, most of all, they could commit themselves fully to their characterizations without fear of being misunderstood. It had really become a different play, and a much better one.

In every way, then, there is simply more going on in a theatrical performance than can be programmed into a script. A symphonic score aims at only one variable—sound. A playscript aims at sound, plus variables of actor, theatre building, lighting, setting, costume, make-up, and even audience. Of course it can make some allowances for all these, but it is impossible to do so completely. A film, on the other hand, runs to the opposite extreme from a symphony. It has far *too many* variables for a scenario to be considered the equivalent of a playscript. A film has all the variables of a play (except the live audience), plus additional ones of camera work and editing. Often these things are not indicated in the scenario at all but are simply added in afterwards. And editing can make a tremendous difference—Robert Altman's *McCabe and Mrs. Miller* was made from a scenario entitled *The Presbyterian Church Wager*; the plot concerned a man forced to build a church as a result of losing a bet in a poker game. In the finished film, one will still see this church, occasionally, as well as several poker games, but the original plot, like the title, has vanished completely. Well along in the shooting, Altman decided that he could make a better film from the same material, primarily through editing it differently.

But even if a scenarist could allow completely for camera work and editing (thus producing a script even bulkier than our hypothetical "score" for *Hamlet*), there is another reason why a playscript cannot be considered to be like a scenario. *The method by which films are made makes directorial control possible to a far greater degree than in a play*. Scenes can be reshot until just the right one is made. Editing can arrange scenes in an infinite number of ways, even adding shots from different films if the director can get away with it. (Movie companies in the nineteen-twenties made money by simply chopping up old Charlie Chaplin films and re-editing them into new ones.) It is often said that film is essentially a director's medium, which is not necessarily so, but which is always at least *possibly* so. In the theatre, for all the talk of the rise of the director, the trend toward the director as creator, and so on, directorial control is simply not possible to the same extent as in film. The stage director can rehearse a scene hundreds of times, but he cannot be sure that the actors will always play it the way they did at the final rehearsal. (Indeed, since the theatre is a live medium he can be sure that in some ways they will not.) He can use stage groupings to provide focus, but he cannot simply move the camera away from an actor who insists on hogging the scene. He can juggle scenes in the playtext, but he cannot edit *after* the performance, maintaining the individual parts unchanged. Each new rearrangement will have to be rehearsed and learned by the actors (assuming they agree to it), who will adapt their performances to the change. But, most important, the director sits in the auditorium during a performance, while the actors go through on their own, night after night. The stage director may be a tyrant during rehearsals, give notes after every performance, and even call postopening rehearsals, but the stage has still come to belong to the actors; the bits and pieces of film after the shooting belong very much to the film director (unless, as used to be the rule in Hollywood, the editor is independent of him). "The arrangement of the incidents," in the full sense discussed in the last chapter, comes in the end under the power of the film director-editor but will always elude the control of a stage director who tries the same approach.

Thus, the trouble with the "concept" approach to stage directing is that the director does not have enough power to impose his concept. In a way, the trouble with most concept productions is that there is not *enough* concept. This is why concept directors notoriously excuse themselves by blaming their actors, their budget, their designer, anything in fact, rather than their own approach to directing, which goes directly against the live and independent nature of stage performance. Somehow, their ideals are never quite realized. If only they had had more money, or could have used the actor they had in mind, or if the sequins had been sewed on in time. Ah, what a performance you would have seen then!

Since, basically, the stage director cannot provide the artistic control necessary for a good performance, the way a film director can, that control must come from the playscript. It is worth considering why scripts were ever invented in the first place. The proponents of the new theatre are quite right in pointing out that, historically, performance preceded written texts. But the conclusion they draw, that scripts are a kind of excrescence, is the opposite of what is obvious—that scripts were found necessary to provide the element of control in production. Of course, good performances can take place without a script. Monkeys typing at random will eventually write all of Shakespeare, and the Rorschach ink blots always look like *something*. But with a playscript one greatly increases the odds. The actors get a fixed basis, rooted in their memory, from which their performances can grow. The performance as a whole can have direction, development, focus. The director's coaching, given at odd times over a long period of rehearsal, is far less likely to provide these things. It is no accident that successful theatres in all times and places have always ended up, even when they began in improvisation, by using scripts. Greek Tragedy, according to Aristotle, began as improvisation; it did not remain so, and, after the experience of Aeschylus, Sophocles, and Euripides, never went back to it. The Atellan farceurs and mimes of the Romans, the early medieval jongleurs and mimes, and the performers of the Italian Commedia dell'Arte similarly came to require the services of playwrights, not because they suddenly acquired a taste for "literature" but because they wanted to make their performances better. To alter a playscript, then, is really a contradiction in terms; to do so is to defeat its basic purpose.

If neither the symphony nor the cinema model is adequate for describing the relationship between text and performance, then how can the relationship be properly described? Susanne Langer has suggested, with regard to musical performance, that the player is as creative as the composer, but that the player *continues* the creative work that the composer began: "Real performance is as creative an act as composition, just as the composer's own working out of the idea, after he has conceived the greatest movement and therewith the whole commanding form, is still creative work. The performer simply carries it on."[2] This is a valuable concept. Applied to the theatre, it maintains the integrity of the script by assigning to it the "commanding form" of a performance; yet, on the other hand, it does not reduce the performer to a slave of the playwright, but rather insists on his importance as a co-creator. In other words, *interpretation and creation are not opposites*. Both are acts of intellect *and* imagination. Playwriting, for example, is not just an explosion of self-expression; the playwright, one could say, *interprets* life, through his imagination, and finds "commanding forms" in it. And anyone who has ever tried dramatic criticism knows that it is a highly imaginative act; the commanding form is not simply there waiting to be picked up and examined but must be discovered, as a function of some interpretive approach, whose very choice involves imagination. (Galileo did not create the moons of Jupiter, but it was creative of him to think of turning his telescope on the heavens.) The director and performer too must come to the script with imagination; interpretation is not simply a matter of following what is written down, as if the script were a blueprint. A construction foreman need not be sensitive to subtlety, nuance, and suggestion in interpreting blueprints (unless they were made by a terrible draftsman!), but a director or an actor or a designer cannot succeed without such sensitivity. Too much in a script is implied indirectly.

Nevertheless, Langer's formulation is still too general. Valuable though it is, her concept fails to distinguish among such possibilities as the traditional production of a playscript, the "updated" production, and the rewriting of a new playscript based on an old one. One could say, for example, that Bertolt Brecht was simply "carrying on the creative work" in his production of *Edward II*, exploring the implications in Marlowe's text and developing them along new lines. Similarly, Richard Schechner, in abstracting elements of tyranny and violence from the text of *Macbeth* (and suppressing almost everything else) for his production of it, could be said to be carrying on the work begun by Shakespeare. In fact, it is hard to think of any example in which the director or performer would *not* be carrying on the playwright's work in some fashion; "carrying on the work" is more an external description than a basis for action.

Actually, the director or the performer carries on the creative work of the playwright, but in a *different* way. Or, one might say, he *interprets* in a different way. The playwright interprets life by selecting and shaping; his method is active. The director and performer may *not* be selective; they must take the playwright's script as a whole and *find* its essence. With respect to the script, the director and performer are *reactive* (which is not the same as being merely passive).

Roger Gross has written of what he calls the "fallacy of neutral performance." This is another way of describing what I have been calling the symphony model, in which the director and performers are passive toward the text. Gross points out that it is impossible to be completely passive toward a playscript when producing it: "The actor's figure, the way he enters the stage, the color of his hair, etc., everything perceived by the audience is interpretation whether it is so intended or not."[3] This is why neutrality is fallacious, why productions that attempt just to follow the text passively (the sort of thing directed by professors in English departments, who want to stop all this tampering with the Great Bard) invariably fail. The opposite extreme, however, might be called "the fallacy of the neutral text," in which the playscript is seen as a kind of dead thing, mere printed words as opposed to the living performance, which need something done *to* them before they can ever come alive. In other words, the fallacy of the neutral text takes an active rather than reactive approach to the text, ignoring the fact that it is not just "words, words, words," but relationships, patterns, a unity.

Here too is the problem with the contemporary playwright who works as just another member of the company, continuously revising the script throughout rehearsal, what Richard Schechner has called "the playwright as wrighter," that is, craftsman or hired hand. There is nothing wrong with playwrights being inspired by a theatre company, writing vehicles for actors, taking ideas from improvisations, even doing *some* revising after rehearsals begin. But there must come a point where the text is fixed. The performers need something tangible to react to; when actors, directors, designers, and playwrights are all trying to be reactive at once, the result is inevitably chaotic. While it is quite true that great playwrights throughout history have all been men of the theatre, with solid experience as directors and even as actors, there is no evidence that any successful playwright has ever written scripts anywhere but at his desk. (Gordon Craig once suggested that Shakespeare wrote his plays by taking well-known stories and asking members of his company to improvise them, a pleasant bit of fancy that of course has no basis in historical evidence.) This is because directors, designers, and performers, as reactive artists rather than active ones, have always sensed the need for a single commanding form, as Susanne Langer calls it, and not just a grab bag of different forms to play with.

There is always a sense in which a good playscript is a finished work. Commanding form, as opposed to a multiplicity of potential forms, is the reason why it is possible to read a play to oneself for pleasure; why it is possible to teach playscripts in a literature class separate from production, even if such teaching is incomplete; why it is possible to write books about playwrights as independent artists, and articles about the structure of their individual playscripts; why it is possible to continue to produce playscripts long after their authors are dead. These are obvious facts; they have been true since playscripts were first written; they will not disappear simply because of some new theories about theatre as a pure art form.

What is happening when we read a playscript as a thing in itself, without regard to production? Bernard Beckerman has written, "On the surface, reading plays seems to require no special preparation, but, in fact, it is as complex a process as reading a musical score and requires as much training."[4] There is an element of truth in this. Nevertheless, the very fact that ordinary people can and do read playscripts, while only specialists read musical scores or film scenarios, suggests that there is a difference. Of course, people may be reading playscripts incorrectly. It is quite possible to come to any literary work with an incorrect or limited set of methods and "read in" things that are not fully supported by the text itself. (Ibsen has probably suffered from this more than any other writer. His playscripts are *still* being read as examples of kitchen-sink Naturalism, a view that a careful reading, or even a careless but unprejudiced reading, will refute completely.) One must read a playscript with an acknowledgement of its form; a playscript is not a novel, any more than a lyric poem is a short story or an essay. It would be ridiculous for someone to say, " 'Ode to the West Wind' is a very bad story. The characterizations are weak, the plot hazy, and there is too much rhyming." But, on the other hand, this does not mean that lyric poems and short stories have nothing in common at all; they are both literary forms and thus share such techniques as allusiveness, symbolism, ambiguity. A playscript must be read with a sense of its unique attributes, but also with a sense of what it shares with other forms. Unique to playscripts is the importance of real space and real time. (Real time is important in music as well, but not in forms of literature other than drama.) With space, for example, a Thomas Hardy novel can start with an entire chapter devoted to a description of a landscape, thus setting the scene in the reader's mind so strongly that he does not forget it throughout the rest of the book. An Ibsen playscript, by contrast, will have only the briefest description of the physical background at the beginning of each act. The reader must be trained to make special note of it, or he may easily forget, for example, that during the first two and a half acts of *Ghosts* it is constantly raining. So too with time: the mad rush leading up to the murder in *Macbeth* and the agonizingly slow but accelerating retribution that follows form an important part of the artistic experience that the reader may easily miss if he has not been trained to be sensitive to the clock when reading a playscript. But, nonetheless, a playscript is a literary work, sharing qualities common to all literature that have already been discussed—complexity, ambiguity, subtlety, structural integrity—plus traditional elements like characterization or plot. It is wrong to ignore the scenario *aspects* of a playscript, but it is also wrong to ignore its differences from film scenarios and its important connections with literature.

In place of the inadequate symphony and cinema models of the playscript-performance relationship, I should like to suggest another, to be called the "sculpture model." Probably no model is completely accurate—ultimately, the playscript-performance relationship is unique to the theatre—but the sculpture model brings out some important aspects that are currently being overlooked. For the purposes of this model, it is necessary to think in terms of sculpting marble statues, and not all the various other types of sculpture that are possible. Consider this: we generally think of a sculptor as an independent, purely creative artist like a painter or a writer, but he is actually far more constrained. The size, shape, color, and texture of his block of marble—and the cost—impose far greater restraints on him than are on, say, a painter. A sculptor cannot carve something that will end up outside the dimensions of the original block; nor should he end up with something much smaller, because marble is expensive. He must find an idea, a "commanding form" that fits his particular piece. One can thus almost think of him as an interpretive artist; Michelangelo wrote of the sculptor "releasing the idea from the stone," as if the statue were there all along, and the sculptor's only job was to find it. The English sculptor Henry Moore has said that in his youth he could only afford odd blocks of marble, pieces that were broken or misshapen. It was necessary to let one lie around the studio for a while, until he found an idea that would fit. Of course, once an idea is found, it is not a matter of just imposing it, mechanically, on the marble; the stone will be found to have variations of color and texture that require revisions from the original plan, and, more important, as the work begins to emerge in reality, it will often suggest things to the sculptor that he had not thought of originally. In the final statue there will thus be an inextricable connection between the idea and the stone, so that it will often be impossible to tell whether certain details came from the sculptor's head or the marble itself. In other words, there is a dynamic rather than passive relationship between the idea and the block; the sculptor does not really *know* his idea completely and consciously until his statue shows it to him.

This interesting example suggests all kinds of analogies pertinent to the theatre. One can think, for example, of the critic as the sculptor, the stone as the playscript, the "idea" as his philosophical approach to it, and the finished statue as his interpretation. His philosophical system (say, Freudian psychology or the principles of versification) clarifies many things about the text, but its close application to the text in turn leads to revisions of his original ideas about it, so that the result in good criticism is never a simple example of some external theory, but rather an *adaptation* of it. (The most interesting part of a critical essay is usually where the theory does not quite fit the work being examined.) Or one can adapt the sculpture model to performance itself. In this case, the director is the sculptor, the playscript the idea, the theatre company (plus budget and performance space) the block of marble, and the finished production the statue. Or, again, the actor can be seen as the sculptor, the character in the text his initial idea, his own body the stone, and his performance the statue. Slowly, through the process of rehearsals, chip by chip one might say, the director releases the idea from the theatre company, an idea that "fits" it. A performance is thus always an adaptation of a text, but the adaptation is to the particular company and stage rather than to the director's ideas about life, politics, modern society, the energy crisis, capitalism, fascism, or any other externality. It is also important, clearly, that the particular playscript be chosen carefully to begin with. Not all playscripts will fit a particular company at a particular time and place; if one does not, it should not be performed at all rather than be strained and distorted. Why not find something that does work, rather than tamper with something that obviously does not? Many of the great theatre companies of the past came into their own when they found a playwright, or sometimes even a single playscript, that was apt for them. Chekhov with the Moscow Art Theatre, Synge with the Abbey, and O'Neill with the Provincetown Players provided the "commanding forms" that breathed life into companies that had hitherto had only desultory successes. This is the connection that every theatre company in North America should be seeking.

In an unsuccessful statue, it is often apparent that the artist was unable to carry through his original idea, because of his lack of skill or because the stone was unreceptive. In a good statue, one cannot distinguish the "commanding form" from the finished product; the statue just *is*. It has an independent life of its own. The final form seems to come from within the statue and be such that it could only be what it is, almost appearing obvious. Similarly, in a good production, there is no distinction between text and performance. The audience should be unable to tell which parts of the production were in the original text and which came from the director, designer, or actors, because performance is not something *added* to a text. Text and performance

have a dynamic relationship, like a partnership in which neither partner's contribution is separable from the other's. In other words, text
and performance have a *functional* relationship, similar to that between a critic's interpretive approach and a text; the director should
not *add* his interpretation to the text any more than the critic adds
his. It is easy to recognize bad criticism of the sort that involves purely
personal interpretation that is not supported by the text; much bad
play production comes from the same kind of approach, in which the
director applies an interpretation that does not fit the text at all, or
fits it only roughly. Like the bad statue that makes us all too aware
of the disparity between the sculptor's idea and the unyielding block
of stone, the bad performance of this sort makes us aware of *two* things,
a concept and a text, in an uneasy combination.

The proper relationship between text and performance can be depicted by a function, D, of the text into performance:

$$D(T) \longrightarrow P$$

Functions can have additional properties: if elements in the second
set are never paired with more than one element from the first, we
call the function "one-to-one." If the first set is "all children," for example, and the second "all fathers," the function connecting them
is *not* one-to-one, since two children can have the same father; if the
first set is "all wives," and the second "all husbands," then (at a given
point in time and excluding bigamists) the "marriage function" connecting them *is* one-to-one, since husbands can have only one wife
at a time. Further, if every element in the second set is the reflection
of *some* element in the first, we call the function "onto." The father-
children function is not onto if dead fathers are excluded but *is* onto
if they are included, since everyone has a father (unless one accepts
the possibility of virgin birth), at least to start with. If a function is
both one-to-one *and* onto, we call it a "one-to-one correspondence."
The marriage function can be considered a one-to-one correspondence
when it has the same exclusions as before. Or, one can think of two
groups of pebbles, with strings running from individual pebbles in
the first group to other individual pebbles in the second. If every pebble
in the second group has a string attached to it, the function is onto; if
no pebble has more than one string attached, the function is also one-

to-one. If both conditions apply, meaning that there is a one-to-one correspondence, that also implies that there is exactly the same number of pebbles in the two groups. (Such models tend to break down, however, in the case of infinite sets.)

We can see, therefore, that what I have been calling the "symphony model" of performance implies a relation between text and performance that is essentially a one-to-one correspondence. Everything in the performance is in the text, and every element (sound) in the performance is a reflection of a single element of notation. (Again, I am speaking of a kind of idealized nineteenth-century symphony, where everything is written down, without ambiguity.) A one-to-one correspondence is not the same thing as identity, but it has all the properties of identity, which is why it is possible to say that text and performance are essentially the same work of art. In the "cinema model," the relationship is not even a function to begin with, since elements in the first set, the scenario, will often not even appear in the second, the finished film. Even if everything does appear, the function is clearly not onto, since many things are added by the director that have no counterpart in the scenario. Nor is the function one-to-one, since, even when elements in the film are a reflection of what is in the scenario, they may reflect it only indirectly. An actor's performance, for example, will be affected in one scene by how his character is described and how he behaves in other scenes. Or the scenarist may provide a lot of background about the characters and situation which the director draws upon, as a whole, for otherwise entirely new ideas. The scenario-film relationship is traditionally a very loose one indeed.

In the case of the theatre, the relationship between text and performance, as I have described it, is definitely a function. Like a symphony, but unlike a film, everything in the text will have some counterpart in the performance, unless the director rewrites the script, in which case the *new* text generates a function. But, for the same reasons as with a film, the function is neither onto nor one-to-one. There will be things in the performance that the text does not and cannot foresee; and a good deal of the work of the director, designer, and performers, while based on the text, will draw upon it indirectly.

There is still a question, however, as to what constitutes an "element" in the text. In a musical score, the elements are simply the notes, plus the other traditional bits of musical notation. But what

about a playscript? Are the elements the words? I have been insisting
that a playtext considered artistically does not consist of piecemeal
elements like words, but of patterns or structures. The Stanislavski
approach, for example, sees the basic unit of a playscript not in individual words or even individual lines, but in "objectives," which incorporate many words and lines. Thus, the true function in a theatrical
performance is not between the text and performance directly, but
between *an interpretation of the text* and the performance. Before and
during rehearsals, the director and performers construct an interpretation of the text, *organizing the text into units that are the elements
reflected in the performance.* We therefore have a double function,
as follows:

$$D[I(S) \quad \rightarrow \quad T] \quad \rightarrow \quad P$$

Here the letter I stands for an intrinsic interpretive function as defined
in Chapter II, while D stands for the performance function that pro-
jects that interpretation into the production P. Such a function is now
one-to-one; it is still not onto, because there may be accidentals of
individual performance which in no way reflect text or interpretation.
These, however, should be minor; we now have something fairly close
to a one-to-one correspondence. Mathematicians say that such a function is an *embedding*; it is a one-to-one correspondence insofar as it is
onto the second set, which is called the function's "range." The script,
we might say, is "embedded" in the performance. In sum, *our notation
shows that a script is realized* (or embedded) *in a performance via an
interpretation, but that that interpretation is not something separate
from the script but rather itself a function on it.*

Note that, with a musical score or film scenario, there is not an intermediate, interpretive function of this sort between text and performance. While I can anticipate thousands of musicians insisting that
there *is* a good deal of interpretation necessary in performing a piece
of music, musical interpretation is nonetheless more a matter of figur-
ing out, in piecemeal fashion, the meaning of individual bits of notation (How soft is "*ppp*"? How fast is "moderato"?) than it is of forming a wholistic function that organizes the entire text. In an idealized,
perfectly precise musical score of the sort I have been postulating, the
"interpretive function" is essentially *identity*; the score is performed

directly. With a film scenario, the inner part of the performance function is like the *extrinsic* interpretive function of Chapter II; the result would look like the following:

$$D[E(T) \quad \rightarrow \quad S] \quad \rightarrow \quad P$$

Strictly speaking, E is not a function here, because, as I noted earlier, it may not operate over the entire text; the director can add and discard parts of the scenario as he wishes. But even if we do consider the film director's work with the text to be functional, it is still extrinsic. The director is not trying to *understand* the scenario; instead, he operates with it as if it were raw material, transforming it into something else instead of seeking its organizational patterns. Instead of assuming the text to be unified, he assumes it to be disunified, a loose collection of characters, events, and ideas that need to be shaped and developed.

The stage director, by contrast, does try to understand the text, must treat it as an already unified complex whose meaning must be divined. He does not perform the text directly, but neither does he transform it into something else. A stage performance is a projection of a text, via an interpretation. And, as I tried to show with my *Macbeth* analysis in the previous chapter, the text is not "words" but a whole space-time complex. A playscript is a performance *in potentia*. The process by which a text is realized is a transformation, but it is essentially a transformation into itself. When a playscript is performed, it is not carried over directly; nor is it altered; it is *fulfilled*.

The values of the functional notation are several. First, the notation stresses that the relation between script and performance is a pairing or, if one considers the intermediate, interpretive set, a triplet. But the pairing is not haphazard; there is a kind of projection or transformation of the initial set into the final one. This projection is neither identical to the script, as in the symphony model, nor independent of it, as in the film scenario model. Instead, it is an orderly transformation, in which every element in the script is first organized via an interpretation and then projected in terms of the resultant structures into the finished performance.

On the other hand, the notation makes clear the well-known fact that, just as there is an infinite number of possible critical interpretations of a text, so too is there an infinite number of possible different productions of a text. This is *not* because a production is something added on to a text as a kind of decoration. It is instead because both the interpretive function and the final set (i.e., the given circumstances of production, such as stage, actors, budget) can obviously vary, which means that the overall production function must vary. The script, however, remains fixed as a starting point. It changes only in the sense that a human being changes in different contexts; I am different with my students than I am with my friends, and different still with my parents, because like all human beings I have a complex personality with many facets. Different relationships tend to draw out or suppress these facets in differing ways, but at bottom I am only one person. A playscript, like a human being, is a complex entity. Like a human, it has a "personality" that will vary in differing production circumstances but which remains at bottom at unity.

Finally, the functional notation stresses the *connectedness* between script and production. Though a given production is only one of an infinite number of possible productions, drawing in turn on an infinite number of textual interpretations, it is nonetheless intimately paired with its playscript. And just as a critical interpretation should be considered only as an overall function, rather than either of its constituent sets (i.e., the generative "system of thought" and the playscript in itself), so too a production must be seen in terms of its overall function. A good production is not script-plus-performance; the audience should not even be aware of script and performance as separate things. A good production is script-*into*-performance, an intimate, point-to-point transformation that moves us only in its wholeness. Script has *become* performance, by pursuing a line of potentiality that had previously been only implicit, and therefore hidden, but which is now actualized in such a way as to seem inevitable.

6

Critical Methods & Metamethods

All this talk about playscript interpretation being a functional relationship leads to an obvious question: What is the function? Just what is the rule or formula by which we can interpret playscripts correctly? Actually, the problem is not that simple. As Roger Gross has pointed out, playscript interpretation is a *heuristic* problem.[1] In other words, *the problem never is just the application of a formula but always includes the finding of a formula.* It is for this reason that script interpretation is always somewhat creative. Contrary to the expectations raised by bright young dramatic critics who publish articles extolling a particular analytical approach, there never has been a fixed and final method that will work for any script, and there never will be one. This does not mean that the analysis and interpretation of playscripts is a mystical, occult process, but it does imply that there will always be imaginative leaps along with logical deduction when one attempts to find out what is happening in a text. The reason for this is quite simple: the human mind abhors a vacuum. It will always seek to find problems that are out of its reach, and, if it cannot find them, it will create them. If playscripts were simple enough to be understood by a single formula, someone would be tempted to write one that went beyond it. Indeed, oversimplification is a common negative judgment made against bad scripts—if a writer merely follows a predictable, standard pattern we consider him a hack. When we say that we want plays to be extraordinary, surprising, or "original," we are automatically implying that the interpretation of playscripts will be heuristic.

An analogy can be found in the games humans like to play. Tic-tac-toe, for example, is a finite game. In fact, once one sees the symmetry of it (starting in any given corner is equivalent to starting in any other), it is easy to evolve a formula for playing it, with which it is impossible to lose. A computer can be "taught" the formula through the simple kind of programming known as an "algorithm," which is just a finite set of fixed instructions. Chess, on the other hand, is an infinite game. One can learn the rules, of course, plus things like standard openings and common situations, and study games others have played. These things, if you like, are algorithms. But there is no single algorithm, no fixed set of instructions, that can be used for all games; it is always necessary to choose, to improvise, to invent. In other words, it is always necessary to create new algorithms for every situation. For this reason, chess is a fascinating game, while tic-tac-toe is trivial—interesting only until one has figured out the formula, and then soon boring. It is possible to program a computer to play chess, but to do so requires a second level of programming. On one level, the programmer feeds into the computer a set of instructions, including the standard openings and so on, which tell the computer what to do in any given situation. But, on a second level, he feeds in instructions about the first level; this second level can alter the instructions at the first level, based on actual experience of playing. The second-level instructions are, if you like, "meta-instructions," or instructions about instructions, and they enable the resulting program *to change itself*. It is as if the computer were learning to play. There is no guarantee that it will always win, no matter how good it becomes through experience, any more than there is a guarantee that a human player will always win. But the computer is far more *likely* to win through a heuristic program than if it stuck to a single algorithm.

The fact that the interpretation of literature is a heuristic problem has led most literary critics today to become eclectic. Fifty years ago it was common to find a critic identifying with a particular approach; today, it is common to find Freudian, imagistic, and anthropological approaches in the same essay, plus additional approaches that are uncategorizable. Like the computer programmed to play chess, the critic is constantly changing himself. The proper choice of method is itself seen as an intellectual problem—each approach is an algorithm, but the critical act is heuristic. Again, this provides no guarantee of success, but the critic is more *likely* to succeed this way than if he had proceeded inflexibly.

In dramatic criticism, however, we still find most often today the oversimplified, algorithmic approach. Drama texts will give a set of simple rules (usually derived from Aristotle's "parts") for playscript interpretation. Or some *enfant terrible* will put forth "Game Theory" as the Final Solution to all textual problems. What they are actually doing is reducing an essentially heuristic problem to an algorithmic one. Surely the test of any critical method should not be whether it is fashionable or original, or even whether it can be easily taught, but rather what it tells us about a particular playscript. In a later chapter I shall be examining a script of Ibsen's through the philosophy of Kierkegaard; it does not really matter whether Ibsen was directly influenced by Kierkegaard (a major controversy during Ibsen's lifetime, since he always vigorously denied it), or that Kierkegaard has become fashionable as an early Existentialist, or even whether his philosophy is a meaningful view of life. It is just that his philosophy provides a set of analytical terms (such as the aesthetic, ethical, and religious levels of the individual life) that illuminate significant patterns in Ibsen's playscripts. Of course, the more profound a philosophy, the more likely it is to be useful in criticism, since both philosophers and playwrights are concerned with understanding life. The choice of Kierkegaard for analyzing Ibsen was not taken at random. But to apply Kierkegaard's philosophy to someone else's playscripts may produce nothing at all of importance; and there may well exist other approaches to Ibsen that will reveal deeper patterns than have ever before been dreamed of, by me or anyone else. The fact that most good criticism has now become eclectic is not because of confusion or lack of commitment, but rather because of a better understanding of the nature of criticism, its goals and techniques.

The advantage of the functional notation, among other things, is that it stresses that a critical approach or method *is not the playscript itself*. The most common error in criticism, particularly dramatic criticism as it exists today, is reification—treating playscripts as if they actually were catalogues of imagery, or psychoanalytic case studies, or "games." Even Structuralism can become reifying when it puts forth a diagram or formula and treats it as if it were the playscript, rather than a *means of understanding* the playscript. Criticism (including its components of analysis, interpretation, and judgment) is not a thing but an *act*. It is ironic that today's playtext jugglers treat the script as though it were infinitely flexible but treat their own critical approach as though it were eternal and perfect. The opposite should be the case—playscripts should be considered as fixed, and critical approaches as constantly evolving and changing. In this way, criticism is analogous to science, which is constantly evolving even though it assumes that its objects of investigation are constant. Matter has not changed over the past three hundred years, but physicists' views of it have continuously changed and deepened. New theories arise that incorporate or supersede the old by their greater profundity. Similarly, criticism of playscripts should be a continuing dialogue. The New Critics rebelled against the Shakespearean criticism of A. C. Bradley, but they could never have come into existence without him—his ideas were not so much false as they were limited, just as the ideas of the New Critics were themselves later to seem limited. The early critics of Ibsen who treated him like a pamphleteer were not wrong either— Ibsen's playscripts do indeed have their social protest aspects. It is just that the social reform approach was inadequate to understanding Ibsen fully; it became a reification, whereby one ended up by talking about women's rights or water pollution rather than the playscripts themselves. More recent critics have tended to treat Ibsen as a poet, which opened up new views of his work, even the scripts of his middle period that seem the most vehemently sociological, but even the poetic approach may eventually be superseded by something else. This is why things like drama journals and critical conferences are so important— it is necessary that criticism be carried on in a day-to-day, continuous fashion rather than only appearing from time to time in the imposing but dangerously reifying form of books. (If Shaw's *The Quintessence of Ibsenism* had appeared as a series of lectures or journalistic essays rather than as a book, it might have been the first word, rather than the last word, in English Ibsen criticism at the time, and our understanding of Ibsen, as well as our productions of his scripts, would have been much better for it.) In the popular jargon of today, we must start to treat dramatic criticism as "process rather than product," which means that it must be encouraged in classrooms, lounges, living rooms, street-

corners, rehearsal rooms, theatre lobbies, journal articles, and letters
to the editor, in addition to the occasional stone tablets from on high
inscribed by distinguished authors.

Nevertheless, the fact that criticism should be process rather than
product does not mean that it need be haphazard. There is a good deal
that one can say about critical methods themselves, without being committed to any particular one of them. As in programming a computer
to play chess, what is needed is a second level of instructions, which
will evaluate and alter critical methods in response to particular problems in individual texts. Listed below are "metamethods," or tests for
evaluating the critical act while performing it. Briefly, any good critical method for analysis, interpretation, and (perhaps eventual) production should

1. Isolate the playscript.
2. Treat it as a space-time complex.
3. Analyze it in detail.
4. Allow for complexity and ambiguity.
5. Find a unifying principle.
6. Test the principle against the text.

It will be seen that these metamethods are drawn from the principles
discussed in the earlier chapters. The important thing here is that they
are not a formula for the criticism of playscripts, but *a formula for
criticizing the criticism of playscripts*. The student of dramatic literature should learn these metamethods if he wants to understand playscripts properly. They are not rules to be applied mechanically that
will always provide a "correct" answer, but rather a means by which
the critic changes himself like the heuristically programmed computer and thus *learns*. Naturally, a student must be taught some basic
critical techniques—it makes no sense to have metamethods without
methods, just as it makes no sense to have a critical method without
any playscripts to apply it to—but he must also be taught that such
techniques, useful as they are at a particular moment, are never the
final word in criticism. Ultimately, what is wanted is a certain *style*
of examining playscripts rather than a set of rules that can be applied
universally. The metamethods are a beginning, rather than an end, to
understanding. Each can be considered in detail:

1. *Isolate the playscript*. This has already been discussed. For pur-

poses of theatrical performance, at least, it seems a fundamental necessity. Criticism that will be of use to the director, designer, or performer must be intrinsic, in the functional sense discussed in Chapter II, for, whatever value there may be in treating a playscript as a historical document or as an example of a particular genre, movement, or "trend," in performance the most use such information can be is as a set of program notes. The critic must therefore get in the habit of always asking himself, "Am I really and truly talking about the playscript itself, or about something else?"

2. *Treat it as a space-time complex.* The dramatic critic must regard a script in terms of its performance potential. This means it cannot be treated as existing outside space and time, like a lyric poem, but rather as being embedded in them, as carrying spatial and temporal implications in its very fabric. The critic must sense the clock ticking away as he reads, becoming aware of such elements as duration, progression, rhythm, tempo; and he must construct in his imagination a vital, ambient space in which the events happen, inferred from stage directions, characters' descriptions, and logical deduction. If he does not do these things, he is not treating the work as *drama*, which is a literary form fulfilled in performance.

But it is not enough just to be aware of the spatial and temporal aspects of a script. They must be treated as *artistic* elements, which means integrated into the overall, unified complex, rather than as something extra or special. Kenneth Burke has defined what he calls "ratios," by which he means connections or transformations (equivalent to what I have been calling "functions") between differing elements of a play. A playscript will imply, for example, a "scene-act ratio" (scene in the sense of setting, and act in the sense of action) in which the setting "both *realistically reflects* the course of action and *symbolizes* it."[2] That is, the setting is not just some decoration to be applied after the fact to please the audience or provide illusion, but instead is part of a unified, aesthetic process, embodying meaning through the construction of a "virtual space" that has specific, telling attributes. Burke gives as an example the setting of the final act of Ibsen's *An Enemy of the People*:

In Act V, the stage directions tell us that the hero's clothes are

torn, and the room is in disorder, with broken windows. You
may consider these details either as properties of the scene or as
a reflection of the hero's condition after his recent struggle
with the forces of reaction. The scene is laid in Dr. Stockmann's
study, a setting so symbolic of the direction taken by the plot
that the play ends with Dr. Stockmann announcing his plan to
enroll twelve young *disciples* and with them to found a *school*
in which he will work for the *education* of society.[3]

This is an excellent example of the vital connection between setting
and action, as well as setting and character. In addition to the "scene-
act ratio," Burke defines numerous other ratios, such as "scene-agent,"
which relates the setting to the characters in it, or "scene-purpose,"
which relates setting to the characters' objectives. In addition, we
might extend Burke's terminology and invent numerous *temporal*
"ratios," such as "rhythm-agent" or "duration-purpose." A lurching
or hesitant rhythm in a character's speech, for example, implies something about that character; it is not just a bit of ornament. The long
duration of the Malcolm-Macduff scene near the end of *Macbeth*, as I
tried to show in Chapter IV, is not an accident and certainly not an
error on Shakespeare's part, but rather both a realistic reflection and a
symbolization of the characters' objectives in the scene; it is a good
example of the use of a "duration-purpose" ratio.

But whether a critic uses Burke's specific terminology is not as important as that he develop the habit of envisioning the script in space
and time, seeing these elements as part of an interconnected whole.
Just as the critic of poetry habitually looks for patterns or "clusters"
of imagery, so the critic of drama must seek clusters of space-time.

3. *Analyze it in detail.* The importance of detail in a work of art
cannot be overstressed. In ordinary, nonartistic writing—a piece of
expository prose like a newspaper article—detail is far less important.
There is even a kind of hierarchy of significance: the smaller the piece
of information, the less important it is. In a newspaper story about a
car crash, what is important is that a person was killed; it is not particularly important what he had for breakfast. The former bit of
information would therefore appear in the headlines and opening
paragraphs, while the latter would appear in a paragraph on the last

page, if at all. In such a newspaper story, the reader follows along as far as he is interested—stopping after the major details at the beginning if he is an ordinary reader, but on and on to ever more minor ones if, say, he is doing research into car accidents.

For analyzing a piece of artistic writing, this habit must be reversed. The student must learn that *every detail in a playscript is of equal significance*. Minor details may even be of *more* significance than major ones, since the major elements of the playscript may have been dictated by the requirements of the story, or by the playwright's sources, while in the minor details the playwright is most free to express himself. In writing a playscript about a car crash, the playwright's use of the crash itself is a foregone conclusion (though of course he is free to write on any subject he chooses); the victim's breakfast may be far more important from an artistic standpoint. The playwright can use such minor details to express subtleties of character (the driver was a nervous type who ate very little, which led indirectly to the crash), or to make a social comment (he gorged himself while millions were starving, making his death a kind of poetic justice), or to express existential horror (his guts were ripped open, spilling his half-digested eggs onto the pavement). A newspaper reporter who tried to write this way would quickly be fired by his editor, who would demand only the most obvious facts and the most direct forms of causal connection: a person was killed because his car crashed; his car crashed because he was speeding. The artistic writer, on the other hand, views life as an interconnected pattern. He is not just concerned with simple, scientific causes, but with associations and reverberations, the *poetic* as well as the linear connections between events.

In our society, which sees science as important and literature as trivial, it is often very hard to make students sensitive to detail in this way. In reading Ibsen's *An Enemy of the People*, for example, the student will usually be impressed by the struggle between progress and reaction, the conflict between civil liberties and economic interests, and thus conclude that it is a moving (or irritating, depending on his point of view) social pamphlet calling for justice and the rights of man. He will not make much of the fact that the hero and his chief antagonist, the Mayor, are brothers or that the representative of economic reaction in the playscript turns out to be the hero's father-in-law. These seem to be just coincidences, as they would appear to be if they were in a newspaper story describing such a situation in real life. But of course, unlike a newspaper reporter, Ibsen had complete *control* over these details—the Mayor and the tannery owner could have been anyone he liked. By making the conflicts family squabbles as well as heroic social struggles, Ibsen was making a statement about the nature of truth—that life is never a matter of simple justice, of good versus evil or truth versus falsity, but that we are always affected in our attitudes toward "facts" by our personal situation and human relationships. Dr. Stockmann, the protagonist, is ironically undercut in the script, by being shown *not* as a disinterested hero who loves truth in the abstract, but rather as an ordinary person who at last has the means of revenge on his smug brother, who has never listened to him, and on his rich father-in-law, who has always had him under his thumb. These are not dominant, major elements in the script, but they are there nonetheless and affect its meaning as a whole. The reader who is insensitive to such detail ends up responding only to Stockmann's view of himself, rather than to the playscript as a whole, which is far more than a simple, social-protest tract.

A proper critical method, then, must involve what is called "close reading," rather than just seeing the play in general terms. Of course, this too can become an affectation, as with Cleanth Brooks and his *Macbeth* essay, so that one does not see the woods for the trees. But, in combination with the other metamethods, close reading is an important principle which need not become artificial. The habit to be developed is constantly to ask, "Why?" Instead of passively accepting the details in a playtext, the critic must constantly say to himself, "What is this doing here? Why this particular detail and not another?"

4. *Allow for complexity and ambiguity.* Any critical approach that gives too many answers should be suspect. A method should allow for the fact that the mysterious, the bizarre, the original, are important aspects of playscripts rather than problems to be solved or questions to be answered. As Kenneth Burke has written, "What we want is *not terms that avoid ambiguity*, but *terms that clearly reveal the strategic spots at which ambiguities necessarily arise.*"[4] A critical method should be open rather than closed; its purpose is to illuminate rather than to explain, and certainly rather than to explain *away*. There is always a temptation, even with the best critics, to come up with a

theory about a script that is too glib, too pat. Such criticism is far more likely to get published, and to get wide attention, than criticism that is more modest. Nevertheless, such temptation must be avoided. The critic must develop the habit of *doubt*.

The equivalent in performance to the glib interpretation in criticism is the "concept" production. Oddly enough, the bizarre concept that has no basis in the text at all is more likely to be successful on stage than the concept which is based on the text, but in an oversimplified way. This is because a wildly updated production is really a brand-new play and thus has at least a random chance of being interesting; the kind of concept production in which the concept is an oversimplification of the text, or an overemphasis of a single aspect of the text, is a new play also, but only in the way that a castrated man is a new person. In the 1973 production of *The Merchant of Venice* at the British National Theatre, which starred Sir Laurence Olivier, the aspect chosen was anti-Semitism. The period was updated to the nineteenth century, to make a connection with modern anti-Semitism; Shylock was played for total sympathy, and the Venetian merchants turned into elegant bigots; the conversion of Jessica to Christianity was depicted as a deplorable sell-out by a shallow, stupid girl. Now, there is certainly a case to be made in the text for all these things. No doubt about it, Antonio, Bassanio, and the other merchants are anti-Semitic; Shylock has genuine grievances; Jessica's conversion is made for a secular reason. The "Hath not a Jew eyes" speech is one of the most poignant exposures of bigotry ever written. Unfortunately for the National Theatre production, however, in the very scene where it occurs there is also the "My ducats and my daughter" business. Shylock is depicted as both sympathetic and avaricious, both tragic and farcical, almost at the same moment. Furthermore, the conversion of Jessica and that of Shylock himself, though both done for improper reasons, are depicted in the script as nothing but good. "Good from evil" might in fact be a better approximation of the playscript's total meaning (it is implicit in the plot of the three caskets, for example) than merely the wickedness of prejudice. The concept production is usually based on the text, but it lifts stones out of the mosaic and treats them separately, rather than as part of a complex pattern. The result is a kind of half play, lacking the richness and excitement that might have been possible with a wholistic approach. Like the critic, the director must also develop the habit of doubt, forming "concepts" of playscripts that are opened instead of closed.

5. *Find a unifying principle.* I hesitated to express this in this way, because of the danger of reification. Paul M. Levitt, in an interesting but often disappointing book entitled *A Structural Approach to the Analysis of Drama*, remarks that "the unifying principle is the operative principle which underlies and governs the place, relation, and function of each scene in a play."[5] This is a risky way of putting it. The unifying principle is not an *element* of a playscript; scripts do not have "operative principles" the way they have characters, settings, and speeches. The unifying principle is a functional relationship between a critical approach and a particular script; it does not exist in the script by itself. Levitt, under the influence of Artaud and Schechner, defines unifying principle as if it were the "real" playscript, the blueprint behind the less important specifics, even insisting that certain specifics can be rejected as not in keeping with it: "To allow that a part or parts of a play are irrelevant is to indicate that we understand the unifying principle which informs the whole."[6] The unifying principle, it seems, does not "govern" except where the critic deems it shall govern. The end result of thinking in this way is to turn the idea of unifying principle into a blank check for whatever interpretation one likes.

Instead, one should define the unifying principle as a *statement* (possibly in the form of a diagram, formula, or phrase) *that enables a person to grasp the significance of a playscript as a whole.* There is no question of its operating on or generating or governing anything. In a sense, it exists "in the eye of the beholder," not like a hallucination but rather like the meaningful organization of a mosaic. It would be better to say that it exists as "a transaction between the eye of the beholder and the thing beheld." A playscript is noumenal, incomprehensible in itself; the unifying principle is a description after the fact, a sounding, an exploration.

The danger of reification is greatly reduced when the idea of unifying principle is taken in conjunction with the other metamethods. Sensitivity to detail is a good safeguard against a unifying principle that is a reductionism. So too are ambiguity and complexity, or openness. As Aristotle put it, a good play is both unified *and* complex. One must find a unifying principle, but its unity must allow for multiplicity, or it is nothing. If it leads instead to deciding that certain parts of a playscript are "errors" or "irrelevant," as the neoclassicists' idea of unity did, or as Levitt's does, then one is behaving like the doctors in Molière's play who would rather let the patient die than to go against medical theory.

An example of the valid application of unifying principle can be found in the criticism of Francis Fergusson. For example, in his book *The Idea of a Theatre*, Fergusson describes the "action" of various classical playscripts in terms of simple infinitive phrases: the action of *Oedipus Tyrannus* is "to find the culprit in order to purify human life,"[7] the action of Racine's *Bérénice* is "to demonstrate the tragic life of the soul-as-rational in the situation of the three passionate monarchs,"[8] while the action of *Hamlet* is "to find and destroy the hidden 'impostume' which is poisoning the life of Claudius' Denmark."[9] The approach is of course drawn from Stanislavski's notion of "the objective" but applied to entire playscripts rather than individual characters alone, and given more intellectual respectability by Fergusson's citation of Aristotle. The phrases are, if you like, unifying principles, but they are not intended to substitute for the actual experience of reading the playscripts or seeing them performed; they cannot even be substituted for the experience of reading Fergusson's book. The approach is merely a way into the playscripts, a tool for understanding, and the phrases themselves are summations of a lengthy critical process, a bit of shorthand notation. Fergusson writes of *Hamlet*, for example: "The contrasts between the visions and the lines of action of the various characters are more important than their overt struggles, and reveal far more about the real malady of Denmark and the attempt to find and destroy it. These *contrasts* are brought out by the order of the scenes, as we shift from comic to tragic versions of the main action."[10] In other words, Fergusson is not just dealing with a few surface events in the text, such as the demand for revenge from the ghost of Hamlet's father or Hamlet's use of a play to catch the conscience of the king, in describing the unifying principle as being "to find and destroy the hidden 'impostume.' " Fergusson interprets this action in a very broad sense and shows how it is realized not only directly in attacks on Claudius, but also in a variety of "comic, evil, or inspired ways."[11] Even Claudius himself attempts to carry out the action, through the agency of Rosencrantz and Guildenstern, or later through the duel with the poisoned sword. For Claudius, Hamlet is the "impostume" that must be found out and destroyed. In every way, then, this unifying principle allows for complexity and ambiguity and stands up under *close* reading.

It goes without saying that Fergusson would not dream of tossing out scenes that do not agree with his unifying principle; in fact, one of the main purposes of his essay is to justify the significance of scenes and parts that *other* critics have found irrelevant, such as "the alternation of the Polonius story and the Hamlet story in Acts I and II— the scenes for which Mr. [T. S.] Eliot says there is no explanation or excuse."[12] Fergusson demonstrates that Polonius too is following the action of trying to purify Denmark, although Polonius's diagnosis of the infection—Hamlet's youth and thwarted love—is very simple-minded. The Polonius episodes are thus not extraneous at all but are a comic variation on the same "action" as Hamlet's. In all this analysis, the unifying principle itself is perhaps less important than how it is worked out. After all, anyone could write a playscript around the "action" as Fergusson has stated it, but the script would not be much good unless this action were carried through with some of the subtlety and variety that Shakespeare gives it. The purpose of Fergusson's "action" is to enable us to see how an apparently very disparate thing, the text of *Hamlet*, actually hangs together. In doing so, it does not simplify the text, or judge it (except in the indirect sense of showing how ingenious it is), or change it into something else. Rather than "governing" the text, Fergusson's unifying principle is *governed by it*.

6. *Test the principle against the text.* In science, it has become standard practice to test a hypothesis experimentally. This was not always so—one has only to think of Galileo dropping weights off the Tower of Pisa. Against the accepted theory of the time, a heavy and a light weight, dropped simultaneously, would reach the ground at the same instant. The respected scientists observing the experiment refused to believe the evidence of their own eyes and explained away the simultaneous landings by vague references to air pressure. A good deal of bad dramatic criticism takes the same approach—one simply ignores the parts of a playscript that do not fit the standard theory, or explains them away as irrelevant. Ibsen has probably suffered from

this more than any other playwright. His play *A Doll House* recently became fashionable again because of the revival of the women's liberation movement. Despite the fact that generations of drama professors have taught it as *the* feminist playscript, directors found that when they went to stage it there really was not very much feminism in it. It seems more an indictment of a particular marriage, or a particular kind of marriage, than of marriage as an institution, and issues like votes for women or equal job opportunity are never even mentioned. Thus, for both the London production and the version filmed in Norway, the script was drastically rewritten. Nora and her husband, both complex characters in Ibsen's version, became a stock heroine and a male-chauvinist villain. Minor characters were similarly rewritten or removed entirely—the London production, with the script adapted by Christopher Hampton, even removed Nora's children (although a few casual references to them were left in), thus softening the most truly shocking element in the play, even for today, which is that Nora walks out not only on her husband, whom she no longer loves, but also on her three children whom she still does love. The result was a coarsening and weakening of a great playscript, to make it into the play that everyone "knew" it was. It is as if a map maker, finding some features of the land that were not on his map, hired some bulldozers to change the terrain itself, rather than change his picture of it.

I have found that a standard test of good dramatic criticism, which can almost be applied mathematically, is the number of quotations and references to the text found in it. Whole books of drama criticism have been written in which playscripts are never quoted at all. Perhaps less exciting to read, but certainly more worthwhile, are critical works that cite the text regularly, giving *evidence* for their view of it. Such criticism may be more tedious than the kind that is written in grand abstractions, but in the long run it will also be more useful to the reader or theatre practitioner. Of course, there is a danger that a critic can get lost in detail and produce an interpretation that does not interpret at all but is only a kind of catalogue. But, at the present time, this danger seems very remote to me in the case of dramatic criticism. Suffice it to say that, just as a good playscript is both unified and complex, so a good work of criticism is both general *and* particular.

There is an equivalent in production to excessive generalization in criticism. Stanislavski talked of "acting in general," by which he

meant a performance in which the actor plays a single, generalized
attitude throughout an entire scene, or even an entire play, without
regard for the contrasts, progressions, and rhythms in the text. Whole
productions can also be "in general." Like the critic who overgeneral-
izes, the director takes a lofty overview of the script—either a private
one of his own or one based on stage tradition—and ignores the nasty,
grainy little details which are the very things that make the script
unique and engaging. Norman Holland once pointed out that Hamlet
is described physically in the playscript as being thirty years old, fat,
and bearded, none of which ever appears in performance. (A more
recent critic was so upset by Hamlet's age that he wrote a lengthy
article in a leading theatre journal to "prove" that it was a mistake.)
Yet what an exciting production could come out of playing Hamlet
in this way, more truly daring than updating him into a Nazi officer
or a Puerto Rican in Spanish Harlem, yet solidly supported *by the text*!
I have heard Hamlet's following speech delivered in about a dozen
different productions of the play, and only once did it make sense:

> Am I a coward?
> Who calls me villain? breaks my pate across?
> Plucks off my beard and blows it in my face? (II.ii.556–558)

In every other case the actor, clean-shaven, roared through the passage in a masterpiece of histrionics, oblivious to what he was actually
saying. The director did not even have the good sense to alter or cut
the line. I have also seen Shylocks who never wore a "gaberdine"
(perhaps we were to believe that, having been spit on so often, it had
been sent to the cleaners), a Macduff who was not even wearing a hat
when Malcolm urged him "Ne'er pull your hat upon your brows"
(IV.iii.208), and a production of *King Lear* in which someone got the
bright idea of playing the title character at about age forty, without
even bothering to cut the line where he states that he is "four score
and upward" (IV.vii.61). I have also directed a production myself in
which, I am ashamed to admit, Macbeth did not draw his dagger when
he said:

> I see thee yet, in form as palpable
> As this which now I draw. (II.i.40–41)

Unfortunately the omission was not pointed out to me until after the production had closed. All such errors result from seeing the playscript in general terms, from not testing a prejudiced vision of a scene against what actually exists there.

But there is more to such testing than simply preventing errors. Theatre, like politics, is "the art of the possible," which means in its case the art of the tangible, the specific, the physical. Critics, directors, or actors who do not like to get close to a playscript are not really suited temperamentally to the art form. Testing an interpretation against the playtext should be second nature for anyone connected with theatre. The close details of a script should not be a cause for impatience, as is the case with far too many critics and theatre practitioners today, but rather a source of inspiration and delight.

These six metamethods are all intended to function together rather than independently and are all in the nature of habits rather than mechanical aids for the interpretation or production of a playscript. Thus it is not particularly important that they be stated exactly as I have them, or even that they be consciously stated at all. Some critics and directors may find them to be just plain common sense, hardly worth bothering to write down; it is only because of the wild turns that playscript interpretation has taken in the past decade that I myself was compelled to think about them. They are important as a *background* for criticism, grounds that should be agreed upon before criticism can begin. In many periods, it would have been unnecessary to express them at all, yet it is by rejecting one or more of them that the theatre finds itself in the quandary that exists today.

In the next three chapters are practical examples of both criticism and performance (drawn from actual productions that I have directed) based on the methods and metamethods I have been developing thus far. These too are not meant to be taken mechanically as formulae. To return to the chess-playing analogy given earlier, it is common in books about chess, after setting down the rules of the game and some standard problems, for the author to provide some examples of actual games. It is unlikely that anyone will ever run into the exact situations found in such games and thus be able to repeat the results found there; rather, the games are important in making the reader "think like a chess player." In conjunction with his own experience in playing, the games aid the reader to develop certain habits of thought and imagination that will greatly improve his chances of success. Similarly, my examples of playscript analysis and interpretation are intended to aid the reader, in conjunction with his own experience as director, critic, or actor, to deal with playscripts. The test of any technique is not only how well a person applies it directly, but also how well he is able to go beyond it on his own. My intention here is to re-orient people in a way that will, I hope, help them to "think like critics," rather than thinking exactly like me.

One further note: in the examples in the next three chapters, as in the examples given so far, I have assumed that the reader is thoroughly familiar with the playscripts under discussion. It would be wise to have copies handy while reading what I have to say about them. Whatever value my remarks may have, they will certainly not mean much in isolation.

7

Shelley's <u>The Cenci</u>

Shelley's *The Cenci* was produced by the Drama Department of the University of Calgary in the winter of 1974 as an example of the Romantic genre. The department attempts to produce plays from all major historical genres of western drama over a four-year cycle; since the productions are intended to be part of the teaching material in dramatic theory and criticism, they are generally done straightforwardly—the veritable "museum pieces" of popular lore—with few if any textual changes, although the productions are not usually historical reproductions. That is, the department accepts, at least implicitly, the functional relationship between text and performance, in which a given playscript can be projected into practically any staging situation. My own belief is that it does not really matter, per se, whether a playscript is produced historically, contemporarily, or some third alternative; those are extrinsic considerations. The important thing is whether the patterns and processes implicit in the script are made explicit on the stage. The question of whether a production should be true or false to history is not, from an artistic standpoint, a relevant one; the real question is whether or not the production is true *to the script.*

In the case of *The Cenci*, the staging situation involved a thrust stage modeled on that at Stratford, Ontario, but smaller in size and having only one exit tunnel down center, rather than two diagonally placed down left and right. The actors available were students from the department, in which it is possible to take extensive acting, voice, and movement over four years, although rather less than would be available at an acting conservatory. In other words, the situation is very much like that at most major university drama departments in North America. The budget available for the production was $2,200, which is rather small for a Romantic play (although *The Cenci* is relatively small in cast and set requirements for a playscript of its type, which is one of the reasons it was chosen). Nevertheless, budget too can be considered one of the artistic variables into which the script must project, so that, within reasonable limits, lack of money should never be offered as an excuse for failure.

The Cenci presents considerable staging problems, testing to the extreme my belief in the nonalteration of playscripts. Although a great theatregoer, Shelley had no experience as a writer for the practical theatre, and the script was never actually performed in his lifetime. Perhaps as a result, the script is full of what appear to be errors of judgment or outright flaws, which Shelley might well have altered had he seen it through production. A striking example occurs in the trial scene (V.ii), in which Marzio, one of Cenci's murderers, is dragged off to be tortured at line 168.[1] A bare eleven lines later one of his guards re-enters to announce Marzio's death; it is hard to conceive how they would have even had time to bind him to the rack. There are many such problems in the script. Perhaps under the influence of Byron, who at the time was touting the French neoclassic drama as a model for English playwrights, Shelley put every bit of action offstage. The story upon which the script is based is a true one, which occurred in Italy during the late Renaissance: Francesco Cenci, a notorious libertine, raped his daughter Beatrice, who revenged herself by having him murdered, and was then found out, tried, and executed. Shelley puts not only the rape offstage (of course no theatre could have shown it then, and very few would now), but also Cenci's other crimes, his murder, the torture of Beatrice's accomplices, their confessions, and her execution. If Shelley's choice of story seemed perverse in the nineteenth century, his *treatment* of it seems perverse now. Even Beatrice's announcement of the rape is in maddeningly oblique terms. She rambles on about the walls spinning around, blood, disease, pollution, scaly reptiles, and "horrible things" for over a hundred lines, but never gives the deed a name. The other characters even remark on this lack of directness—when Giacomo, Beatrice's brother, asks Orsino, her would-be lover, what outrage has been perpetrated, Orsino replies:

> That she speaks not, but you may
> Conceive such half conjectures as I do,
> From her fixed paleness, and the lofty grief
> Of her stern brow bent on the idle air,
> And her severe unmodulated voice,
> Drowning both tenderness and dread; and last
> From this; that whilst her step-mother and I,
> Bewildered in our horror, talked together
> With obscure hints; both self-misunderstood
> And darkly guessing, stumbling, in our talk,
> Over the truth, and yet to its revenge,
> She interrupted us, and with a look
> Which told before she spoke it, he must die. (III.i.349–361)

"Obscure hints," indeed! Regardless of the conventions of the nineteenth-century Romantic stage, or even the seventeenth-century neo-classic stage, nothing required Shelley to be so vague in the *reporting* of the deed. If he was squeamish, he might at least have had Beatrice say something like, "My father did something to me so horrible I dare not name it." Instead, Shelley almost seems to go out of his way to be imprecise, even calling into question whether the rape actually took place at all. Perhaps Beatrice imagined the whole thing; earlier on, in II.i.64–76, she was established as a semihysteric, accusing her father of having trampled her, made blood stream down her cheeks, given her "ditch-water" to drink and "the fever stricken flesh of buffaloes" (!) to eat, but as she calms down admitting that

> He only struck and cursed me as he passed;
> He said, he looked, he did;—nothing at all. (II.i.75–76)

Perhaps the rape incident too was "nothing at all," just another fantasy of a neurotic girl; since we are dealing with a playscript rather than the historical record, there is really no way of telling. One can certainly say, however, that the script makes the act questionable.

The speeches in the script are full of anticlimaxes like that in this one, which is another problem with the play. For all of Shelley's announced intention of writing a verse that would be dramatic rather than "mere poetry,"[2] it is rarely dramatic in the popular sense of being emotionally striking. Even critics in Shelley's time, when they were not denouncing the work for being disgusting and immoral, attacked it for being so low keyed and understated, as in Beatrice's final speech:

> Here, Mother, tie
> My girdle for me, and bind up this hair
> In any simple knot; ay, that does well.
> And yours I see is coming down. How often
> Have we done this for one another; now
> We shall not do it any more. My Lord,
> We are quite ready. Well, 'tis very well. (V.iv.159–165)

Putting her hair up was not the sort of thing a tragic heroine was supposed to do on her way to her execution. The script is written entirely in blank verse, but unlike that of Shelley's Jacobean and neo-classical models, the tone is almost always calm, pensive, and colloquial; even when spectacular events are described, the description itself is usually blunt and unadorned:

> For Rocco
> Was kneeling at the mass, with sixteen others,
> When the church fell and crushed him to a mummy,
> The rest escaped unhurt. Cristofano
> Was stabbed in error by a jealous man,
> Whilst she he loved was sleeping with his rival;
> All in the self-same hour of the same night. (I.iii.58–64)

The repeated, and often lengthy, understatement in the script foreshadows the Naturalism of the later part of the century rather than providing an especially good example of dramatic Romanticism, which more than once made me feel we had chosen a bad script for pedagogic purposes, as well as for theatrical ones.

The experiences of other directors with the script were not of much use. Although not performed until 1886, it has been done fairly often since then, but I was unable to find any production that did not alter the text drastically. The director of the Old Vic production in 1959, Michael Benthall, started with the assumption that the script was flawed and announced his intention "to draw out enough of the gold to cover up the dross."[3] He made few cuts in the text, but he tried to bring out the spectacular elements, in particular putting the torture of Marzio on stage during the trial scene. The production was a flop. Artaud's version of the script, which is now probably better known than Shelley's, made drastic cuts and translated Shelley's already understated verse into an even flatter prose. In the preface to his version, Artaud expressed his usual doctrine that meaning can be separated from its expression: "Shelley added to nature his own style and that language of his which resembles a summer night bombarded by meteors, but personally I prefer nature in the raw."[4] Artaud held the erroneous but all too common belief that poetry is something that is just "added" to a script, a form of decoration rather than an embodiment of meaning. His "raw" version, which claimed the influence of Stendahl's version of the story as well as Shelley's, stressed the elements of spectacle through elaborate stage directions, reflecting Artaud's belief in the importance of the *mise en scène*, and put the torture of *Beatrice* on stage. And there is no nonsense about the rape; while it is not shown, Beatrice says, quite straightforwardly for an author who was suspicious of language, "Cenci, my father, has defiled me."[5] Artaud's production, in 1935, has subsequently had unquestioned influence on the French stage, but it too, like the Old Vic production, was a flop at the time.

Given these bits of history, I felt that there was nothing to be gained by altering the text. The glaringly obvious change, which seemed to cry out to be done, was to liven up the text by putting some of the action on stage, but this approach had not particularly helped my predecessors. I decided instead to stick with a Structuralist approach, in which the text is presumed innocent until proven guilty. Unity was assumed. In particular, I assumed that there was some purpose behind Shelley's oblique treatment of the story's action (besides the possible extrinsic one of wanting to imitate neoclassic tragedy), even if I could not for the life of me see what that purpose was.

The first approach to the text that I attempted was through the analysis of imagery. I was impressed by the success of the New Critics with Shakespeare and was convinced that their approach had never had an adequate trial in the theatre. Furthermore, there was no doubt that Shelley was influenced by Shakespeare and his contemporaries: the period of the playscript is Elizabethan; the locale and story recall the Italianate tragedies of Ford or Webster, with all their incest, blood, and horror; and the script resounds in echoes of all of Shakespeare's major tragedies. Both the banquet scene and the murder scene are clearly modeled on *Macbeth*; the simple "bind up this hair" ending recalls Lear's "Pray you undo this button"; Cenci's gleeful wickedness recalls Richard III, while Orsino's introspection makes him, in Stuart Curran's words, "a diluted Hamlet."[6] The blank verse, despite its often conversational tone, is not devoid of imagery—in fact, as the New Critics used the term, imagery arises wherever there is a description or a comparison of any kind, which makes its analysis possible even with expository prose. Finally, Curran in his book maintains that "the claim could be made . . . that in *The Cenci* Shelley has created the only poetic drama in English after Shakespeare in which extensive patterns of imagery achieve a meaningful and organic unity";[7] Curran develops several of the images, particularly those relating to light and darkness. From using his book, as well as by reading the script numerous times, I was able to discern quite a few image clusters. The following are only some of them:

FATHERS

I.ii.47	II.i.47	III.i.36–37
I.ii.54	II.i.55	III.i.39–40
I.ii.72	II.i.59	III.i.44
I.iii.22–23	II.i.93	III.i.69
I.iii.101	II.i.132	III.i.73–74
I.iii.118	II.ii.6	III.i.144
I.iii.125	II.ii.20	III.i.288
I.iii.139	II.ii.31–33	III.i.340
I.iii.149	II.ii.47	III.ii.52
II.i.10	II.ii.55	IV.i.104 ff.
II.i.16–17	II.ii.73	IV.i.126
II.i.24	II.ii.80	IV.iii.18 ff.
II.i.35	II.ii.148	IV.iii.32

IV.iv.101	V.i.11	V.iii.12
IV.iv.112–	V.i.45	V.iii.82
113	V.ii.75	V.iii.83
IV.iv.146	V.ii.87	V.iii.100
IV.iv.148	V.ii.106	V.iii.104
IV.iii.51	V.ii.120	V.iv.10
IV.iv.21	V.ii.128	V.iv.17
IV.iv.55	V.ii.157	V.iv.20
IV.iv.98	V.ii.188	

CHILDREN

I.i.40	II.i.58	IV.i.21
I.i.43	II.i.85	IV.i.40
I.i.61	II.i.133	IV.i.78
I.i.63	II.ii.10	IV.i.107
I.i.130	II.ii.22	IV.i.139 ff.
I.ii.78–79	II.ii.32	IV.iv.36
I.iii.27	II.ii.127	IV.iv.98
I.iii.35	III.i.211	IV.iv.103
I.iii.105	III.i.291	V.ii.14
I.iii.109	III.i.316	V.ii.18
I.iii.125	III.i.327	V.iii.47
II.i.8	III.i.348	V.iii.103
II.i.16	III.ii.5	V.iii.106
II.i.37	III.ii.82	V.iv.92

BLOOD

I.i.38	III.i.95	V.ii.133
I.i.113	III.ii.18	V.ii.150
I.iii.11	III.ii.66	V.ii.166
I.iii.36	IV.i.114	V.ii.171
I.iii.87	IV.i.116	V.iii.45
II.i.40	IV.i.163	V.iii.64
II.i.55	IV.ii.23	V.iv.33
II.i.65	IV.iii.45	V.iv.96
III.i.2	IV.iv.75	V.iv.125–126
III.i.13	V.ii.83	

WHITENESS

I.i.39	III.ii.21	V.i.11
I.iii.101	III.ii.25	V.i.68
I.iii.157	III.ii.69	V.ii.8
II.i.39	IV.i.19	V.ii.169
II.ii.39	IV.i.96	V.iii.24
III.i.71	IV.ii.20–23	V.iv.23
III.i.83	IV.iii.36	V.iv.139
III.i.351	IV.iv.124	

GOLD

I.i.6	III.i.162	IV.iii.27
I.i.127	III.i.185	IV.iii.48
I.iii.74	III.i.289	IV.iv.84
II.ii.68	IV.i.6	V.ii.26
II.ii.130	IV.i.56	

A statistical exercise such as this can be valuable in developing the habit of discerning repetitive patterns, a sensitivity to relationships in the script that are not directly connected to the more obvious elements of story and character. Statistics also force one to look at the script in solid, factual terms; one can dispute indefinitely Cenci's motives, Shelley's philosophy, or the place of this work in the history of western drama, but the facts that there are 64 references to fathers in the script (an average of once in every 37 lines) and 29 references to blood (once in every 81 lines) are concrete and indisputable. No one could deny that fathers, children, blood, whiteness, and gold are important to this playscript. The associations they evoke are clearly a major part of the verbal ambience surrounding the action.

Nevertheless, a simple list or catalogue is of no use at all until one considers the *significance* of the sets of images; the analytical work of taking the script apart must be complemented by the interpretive or synthetic work of seeing the parts in relation to the whole again. Statistics prove nothing by themselves. The large numbers of references to fathers and children, for example, are not surprising considering the subject matter of the playscript; it is hard to imagine a script about the Cenci story that would not contain many such references. In rein-

tegrating the imagery into the text, the principle of *choice* must be
considered; imagery of this sort is not what critics call "free" imagery,
and the analysis of it by itself is unlikely to provide insight into deep
structure. Far more significant in this script, because they are more
inherently free, are the many references to relatives in general:

RELATIVES

I.i.16	II.i.62	IV.i.109
I.i.18	II.i.63	IV.i.132
I.i.28	II.i.84	IV.iv.34
I.i.43	II.i.88–90	IV.iv.63
I.i.61	II.i.95–98	IV.iv.70
I.i.63	II.i.99	IV.iv.113
I.i.135	II.i.121	IV.iv.158
I.ii.49	II.i.161	V.iii.9
I.ii.56	II.ii.46	V.iii.12
I.ii.58	II.ii.148	V.iii.14
I.ii.69–70	II.ii.150	V.iii.46
I.ii.78–79	III.i.58	V.iii.48
I.iii.1	III.i.300	V.iii.58
I.iii.31	III.i.305 ff.	V.iii.100
I.iii.34	III.i.355	V.iii.103
I.iii.105	III.i.369	V.iii.117
I.iii.121–123	III.i.380 ff.	V.iv.19
I.iii.126	III.ii.5	V.iv.24
I.iii.153	III.ii.54 ff.	V.iv.90
II.i.7–8	III.ii.80	V.iv.117
II.i.13	IV.i.24	V.iv.134–135
II.i.17		

There are as many references to relatives as there are to fathers; we
hear of nephews, uncles, brothers, sisters, mothers, and "kinsmen,"
again on an average of once every 37 lines, but more important than
this bare statistic is the fact that here Shelley had considerable freedom
of choice. It was not necessary for him to make Cardinal Camillo the
Pope's nephew, or for the banquet to be given for the Cenci kin (in
Artaud's version, for example, the visitors are referred to only as

"friends" or "noble guests"). The script thus makes an indirect statement about the nature of human relationships, which is perhaps most
explicit in the following. Beatrice and Bernardo have been talking with
their stepmother, Lucretia, about their father's tyranny:

> *Beatrice.* Did you not nurse me when my mother died?
> Did you not shield me and that dearest boy?
> And had we any other friend but you
> In infancy, with gentle words and looks,
> To win our father not to murder us?
> And shall I now desert you? May the ghost
> Of my dead Mother plead against my soul
> If I abandon her who filled the place
> She left, with more, even, than a mother's love!
> *Bernardo.* And I am of my sister's mind. . . .
> Oh, never think that I will leave you, Mother!
>   (II.i.89–103)

Though Lucretia is only a stepmother to Bernardo and Beatrice, she
is a more genuine parent than their biological parent, Cenci. This is
all the more ironic when one considers that the stepmother is a traditional evil character in literature; Shelley is reversing our standard
attitudes toward human relationships. For him, blood ties, like the
social and legalistic bonds represented in the playscript by the power
of the Church, are merely arbitrary. Beatrice's father abuses and
ravishes her; her kinsmen, both at the banquet and later, ignore her
plight; her Church first refuses her aid and then, when she takes matters into her own hands, tortures and executes her; but her stepmother
protects and loves her. Love is not dependent on formal structures like
Church and family, but rather on individual behavior in each particular case. In this regard, the images relating to blood take on a special
significance, since the word has two possible meanings, one denoting
violence and the other kinship. In this playscript the two meanings,
which seem as far apart as possible, are equated.

Thus it is in the interaction among images that their true significance becomes clear. Again, the color words—white, gold, and blood—
suggest a powerful visual imagery that might be of considerable value

in designing the set for the production. But it would not do merely to splash white, gold, and red paint about the stage indiscriminately, without regard to the context of the imagery. In most cases in the script, white and gold are associated with evil. Gold is referred to primarily as a source of bribery and corruption:

> *Giacomo.* My friend, that palace-walking devil Gold
> Has whispered silence to his Holiness. (II.ii.68–69)

Whiteness, on the other hand, is generally associated with hypocrisy. Camillo says to Cenci:

> *Camillo.* How hideously look deeds of lust and blood
> Through those snow white and venerable hairs!
> (I.i.38–39)

Cenci is a kind of "white devil," the devil with a fair outside that is such a popular figure in Jacobean tragedy. In a similar vein, the Pope is twice described as having white or hoary hair (II.ii.39 and V.iv.23); also, the word *white* is twice associated with torture (V.ii.8 and V.ii. 169) and once with death (V.iv.139). Again, Shelley is reversing our standard attitudes, since white is usually associated with innocence or goodness, setting up a perverse ambiguity that in its own subtle way is more effective than if he had actually shown Cenci's crimes. (Needless to say, the whiteness imagery has been removed in Artaud's version.) In our production, then, the evil characters—Cenci, the "smooth and ready" Orsino, the judges in the trial scene—were all given white costumes. Cenci's even had a red lining, suggesting blood underneath whiteness like the image in Camillo's speech above. It should be clear that what we were preparing was not some kind of color code, so that the audience after two or three scenes might say, "Aha! Whiteness means evil," but rather something that would work subliminally, like the images in the text, so that the audience's standard expectations would be inverted and a feeling of uneasiness engendered.

At this point, then, I had arrived at a unifying principle that could be expressed as something like "an inversion of traditional values." In the text, whiteness implies wickedness rather than goodness;

parenthood is destructive rather than creative or protective; the act of love has become an act of hate; the Church is an instrument of evil. The evil characters—Cenci, Orsino, the judges, and the unseen Pope— are confident, vigorous, active; the ethically good characters—Lucretia, Bernardo, Giacomo, Cardinal Camillo—are hesitant, doubting, fearful, passive. The unifying principle, then, provided important information for preparing the production. The actors playing the evil characters, in addition to being costumed in white, were instructed to speak smoothly, to move vigorously, to smile and exude confidence, to be in every sense the opposite of skulking villains. I recalled Stanislavski's remarks about Iago, another "white devil" character: "His external appearance is rough, good-natured, sincere, honest. . . . There are two personalities in Iago: The one is what he appears to be, the other what he actually is. The one is pleasant, rather unrefined in manner, good-natured, the other wicked and repulsive. The exterior which he has assumed is so misleading that everyone (to a certain degree this includes his wife) is convinced he is the most sincere and best-natured of men."[8] Frank Finlay, in the 1964 National Theatre production of *Othello* that starred Sir Laurence Olivier, perfectly created Iago's good-natured, sincere façade (every other major character in the script calls Iago "honest"), much to the horror of conservatives who would have preferred the traditional swaggering blackguard to the character Shakespeare actually created. I felt that the villains in *The Cenci*, while not "rough," must similarly be played for pleasantness and sincerity. The actors chosen for the evil roles were handsome, sympathetic people. Cenci himself was played with an air of dignity and vitality, so that lines like "I never saw such blithe and open cheer / In any eye!" (I.iii.17–18), spoken of him by one of the guests at the banquet, were readily acceptable. It was only when he was alone with his family that he displayed the more ominous side of his character. It is interesting in this regard that Shelley makes Cenci a devout Catholic, who believes that "Heaven has special care of me" (I.iii.65); the historical Cenci was a notorious atheist, but Shelley here exercises the principle of choice in order to make the character decent, respectable, and righteous—in externals.

Conversely, the "good" characters were costumed in drab colors and moved and spoke in tight, hesitant ways. Lucretia developed a whining voice which undercut her pious declarations with bitter irony:

> Trust in God's sweet love,
> The tender promises of Christ: ere night,
> Think, we shall be in Paradise. (V.iv.75–77)

This speech delivered normally could have considerable force, but when given with a feeble hesitancy it expresses its opposite, denying all Sunday School notions of divine justice or an afterlife. Lucretia is not religious, but merely pathetic. Beatrice's brother Bernardo, another of the feeble/good characters, of whom Beatrice says, "the rust / Of heavy chains has gangrened his sweet limbs" (II.i.70–71), was played with a hunched back and a limp. The guests at the banquet were given a stylized, slow-motion tempo for their speeches and were rooted to their positions during their expressions of righteous outrage, so that lines like

> Thou wretch!
> Will none among this noble company
> Check the abandoned villain? (I.iii.90–93)

expressed only impotence. The actor delivering these lines spoke as if he were talking in his sleep, which contrasted strikingly with Cenci's firm, clear speech.

There is ample evidence for such contrasts in the imagery of the script: images of *flow* are contrasted with images of coldness, hardness, *frozenness*. Flow is invariably associated with the vigorous/evil characters, as when Cenci says, in one of the "blood" passages:

> My blood is running up and down my veins;
> A fearful pleasure makes it prick and tingle:
> I feel a giddy sickness of strange awe;
> My heart is beating with an expectation
> Of horrid joy. (IV.i.163–167)

Frozenness, on the other hand, is usually associated with the feeble/

good characters, like Cardinal Camillo, who says in the trial scene:

> What shall we think, my Lords?
> Shame on these tears! I thought the heart was frozen
> Which is their fountain. (V.ii.59–61)

Shelley appears to be developing a scale of values in the playscript similar to those of modern Existentialists, for whom a vigorous, committed evil (doing one's "thing," even when it is outside the boundaries of conventional morality) is preferable to pious but passive moralism. In this regard, Rolf Hochhuth's playscript *The Deputy*, in which an impotent Pope is depicted as more wicked than Hitler, even though the Pope is conventionally religious, is a modern counterpart to Shelley's *The Cenci*. In Shelley's script, Cenci really is morally preferable to his adversaries, because their response to his evil is so fitful and inept; better to be an energetic villain than a pious moralist whose morals are nothing but slogans.

The setting for the play continued the "inversion" principle. At the back was an enormous triumphal arch, through which Cenci could make heroic entrances; the weak characters generally slipped in through the sides or from the tunnel down center. There was no attempt whatever to reproduce nineteenth-century scenic conventions. The setting was fixed, with different areas of the thrust used for different scenes, with small furniture props brought out between scenes as necessary. The central and side arches at the back could be "plugged" to suggest greater confinement in some of the smaller scenes, but, beyond that, there was no creation of illusion. Instead, the designer developed religious motifs, suggesting the evil Church which always lurks as a background to the action. The stage floor (easily visible to the audience, who sit in steep tiers above it) was rebuilt in the shape of a cross. The banquet scene was staged as a mass, in keeping with the connection that Cenci himself makes:

> (*Filling a bowl of wine, and lifting it up*) Oh, thou
>   bright wine whose purple splendour leaps
> And bubbles gaily in this golden bowl
> Under the lamplight, as my spirits do,

To hear the death of my accursèd sons!
Could I believe thou wert their mingled blood,
Then would I taste thee like a sacrament. (I.iii.77–82)

We used an altar table at stage center; candles that servants, like aco-
lytes, lit onstage; and a wine glass like a chalice that Cenci elevated
during the above speech. Finally, we planned for a crucifix to hang
above the stage throughout the play, but this was cut for production—
one of several mistakes I was to make with the play.

Thus, the imagery approach provided a powerful stimulus for me
and the others working on the production. Its effect was not merely
negative—ensuring against mistakes—but also positive in that it actually channeled our imagination, suggesting original and striking
solutions to staging problems that we otherwise would not have conceived. The method is simple enough in theory: it is just a matter of
cataloguing the recurrent images, and then considering their significance in terms of the play as a whole. In practice, it is not so cut and
dried. One must be sensitive enough to spot the images that do recur,
and ready to make choices that some might find arbitrary. For example, I decided early on that words like *hoary* and *pale*, which occur
quite frequently in the script, should be included under images of
whiteness; the final list, then, was not one that could be made mechanically but one in which there was already an element of imagination.
Furthermore, many of the image clusters did not seem, to me at least,
to have any particularly significant function. There are some twenty-
one allusions to animals in the playscript; I leave it to future critics
to discover why. For some reason, there are many references to hair
as well: Cenci, the Pope, and old men in general are spoken of in
terms of their "hoary hair" (perhaps only for alliterative purposes?),
and there are several references to Cenci dragging Beatrice around by
the hair, as in "Might I not drag her by the golden hair?" (IV.i.6).
I am not sure what all this means, either, but I did not cut these
passages from the play, and I even went so far as to have the actress
playing Beatrice bleach her hair to appear "golden." Again, I believe
that a director, and a critic too, should develop a habit of modesty
toward a playscript; instead of automatically thinking, "I know better.
Chuck this out," one should always assume that the playwright knew
what he was doing, even (or perhaps especially) where the script

seems difficult or obscure. I am not a particularly modest person, as
will be seen from this book, and I am also fully aware that Shelley
was not some kind of god creating a sacred text but a fallible human
being; but nonetheless I did not feel that in the long run *my own purposes* would be well served by tampering with Shelley's script. For
one thing, a work of art that contains no element of the irrational or
inexplicable is usually tepid and dull; for another, artistic creation is
as much an unconscious as conscious process, so that theatre practitioners may well be influenced by a script in important ways that they
are completely unaware of. The purpose of a critical method is not to
explain everything in a playscript, but instead often to make it clear
that one does *not* understand certain elements. These days, when
every university bookstore sells trots that purport to give us Shakespeare "without tears," or *Hamlet* "made simple," it may be healthy
to consider the opposite: a playscript "made difficult."

Despite this, however, I still did not feel that the imagery approach
went far enough with *The Cenci*. Major problems remained, such as
the lack of onstage action, or the character of Beatrice, who did not
seem either good or evil in the way that the other characters are easily
categorizable. I did not feel that I had solutions for these problems or
had even clarified them enough as unanswerable questions. I believe
that good works of art always contain elements of the mysterious, but
one should be clearly aware of them as such; that is, one should ideally
always be able to say categorically either "this is the reason" or else
"there is no reason." Mysteriousness should not be used as an excuse
for fuzzy thinking or wild interpretation.

I began to look at the plot of the play in the temporal way I have
already discussed in Chapter IV, in terms of choice, sequence, progression, and so on. The imagery approach is basically static; it treats the
images "spatially" as everywhere simultaneously present, with no
special importance attached to the immediate context in which a
particular image occurs, or to its place in the sequence of events. In
my discussion of the imagery of *The Cenci* so far, I have occasionally
discussed the context of an image, but I have attached no importance
to where it appears in the overall progression. My point about Cenci
being a white devil, for instance, which I supported by quoting
Camillo's speech at I.i.38–39, would have been the same had Shelley

placed the passage in the last act instead of the first. But in several places, Shelley provides a sequence of whiteness images to suggest a progression, as in the following where one whiteness leads to another:

Marzio.   Your cheeks are pale.
Olimpio. It is the white reflection of your own,
              Which you call pale.
Marzio.   Is that their natural hue?
Olimpio. Or 'tis my hate and the deferred desire
              To wreak it, which extinguishes their blood.
                                        (IV.ii.20–24)

Whiteness spreads here like an infection, from Marzio's face to Olimpio's, or, as Olimpio then suggests, from his own inner hatred to his outer complexion. The same sort of thing occurs earlier, when Giacomo is describing Cenci, whom he thinks has just been murdered:

                    Ha! 'tis the blood
Which fed these veins that ebbs till all is cold:
It is the form that moulded mine that sinks
Into the white and yellow spasms of death:
It is the soul by which mine was arrayed
In God's immortal likeness which now stands
Naked before Heaven's judgment seat! (*A bell strikes.*)
                                        One! Two!
The hours crawl on; and when my hairs are white,
My son will then perhaps be waiting thus,
Tortured between just hate and vain remorse. (III.ii.18–27)

Whiteness, and thus hatred, murder, or evil in general, is infectious, passing from one character to another almost like a disease, or, in Giacomo's case, by heredity; and, when Giacomo's "hairs are white," he may pass the pollution on in turn to *his* son.

The infection sequence occurs with many other whiteness images, as in the following:

> *Lucretia.*   Could it be worse
> Than when he [Cenci] smiled, and cried,
>   "My sons are dead!"
> And every one looked in his neighbor's face
> To see if others were as white as he?
> At the first word he spoke I felt the blood
> Rush to my heart, and fell into a trance. (II.i.36–41)

Here Cenci's whiteness (and he has been specifically described as
"white" three times by this point) spreads to the entire banquet party,
including Lucretia, whose blood, like Olimpio's later, rushes from her
face. Looking at the playscript as a whole, I noticed that the early
images of whiteness refer to Cenci, but as the action proceeds they
are attached to many others: the banquet guests described in this passage, the Pope, the murderers, abstractions like "the truth" and "innocence," and finally, in the last example in the script, to Beatrice.
Bernardo has just had his final appeal rejected, and he realizes that
the prison guards have arrived to carry out the execution of his sister:

> *Bernardo.*   They come! Let me
> Kiss those warm lips before their crimson leaves
> Are blighted . . . white . . . cold. (V.iv.137–139)

It is surprising to find an image of whiteness (and again in the sense
of blood leaving the face) applied here to Beatrice; in its immediate
context it is natural enough as a means of describing death, but by
accretion the image has developed up to this point to have a strong
association with evil, and Beatrice is not an "evil" character. Or is
she? I recalled that she *is* her father's murderess, and her bold lies
about the deed, combined with her scorn for her weak accomplices, are
reminiscent of Cenci himself. The playscript begins, in the first scene,
with the "hushing up" of a murder committed by Cenci, about which
he had not the least remorse. In fact he, like Beatrice at the end, is
scornful of those who feel pangs of guilt:

> *Cenci.* All men delight in sensual luxury,
> All men enjoy revenge; and most exult
> Over the tortures they can never feel—

Flattering their secret peace with others' pain.
But I delight in nothing else.....

.   .   .   .

And I have no remorse and little fear,
Which are, I think, the checks of other men. (I.i.77–85)

In many ways, Beatrice is her father's true daughter: she shows some
of his spirit from the beginning, when she is the only one who will
stand up to him, and she resorts to one of his typical methods—venge-
ful murder—after she is raped. One of the blood images is significant
here: she tells her father, through the intermediary of Lucretia, that
she sees "a torrent / Of his own blood raging between us" (IV.i.113–
114). The two meanings of "blood"—violence and heredity—are both
suggested. Cenci reinforces the second meaning by referring to his
daughter two lines later as "this my blood, / This particle of my divided
being" (IV.i.116–117), and he is more right than he imagines. In the
same scene, Cenci repeatedly curses Beatrice, vowing to "make / Body
and soul a monstrous lump of ruin" (IV.i.94–95), and, while it seemed
to me at first that his curse does not come true, I later realized that it
does, after a fashion. The curse is a reiteration of the "infection" motif;
Cenci infects his daughter with his own wickedness, through his curses
and his ravishing her, though with a result that is different from what
he intended!

The flow imagery I mentioned earlier suggests the spread of pollution, and, like the whiteness imagery, the flow imagery progresses
through the script from Cenci to Beatrice. The first three examples of
fluidity are expressed by Cenci (I.i.112–113, I.iii.77–78, and I.iii.164–
165), who compares the tears of his enemies to the sweat of Christ,
and the wine he pours in the banquet scene to his dead sons' blood,
while his own excitement he attributes to his brain "swimming
round." Later, he describes the act of rape he is about to commit in the
following terms:

'Tis an awful thing
To touch such mischief as I now conceive:
So men sit shivering on the dewy bank,
And try the chill stream with their feet; once in . . .
How the delighted spirit pants for joy! (II.i.124–128)

> *Lucretia.*   My sweet child,
> You have no wound; 'tis only a cold dew
> That starts from your dear brow. (III.i.3–5)

Beatrice then refers to her undone hair flowing down, and then echoes Cenci's earlier reference to his swimming brain by describing her own dizziness:

>   How comes this hair undone?
> Its wandering strings must be what blind me so,
> And yet I tied it fast.—O, horrible!
> The pavement sinks under my feet! The walls
> Spin round! (III.i.6–10)

Again, the flow images, like those of whiteness, seem to transfer from Cenci to his daughter, in a grotesque kind of "heredity." One of the striking ambiguities of the playscript is that it seems to say on the one hand that kinship is meaningless (hence the importance of the stepmother Lucretia being a "true" parent as opposed to the false Cenci), but on the other hand that heredity, in an indirect and pernicious way, is the driving force behind the world. No doubt reflecting Shelley's ambivalent feelings toward his father, his two wives, and his dead son, heredity in the script carries opposite meanings, both of which must be accepted simultaneously. A scientific person would find this frustrating, yet science has never really resolved the problem of "heredity versus environment," which is a variation on the older problem of man's free will. The characters in this playscript seem both free and determined, both responsible for their acts and yet subject to malevolent forces beyond their control. Just as in real life, it is impossible to categorize their actions as purely free or unfree; the "law of the excluded middle" does not apply.

Using the flow imagery, I was able to see at last the significance of the final interchange between Beatrice and Lucretia, in which Beatrice talks calmly about their hair coming down. By itself this passage is nothing, a little slice of life that would seem out of place in a serious tragedy. But nothing demonstrates better the danger of atomizing a script than looking at an incident like this out of the context of the whole. The action of adjusting their hair recalls Beatrice's earlier action, cited above, immediately after the rape; furthermore, the flowing hair itself is a culmination of a series of flow images that "flow" themselves from Cenci to Beatrice and ultimately to the entire world, even in its most minute and apparently meaningless incidents. In other words, a principal *image* of the playscript is also the principal *action* of the playscript. And the final event in the script, the simple falling down of some locks of hair, which many directors would be tempted to alter or leave out (as Artaud did, of course), is actually the *culmination* of that action.

The major element of plot progression, then, is an infection, the flow of Cenci's vigorous evil into a passive world. Cenci pollutes not only Beatrice, but also his son Giacomo (who suggests in his speech quoted earlier that he will pass on the pollution to *his* son), his kin (represented by the guests at the banquet), the Church through his gold, Orsino through envy of Cenci's wealth and power, and, ultimately, as Beatrice herself puts it, the entire world:

> For was he not alone omnipotent
> On Earth, and ever present? Even though dead,
> Does not his spirit live in all that breathe,
> And work for me and mine still the same ruin,
> Scorn, pain, despair? (V.iv.68–72)

The unifying principle, "evil infecting goodness," is temporal as well as spatial; it is also more precise than, yet inclusive of, the earlier formula, "an inversion of traditional values." This unifying principle explains why Shelley downplays the rape in the script; the rape itself is merely one aspect of a far more general movement. Instead of presenting us with a case study of rape, in the manner of a modern television writer, Shelley is demonstrating the functioning of a Manichaean universe, in which evil is at war with good and appears to destroy it.

In production, we tried to show this progression in many ways. Naturally enough, we had Beatrice change costume as her character changed; as she moved from good to evil her costume changed from black to white. We also tried to suggest the continuation of Cenci's spirit after death through parallel costuming; his white robe was imitated in the judge's robe and in the "rich mantle" that Beatrice gives to Marzio after the murder. The same purpose was served through parallel staging, such as the use of the triumphal arch for the entrance of the judges in the trial scene, in the same manner that Cenci had entered earlier. But most important were the demands upon the actress playing Beatrice, who must show change and development from a pious, gentle character to some kind of avenging angel. Beatrice really becomes the heroine of the play (it is noteworthy that the title, *The Cenci*, is plural, referring not to her father alone but to the two of them), both in the sense of becoming its active agent and of taking on her father's characteristics. More time (and money, in the case of a professional production) should be spent on casting this part than on even that of Cenci, who is a static character, unchanging in himself.

As we rehearsed the play, I became more and more aware of the scene "ratios," in the Kenneth Burke sense, and realized I should have paid far more attention to them earlier, especially since a major problem with the script is Shelley's invariable choice to put major action offstage. As a result of the "evil infecting goodness" principle, I was convinced that Shelley did not put the rape offstage out of mere fastidiousness, but rather because he was more interested in exploring the causes and effects of this act than in making it sensational. Nevertheless, this still did not seem explanation enough. If Beatrice is brutalized by the rape, why is she so fastidious in talking about it? As we staged each scene in rehearsal, I came to realize not only that major events are offstage, but also that many minor events occur there as well. In fact, in thirteen out of the fifteen scenes, something is happening offstage *simultaneously* with the action onstage. (One becomes unavoidably aware of such things when the actors start moving through real space and speaking their lines in terms of meaning rather than abstract images, but one should develop the habit of being alert to such striking uses of scene even in reading.) Sometimes the offstage occurrences are minor and subtle, as in the opening scene when Cenci's servant, Andrea, announces:

> *Andrea.* My Lord, a gentleman from Salamanca
>   Would speak with you.
> *Cenci.*   Bid him attend me in
>   The grand saloon. (I.i.121–123)

We never see this "gentleman" or hear of him ever again; he is probably supposed to be the bearer of the letters announcing the deaths of Cenci's sons (cf. I.iii.39 ff.), but his main function here is to remind us that there is more to the world of the play than the part we can see. Other offstage events are more striking, like the murder of Cenci, the torturing of Marzio, or Bernardo's desperate entreaties to the Pope during the final scene. There is also a scene (IV.i) in which Cenci repeatedly sends word, via Lucretia and the servant Andrea, to Beatrice that she should

> . . . come hither, and before my mood
> Be changed, lest I should drag her by the hair. (IV.i.29–30)

Four times during this scene Cenci sends for her, and four times she sends back her refusal. Why does he ask so many times—why not simply drag her in as he first intended? Repeatedly, insistently, the scene reminds us that Beatrice is offstage, until she becomes the focus of our attention, more noticeable by her absence than she would be if present.

Shelley is again anticipating the achievements of the Naturalistic dramatists, here by creating an important offstage world, so that the stage becomes a "slice of life" that extends off into the wings rather than existing as a self-contained entity. Such treatment of scene is extremely rare before the late nineteenth century. There is nothing particularly new or remarkable about characters discussing offstage events, but in most earlier drama those events occur in the *past*; here, events are occurring offstage *at the same time* as the events that the audience sees, and are continuously interacting with the onstage events. This almost never happens in Shakespeare, for example; one of the few cases I can think of in which Shakespeare creates two parallel, continuing actions, one on and the other off, occurs in the scenes leading up to and including the murder in *Macbeth*—the playscript that obviously had the strongest influence of any upon *The Cenci*.

It thus became clear to me that the mysteriousness of this offstage world *is a part of the play* in performance, rather than being a regrettable fastidiousness on Shelley's part. In Kant's terms, the offstage world represents *noumena*, which can never be known directly, while the onstage world represents *phenomena*, the sense impressions we receive from which we try to deduce the truth about noumena. We are, in Giacomo's words, "as one lost in a midnight wood" (II.ii.93), reacting to strange phenomena that seem just ordered enough to suggest some underlying pattern, yet not ordered enough to convince us that the pattern is meaningful or good. That is, the pattern is an *essential mystery*. Consider cause and effect in the playscript: What is the cause of Beatrice's moral degeneration? Her father. But, behind him, we see a further cause in the Pope and the Church, who wink at Cenci's crimes and fail to protect her from him. Already we are at an unseen level, since the Pope, although important for the play's action, never appears onstage. Yet behind the Pope is God, who must bear the blame for allowing such a Pope and Church to exist. There is a hierarchy of fathers in the playscript through whom the infection is spread, from God, to the Pope, to Cenci, to Cenci's children. (And Giacomo implies that it will in the future be spread to *his* son.) The noumenal offstage world is portentous and terrifying, the ultimate source of evil in the play. God seems totally remote and cold, either a Deist figure who does not care about the world he has created, or a Manichaean demon radiating evil, or a mere figment. Lucretia, ever pious in her simple-minded way, implores Beatrice, against all the evidence to the contrary, to "trust in God's sweet love" (V.iv.75), to which Beatrice replies:

> You do well telling me to trust in God,
> I hope I do trust in Him. In whom else
> Can any trust? And yet my heart is cold. (V.iv.87–89)

Ultimately the play focuses all our attention on this "God," who both is and is not.

The noumenal quality of the offstage world may be the reason for the repeated "eye" imagery in the script. There are twenty-one references to eyes and seeing, of which the following is the most striking:

> The all-beholding sun yet shines; I hear
> A busy stir of men about the streets;
> I see the bright sky through the window panes:
> It is a garish, broad, and peering day;
> Loud, light, suspicious, full of eyes and ears. (II.i.174–178)

Note the twofold nature of the imagery: Cenci is watching and feels that he is being watched. The characters in the play always seem aware of the background to their actions, both hoping and fearing that they are being watched, yet unable to see for sure in the blackness.

I thus reached a final formulation of the unifying principle: "the flow of evil from noumena into phenomena," with all that those technical philosophical terms had come to signify from my long exploration of the script. In production, this worked very well for the visual elements—although more by coincidence, I must admit, than by insight on my part, since by this time we were practically ready to open. We had planned very specific lighting, so that the characters were usually in a sharp pool of light surrounded by blackness, suggesting the phenomena-noumena dichotomy. Parts of the stage (the side arms of the cross) slid back to reveal huge, gaping black holes, through which Cenci entered at the beginning and the victims descended at the end, suggesting again the noumenal world that is triumphant in the play. Large mirrors in the banquet scene—originally intended to suggest the two-faced natures of the guests—turned out to be very wavy and mysterious in their reflections, which in this case was all to the good. Music originally intended only for Beatrice's song at the end of V.iii was used in several other places under the action, melodrama style. It was simple and atonal, and since it was played underneath the stage it seemed to come from everywhere or nowhere; it was thus probably the most successful element in creating the illusion of an enigmatic, malevolent background.

The acting in the production, however, was generally less successful. The marriage between the generating idea and the theatre company was not really consummated, largely because of my own failure to articulate the idea with a proper unifying principle soon enough. Many of the actors were never really happy with the static quality of the play, of the necessity for a stillness in which slight movement or subtle nuance of voice must convey everything. The production should have been more like a Japanese Noh play than a traditional western performance. Furthermore, I did not spend enough time in setting up an offstage world for the actors, through improvisation and discussion, which would have made it easier for them to work with their attention offstage rather than on. In short, the production was underrehearsed. This is a far more common occurrence, even in university theatre, than is generally realized. Of course the sets were finished, the actors knew their lines, and the performance progressed smoothly. But, as is often the case, the playscript was of such complexity and difficulty that we only began to understand it at the end. Of course, had I been more perceptive about the script before rehearsals began, the extra time would not have been necessary; but, on the other hand, I see no reason why a rehearsal should not be an *exploration* rather than just the working out of a preconceived interpretation, or why critics or directors cannot be allowed to learn about a playscript from watching it in real space and time rather than just in their own heads. In the real world, human beings are fallible and playscripts difficult, and the more that is going for you the better. The possibilities of a *theatrical* approach to dramatic criticism, where one learns about a playscript from producing it, have hardly been explored.

Certainly, from this production, I learned a great deal about Shelley's *The Cenci*. Whatever else it was, the production was instructive. Furthermore, despite my lapses, I was impressed by how the play showed through. The production had a strange beauty and mystery that seemed to be correct; there was a firmness and direction that convinced me that Shelley's script, far from being riddled with errors, is the most theatrical of the versions of the Cenci story. Apparent mistakes, like Marzio's hasty death, were seen in performance to be actual strengths. There was no laughter when the guard announced that Marzio had died (although I had laughed when I first read it); instead, it seemed a typically mysterious occurrence in an offstage world that had already been established as enigmatic and terrifying. Shelley took a bizarre and sensational story from real life, but, unlike his successors who focused on the story's sensationalism, he found within it something deeper and more profoundly dramatic.

8

Ibsen's <u>A Doll House</u>

Henrik Ibsen's *A Doll House* was produced in March of 1975, again as part of the University of Calgary major production season, with the same staging parameters as the production of *The Cenci*, except that the stage itself was in a small experimental theatre that is really nothing more than a bare room about forty feet square. The room is equipped with an electronic lighting board and a lighting grid covering the entire space, so that one can place the audience and acting areas wherever one wishes. Most universities now have a studio theatre space of this kind; the main thing that differentiates the one at the University of Calgary from most others is the unfortunately low ceiling (about 12 feet high), which creates problems in both lighting and acoustics.

I had long been interested in producing *A Doll House*, even before the revival of the women's liberation movement made it once again fashionable. As I shall try to show here, it is far more than a mere propaganda tract; instead, it is a genuine modern tragedy of considerable grace, subtlety, and power. It is instructive to consider it in the context of this book, because there is a kind of prejudice against playscripts of this kind, a feeling that however well Structuralism might work with poetic dramas like those of Shakespeare or Shelley, it could be of no use with blunt, straightforward, shallow, Naturalistic playscripts like those that Ibsen is supposed to have written. This attitude is wrong. Since Structuralism is not a simple formula but a "metamethod," it is valuable in the interpretation of any kind of playscript. Moreover, Ibsen's scripts are far more difficult than is popularly imagined, making a Structuralist approach almost mandatory for any real success in producing them.

Despite a revaluation of Ibsen going back some thirty years, from M. C. Bradbrook's *Ibsen the Norwegian* through other excellent critical works by G. Wilson Knight and John Northam, plus fine new translations by Rolf Fjelde and Michael Meyer, there is a widespread prejudice against Ibsen in the theatre. It is manifested by alteration of texts (the most popular version of *A Doll House*, among the many hundreds of productions in the past few years, has been the vulgarized "adaptation" by Christopher Hampton for the London production of 1973) and, worse, by shallow productions that do not even begin to deal with the complexities of the script, when it is produced unaltered, because neither director nor actors ever imagined that such complexities might exist. It is almost as if a conspiracy existed to prove, by giving them simple-minded productions, that Ibsen wrote simpleminded playscripts.

Part of this prejudice is derived from a prejudice against Naturalism itself. The Naturalistic dramatist, it is held, merely records the surface events of life, like a newspaper reporter or a sociologist making a case study; therefore, his playscripts can hardly have any deep structure at all. Of course this is nonsense. For one thing, science itself has changed in our century, so that even scientists are no longer solely concerned with easily observed surface phenomena. For another, it has been clear since Kant that it is impossible to record life *directly*. The reason we think that the Naturalistic playwrights were doing so is because that is how they themselves described their work. They were mistaken. Instead of reporting totally objective "data," they were, like any other artists, abstracting from their experience and projecting that abstraction into a set of conventions. These conventions were somewhat different from those prevalent on stage at the time, but they were no more, and no less, close to "life itself" than any other conventions.

The Naturalistic conventions derived from a belief in the importance of phenomena, in the Kantian sense. The Naturalistic dramatist sees the phenomenological world as complete and self-contained in cause and effect. While the world of "noumena" obviously must exist, it is not remote or mysterious as in *The Cenci*; the Naturalistic dramatist accepts the empiricist belief that all we really need to know can be gained through the senses. Phenomenological events are always to be explained in terms of other such events, rather than of something unknowable behind them. This belief generates a set of dramatic conventions based on *continuity*—since there is no mystery in such a world, there can be nothing missing; nor can there be any boundaries which would imply an unknowable world beyond them. The Naturalistic stage world is one with no gaps and no ends. The stage is a slice of life that continues off into the wings. The setting creates an environment for the characters; they form a continuous fabric with it, rather than, as in earlier settings, standing isolated in front. The set itself is not just a collection of discrete parts: if there are a door and a window, there must be a wall connecting them; scene designers, often to their frustration, must consider connecting elements like rugs and ceiling pieces, as well as details like doorknobs, crockery, pictures, books, lamps, wallpaper, molding. No part of the setting or the action may seem empty. The plot of the play must be part of a long flow of continuous history, so that the characters' lives appear to continue into the past and future in the way that the set must appear to continue into the wings. The characterizations must have no gaps either: every aspect of a character must be shown to have a cause or "motivation." Lady Macbeth may not be depicted as a demon at the beginning of the play and a contrite penitent at the end without showing the continuous process (which Shakespeare, not being a Naturalist, failed to show) by which she changed from one state to the other.

A Doll House provides excellent examples of all these conventions. The setting—a living room—opens into a hallway, which opens (through the door with the letterbox) into the outer hall of the apartment building; downstairs is another door (which provides the famous door slam) to the outside. There are doors to other parts of the apartment—Helmer's study, the kitchen, the bedrooms. Upstairs is another apartment where the Helmers attend a party in Act III. We hear constantly of important locales outside the apartment building—Krogstad's room, Dr. Rank's offices, the river where Nora intends to drown herself, the small town where Mrs. Linde used to live with her husband, and Italy where Helmer and Nora lived for a year to cure his consumption. All these locales are not just "off"; they are essential to the action, constantly interacting with the events we see onstage. As with space, so too with time: We learn of Nora's upbringing, her education, her childhood friendships, her marriage, her trip to Italy with her husband, and of course her forged note, all of which are causes of what we actually see. Likewise, the action continues into the future, as we wonder, after the door slam, what will become of Nora in that cold, harsh world outside. Within the part of this continuous world that we actually see are a wealth of Naturalistic details to fill it up—props that would have rarely appeared onstage before, such as hats, coats, gloves, canes, a stove, a lamp, chairs, tables, Christmas presents, a Christmas tree, letters, newspapers, embroidery, a piano which is actually played, cigars which are actually smoked, candles which are actually lit, macaroons which are actually eaten. It is interesting to compare the prop list of *The Cenci*, which is twice as long and has a dozen locales, with that of *A Doll House*: the production of *The Cenci* required eleven pieces of furniture and some fifteen props; *A Doll House*, fourteen pieces of furniture and nearly a hundred props. This, despite the fact that *The Cenci* depicts numerous events over several years, while *A Doll House* depicts one basic event spread over a day and a half. During that day and a half, all activity is either shown directly or, after short gaps between the acts, immediately sketched in by exposition, as when Krogstad says to Mrs. Linde at the beginning of Act III, "I found a note from you at home. What's back of all this?"[1] Ibsen has created a world which, unlike that of previous drama, is continuous in both extension and enlargement, so that there are no ends as one moves offstage or outside the play's time span, and no gaps if one looks closely onstage.

It must be understood, however, that Ibsen is not doing this out of a desire for novelty—the "thrill" of seeing someone doing her embroidery onstage—or merely as a means of creating verisimilitude. His technique arises out of a vision of the world as being structured in a certain special way. This vision will seem more "real" than that of a Romantic like Shelley if it accords with one's own view of how that universe works, but that is all. By itself, the continuity technique is neutral, no less and no more conventional than the Romantic technique of depicting the world in separate chunks.

Nor does Naturalistic continuity preclude the use of artistic tech-

niques common to all good drama—the symbolism, the hidden patterns, the complexity and ambiguity. It is just that these aspects will
be organized in a different way. A simple example is the famous door
slam at the end of the play. Ibsen loved spectacular climaxes, ending
Brand (written in the Romantic style) with an avalanche that destroys the hero and a companion as they struggle to reach the peak of
a mountain. The avalanche is suggestive of many meanings—the
hopelessness of Brand's quest, the ruthlessness of nature, the mortality
of man. It also culminates, in a physical way, the "submersion" motif
that is developed throughout the work, the conflict between individu-
ality and mediocrity that is at the core of the play's meaning. But the
point is that, since *Brand* is not a Naturalistic play, Ibsen was not
required to give the avalanche itself any real justification. It appears
to be "caused" by a mysterious hawk at which Brand's companion has
been shooting, or it may even, it is suggested, *be* the hawk itself transformed into an avalanche by magic. In other words, it is not caused
by anything in the world itself but by something hidden and inexplicable behind it, a mysterious deity of some sort. For this reason, the
symbolic nature of the avalanche is obvious; it is made to stand out
from the fabric of the play, almost like proclaiming "symbolism" with
flashing lights. The door slam in *A Doll House* is in many ways equivalent to the avalanche in the earlier play: it too suggests many meanings beyond its immediate function of punctuating Nora's exit, such
as the end of a way of life, the "gulf" between Nora and her husband
that Helmer talks about (p. 113), and perhaps a crashing chord in a
musical finale, since we only hear the door slam without seeing it,
and the play has contained a great deal of music up to that point. The
difference between this and the avalanche is that, while it is a symbolic act, it is also completely motivated: Nora has to go out the door
to leave the house, and she slams the door as an expression of her anger
and resolution. To the naïve audience member, the event does not
even seem to be a symbol but rather the simple continuation of a
linear progression of action. Nevertheless, it is no accident that this
door slam has come to stand, in the public's mind, for the play itself
(one famous teacher always used to tell his classes that "when Nora
slammed the door at the end of *A Doll House*, she opened the door on
modern drama"); everybody remembers the slam because it really
does sum up the meaning of the play. The slam is a symbol, but it is

what might be called an "integrated" symbol rather than a detached one like the avalanche.

It is important that symbolic elements in a Naturalistic masterpiece like *A Doll House* not be overlooked, because of their integration into the action. I have seen productions in which the final door slam sounded as if someone had tripped over a piece of scenery backstage. This was a serious mistake. If anything, such symbols should even be a bit exaggerated with Ibsen, because, as we shall see, he often exaggerated them himself, struggling against the Naturalistic convention rather than completely submitting to it. In our production, the final sound was almost like the slamming of a bank vault, and Helmer, onstage, reacted to it almost as if he *were* hit by an avalanche. In our production generally, we were very careful to construct a continuous, Naturalistic façade. We researched the period in order to make historically accurate props and costumes. There were a real Christmas tree, real lamps, a stove that glowed when real coal was put into it, real children and a real baby (often cut from productions for expediency), real embroidering, real knitting, real cigar smoking. We carefully worked out, at the beginning of rehearsals, a blueprint for the entire apartment house, a map of the town, and its location in Norway. We got books and pictures of Italy and discussed what Nora and Helmer's trip there might have been like. We improvised important scenes from the past, before the play begins: Krogstad courting Mrs. Linde, Helmer in his illness being examined by Dr. Rank, Nora borrowing the money from Krogstad. One long improvisation was simply a day taken at random out of the Helmers' lives—the maids cleaning and working in the kitchen, Helmer working in his study, Nora playing with the children and doing her embroidery. (Since the seats for the audience were not yet in place, there was enough room to lay down the entire floor plan of the Helmers' apartment in the theatre.) The purpose of all these exercises was to develop "relating" in the Stanislavski sense, establishing connections between the actors and each other, as well as between the actors and their surroundings. It was important that the actors behave as if they knew one another, were used to each other's presence, were in some cases intimate with one another, and were in surroundings that were very familiar, filled with memories of the past. On a basic level, it is always important when, say, two actors must gesture offstage to the kitchen that they point in the same direction, but for this play I wanted far more, so that the characters would seem embedded in their environment. The maids would practically know every board in the floor from cleaning it, Helmer every scratch in his desk from working there, Nora the exact workings of the living room stove, to which she must add coal during the play. All these continuity-generating exercises are essential in producing Naturalistic drama.

Yet they are nothing new; for most good directors, such techniques have become standard practice. My point here is that *by themselves they are not enough.* Continuity is, if you like, the "unifying principle" for all Naturalistic drama, taken as a whole. It does not by itself provide a unifying principle for an individual play. In production, continuity is only a starting point, a means to an end and never an end in itself. In our *A Doll House* production, I was concerned that the playscript's deep structure, as well as its surface structure, be presented in performance. I had seen too many productions of Ibsen, some by brilliant directors, that were rich in Naturalistic detail, had superb ensemble performances, and an overall façade as smooth as glass but still were not plumbing the depths of the script. Had they been doing Shakespeare, these directors would never have dreamed of restricting themselves to pretty costumes, pleasant voices, and an attractive set, but because of Ibsen's reputation as a "Naturalist" they were doing the equivalent with him.

It is interesting to consider the shape that anti-Ibsen prejudice takes in the theatre. There are striking contradictions. On the one hand, *A Doll House* is supposed to be an ardently feminist playscript; yet, on the other, it is rarely performed anymore without its feminism hyped up. On the one hand, the playscript is ridiculed as simple, kitchen-sink Naturalism; on the other, it is ridiculed (often by the same people!) for being clumsy and *un*natural. The character Krogstad, I was told, is a villain out of the cheapest melodrama, and his sudden conversion at the end a fatuous sentimentality. The trip south to save Helmer's life, which caused all the trouble in the first place, is a feeble contrivance—as if a vacation on the Mediterranean could have transformed a dying man into the healthy, vigorous individual we actually see onstage. Dr. Rank is an obvious death symbol, and symbols are something that Naturalism was supposed to have got rid of. And, as for all the nonsense with the letters and the letterbox, it is a bit of stage hokum that even Ibsen does not seem to believe in, because, after he finally has manipulated Krogstad to the point where he is willing to take his damning letter back unread, Mrs. Linde tells him not to, and he doesn't! But worst of all, Nora's famous decision to walk out is poorly motivated; she has been characterized until then as frivolous and naïve, and to have her leave her husband, and especially her children, after a little spat, is hard to believe.

Now obviously, the anti-Ibsenites cannot have it both ways—condemning the playscript for being too Naturalistic and at the same time for not being Naturalistic enough. The existence of these contradictions is evidence that people have been looking at the playscript in the wrong way. A genre approach does not work with Ibsen. "Naturalism" as a slogan may work with lesser playwrights like Zola or Brieux, but Ibsen, like all great writers, transcends the style in which he is operating. It is worth recalling that he began as a poet and verse dramatist, writing many plays in the Romantic style, before turning to Naturalism with *Pillars of Society*—his fifteenth play, written when he was forty-nine. The "flaws" in *A Doll House* are revealed to be no flaws at all when one takes a critical approach that is suitable to it. Because of this, I was convinced that we could produce the play without altering the text and without making the usual qualifications and apologies about it that have become common from so many directors.

The approach taken to the text was through the philosophy of the Swedish philosopher Søren Kierkegaard. I need not here go into the reasons for this choice. The influence of Kierkegaard on Ibsen has been a controversial topic since Ibsen's lifetime—Ibsen himself repeatedly denied any Kierkegaardian influence at all—and is still a topic of interest to scholars of both men. The important thing for us, however, was how well the Kierkegaardian philosophy served to illuminate Ibsen's work. That is, for staging purposes, it does not matter whether the Kierkegaardian patterns in *A Doll House* are the result of conscious imitation, unconscious influence, or sheer coincidence. In analyzing a playscript for production, we are concerned with the Structuralist question of how it works, rather than the historical question of how it came to be written.

Basically, Kierkegaard identified three stages of individual existence: the aesthetic, the ethical, and the religious. The first two are described extensively in his two-volume work *Either/Or*, written in 1843, and the third in his book *Fear and Trembling*, completed the same year. Although each stage of life is higher and better than the previous, each has its own purpose and validity. The aesthetic person lives for self-gratification; the ethical for duty; the religious for faith. The religious level, although an important idea in several other of Ibsen's playscripts, is not at issue in *A Doll House* and thus need not concern us here, but the aesthetic and ethical levels, and the relation between them, are very important to this particular script.

The aesthetic person lives for pleasure; he is literally amoral, though not necessarily *immoral*. His philosophy of life, if it can be called that, is *carpe diem*, seize the day, live for the moment. "Time flows, life is a stream, people say, and so on. I do not notice it. Time stands still, and I with it," writes Kierkegaard in an aesthetic persona.[2] A prime example of this type is the artist, in the nineteenth-century sense of the Bohemian lover of pleasure and beauty; hence the term, "aesthetic." Yet the pleasures need not be entirely selfish ones; love of family or friends, for example, in the direct and simple warmth of an animal or child rather than the mature and responsible manner of an an adult human being, is possible for this type.

The ethical person, by contrast, lives for duty and personal vocation. Duty for him is not merely an externally imposed obligation, an onerous necessity, but part of his very being, an inner compulsion: "He has clad himself in duty, for him it is the expression of his inmost nature," writes Kierkegaard.[3] The ethical person loves "the universal," in the Kantian sense of the categorical imperative, where each human action must be weighed as though it were a universal principle. As the title character in Ibsen's *Brand* says, "I know but one law for all mankind. / I cannot discriminate."[4] There are no exceptions, no special cases, not even, as in Brand's case, for one's own family. A prime example of this type is found in the Bible, in the character of Job.

In Kierkegaard's philosophy, these stages are to be considered totally separate; development from one to another is a matter of a great leap rather than a gradual change. The aesthetic man does not, say, grow bored with a life of pleasure, donate a few dollars to the Red Cross, and coach a basketball team on Saturdays, and thus gradually turn into a Job. The transformation is sudden and total, usually in response to a great challenge. Nevertheless, the fact that gradual development is not possible does not mean that intermediates do not exist. But these intermediates are not stages of life in the same sense that the aesthetic, ethical, and religious are, because they lack validity. They are a kind of shadowy, half existence, even worse than the stage halfway below. Kierkegaard described the state between aesthetic and ethical as "ironic," and between ethical and religious as "humorous," the words denoting the ludicrous, counterfeit nature of such existence. An ironic person is a hypocrite, presenting a pious ethical façade to the world while actually being venal and self-serving. The intermediate levels, then, are definitely not to be thought of as halfway houses for the validly developing individual; such a person leaps over them.

The important elements of Kierkegaard's philosophy for the understanding of *A Doll House*, then, are the aesthetic and ethical stages of life; the intermediate, hypocritical, ironic level; and the idea of a sudden transformation or leap. The principal event in the play, which is Nora's walking out on her family at the end, can be clearly seen as an example of a leap to an ethical stage of existence; but the Kierkegaardian scheme pervades the entire playscript, providing it with a unifying principle. Consider the characterization of Nora. From the beginning, she is treated symbolically: The play begins with her entrance, as she comes in humming and carrying Christmas gifts for her children. A delivery boy follows with a Christmas tree. Nora pays him, adding a large tip (which we soon discover she cannot afford). As soon as he leaves, she reaches into her pocket for some macaroons, which she eats greedily. Hearing her moving about, Helmer calls to her from his study, "Is that my little lark twittering out there?" (p. 43). He is in the habit, it seems, of calling her names of small animals as terms of endearment; he later repeatedly calls her a bird, a squirrel, a lark, a dove. Nora's love of music, her extravagance, her appetite, her association with animals—all establish her as an aesthetic character, as do her love of her family, her shameless lying, her dancing the tarantella. Her transformation at the end is thus a straightforward Kierkegaardian leap from the aesthetic to the ethical stage of life; it *is* weakly motivated, but then one must remember that Kierkegaard's theory of the individual, being discontinuous, is essentially unnaturalistic. Behind the Naturalistic façade of *A Doll House* is a theory of characterization that is actually Romantic. Nora herself, while having

many of the "well-rounded" features we have come to expect in a
Naturalistic playscript, is depicted basically in terms of two conven-
tionalized types.

Helmer, Nora's husband, is depicted in contrast with her, being
characterized through the first two and a half acts of the playscript as
strongly ethical. Nora is particularly impressed with his high moral
character:

> Being a lawyer is such an uncertain living, you know, espe-
> cially if one won't touch any cases that aren't clean and decent.
> And of course Torvald would never do that, . . . (P. 49)

They have had to live frugally as a result of Helmer's ethics, which
necessitated the loan with the forged signature that Nora obtained
when his illness required a trip south. Helmer himself would never
have gone into debt:

> No debts! Never borrow! Something of freedom's lost—and
> something of beauty, too—from a home that's founded on
> borrowing and debt. (P. 44)

Helmer has a natural bent for preaching like this—to others. He turns
every scene with Nora, until the final one, into a little moral lesson,
against debt, against extravagance, against lying, against hypocrisy.
But, although he seems a bit of a prig, we do not suspect (nor does
Nora) that his morality is a mask. When he finally learns of Nora's
forged note, he at first acts true to form:

> I should have suspected something of the kind. I should
> have known. All your father's flimsy values— Be still!
> All your father's flimsy values have come out in you. No
> religion, no morals, no sense of duty— (P. 105)

This is just the sort of thing Nora expected. She accepts it calmly and
is even resigned to committing suicide, by jumping into the river. (A
common motif that Ibsen often associates with the aesthetic character
is that of drowning or dissolving.) But almost immediately Helmer's

façade begins to crumble. He is more concerned with his own career, it turns out, than with Nora's moral character:

> Now you've wrecked all my happiness—ruined my whole future.
> Oh, it's awful to think of. I'm in a cheap little grafter's
> hands; he can do anything he wants with me, ask for anything,
> play with me like a puppet—and I can't breathe a word. I'll
> be swept down miserably into the depths on account of a feather-
> brained woman. (Pp. 105–106)

The phrase "swept down miserably into the depths" and the word *puppet* (remember the title of the play!) both ironically suggest that *he* is now at the aesthetic level. Where Nora had just been about to plunge into the depths literally, by committing suicide, he has unwittingly plunged down morally, in her eyes as well as the audience's. His moral downfall parallels Nora's moral rise, although in Nora's case it is a genuine change while in his it is merely an unmasking; he has been a hypocrite all along.

A new letter suddenly arrives from Krogstad. Enclosing the forged note, he announces that he is ashamed of his former ways and is turning over a new leaf. Helmer's reaction exposes his own moral weakness—he tears up both letters as well as the note and burns them, delighted that the whole affair has blown over and that his life can return to normal. The moment is extremely theatrical, in a miniature way reminiscent of similar climaxes in Ibsen's earlier, Romantic plays, like the avalanche in *Brand* or Peer Gynt dying in Solveig's arms as the sun rises in *Peer Gynt*. The papers burn, a little glow spreading through the room, while a "frozen look" (p. 107) comes over Nora's face. This moment is the turning point in the play, which is often overlooked or underplayed in performance because of the famous "discussion scene" that follows. But the discussion is merely the working out of what has already happened—the vast yet almost instantaneous transformation of Nora, precipitated by the equally sudden change in the opposite direction of Helmer. Of equal importance with the discussion is the action that accompanies it. Nora changes from her dancing-girl costume (a souvenir of the trip to Italy) into regular clothes, symbolizing her change in character from the aesthetic to the ethical. She then proceeds not so much to "discuss" things with her husband as to *preach* to him—as he used to preach to her—telling him solemnly that "right from our first acquaintance, we've never exchanged a serious word on any serious thing" (p. 108), that she has been a doll-wife to him, that she now feels a "duty" to herself to find out what is morally genuine in life. Helmer's words, by contrast, are now all of love, family, children—Nora's former obsessions. But he learns that it is of no use, recognizing the Kierkegaardian separation between their states of existence with the characteristic phrase, "There's a gulf that's opened between us" (p. 113), a gulf that is further emphasized at the end by the slammed door.

Thus, Helmer and Nora reflect one another in reverse. In fact, all the characters in the script (including one who does not even appear onstage) can be arranged in a Kierkegaardian scheme, reinforcing and contrasting each other:

Aesthetic	*Ironic*	*Ethical*
Nora (Acts I, II, beginning of III)		Nora (end of Act III)
Helmer (end of III)	(Helmer throughout)	Helmer (I, II, beginning of III)
Krogstad (I, II, beginning of III)		Krogstad (end of III)
The Helmer children		
Nora's father (unseen)		
Delivery boy		
Anne-Marie (nursemaid)		Helene (maid)

Helmer, as can be seen, is a special case, since his *true* character throughout is at the intermediate, hypocritical, ironic level. We see the ethical side of him through the first two and a half acts and the aesthetic side at the end.

This scheme also clarifies the position of Krogstad. His reformation is indeed stagy, in Naturalistic terms—but then so is Nora's. The important factor in terms of the structure of the playscript is that his change exactly parallels hers; the situation is like plot and subplot in

Shakespeare, one of Ibsen's most important literary influences. In fact, there is a third character whose history parallels that of Nora and Krogstad—Mrs. Linde, Nora's former school companion. Originally (before the play began), we are told, Mrs. Linde married for money in a meaningless marriage—another doll, another house. After the death of her husband, she changed drastically, taking on the responsibility of supporting her bedridden mother and her two young brothers. She began working for her living and generally leading an independent life. Nora does not even recognize her when she arrives, because she has changed so dramatically (p. 48).

Mrs. Linde is one of the catalysts for transformations in the play. She provides part of the inspiration for Nora's eventual change, by proving that a woman can function on her own. Mrs. Linde is also instrumental in the transformation of Krogstad; the two are paired off at the end, with the implication that they will marry. Their marriage thus serves as a contrast to the two bogus marriages in the play, incidentally showing that Ibsen was not opposed to *all* marriage, but only marriages that had no ethical foundation. *A Doll House* is Ibsen's most straightforward study of the ethical life.

As rehearsals for the play progressed, we found that the aesthetic-ethical polarity operates even at the level of the minor characters. There are two maids in the Helmer household, both of whom for some reason have French names—Anne-Marie and Helene. Anne-Marie, it turns out, had an illegitimate child in her youth, which she gave to strangers (p. 73); she then came to be Nora's nursemaid when Nora was a child, and is now nursemaid in turn to Nora's own children. Being established as amoral, and closely associated with children, she is an example of an aesthetic character. The other maid, Helene, is less completely characterized, but it is apparent from the tasks we see her do—lighting lamps, answering the door, delivering messages—that she is far more involved than Anne-Marie in the actual running of the household. That is, in a rather sketchy way, she is an ethical character. We tried to show this contrast in the casting, makeup, costuming, and performance of the two roles. Anne-Marie was warm, friendly, rather heavy-set, and a bit vague and rambling; Helene was thin, austere, brisk, efficient.

In general, the Kierkegaardian scheme was of great help to the actors in production. It enabled us to avoid the pitfalls of the usual feminist approach to the playscript. That is, the play becomes richer and more interesting if Helmer is *not* characterized as a male chauvinist pig with Nora as his noble, suffering captive. In our production, we made it clear that Nora had married for love and took great delight in her family. The important thing, in Kierkegaardian terms, is that she *changes* in the course of the play, suddenly and drastically. If she is played heroically from the beginning, we wonder why she never left her husband long ago—indeed, why she ever married him in the first place. Through the first three-fourths of our version, the actress instead did everything possible to suggest an animal or a child, rather than a mature adult. She pranced about the stage like the squirrel Helmer always compares her to; when she played with the children she giggled and rolled about the floor even more enthusiastically than they did; she danced the tarantella wildly; and, in the serious scenes, she whined and pouted like a child who had been caught at the cookie jar. In the final scene, however, she became a different person. Her hair, formerly in pigtails or, when she was in her tarantella costume, hanging loosely, was now drawn back severely. Her costume had straight, hard lines, hiding the curves of her body, and was colored a plain, dark gray. She lowered her voice in pitch and spoke to Helmer harshly and brusquely, often interrupting or "topping" his lines in her replies to him. Rather than a sentimentalized cliché of a liberated woman, she became something hard, cold, a bit unpleasant. Recalling that, for Kierkegaard, the *religious* rather than the ethical life is the highest, we made clear that there were drawbacks to her new character just as there had been to the old. This in turn made many elements of the play clearer to the audience—why she would so callously leave her children; why Helmer's traditional methods of controlling her, such as offering her protection or sex, no longer worked; and how she was going to survive in the cruel world outside that had been so vividly described earlier by Krogstad and Mrs. Linde.

As for Helmer, he does not change in the play, but he is *exposed*. We tried to have the audience always see him through Nora's eyes, so that his behavior at the end was a genuine exposure, rather than merely a confirmation of what everyone was thinking about him all along. His little sermons to Nora, for example, were spoken with simple conviction, as if he genuinely believed them. He was relaxed rather than pompous, pleasant rather than brutal. In terms of his society, he was a *good* husband, not a lout. He acted in a genuinely protective way toward his wife; he did not want to "exploit" her, any more than one wants to exploit one's child or pet, but neither did he treat her as his equal. At the end, the difference in his character was striking—a complete surprise to Nora (later she actually says that she never dreamed he would act the way he did, but in many productions there is no contrast at all, because Helmer is established as a phony from his first entrance). A whining note came into his voice, and his firm posture became a cringe. During the time Nora was changing out of her tarantella costume, he too began to undress— loosening his tie, removing his coat, unbuttoning his vest—reflecting the moral stripping that had just taken place. The contrast at the end between the fully, even overly, dressed Nora and the disheveled Helmer was telling.

The aesthetic-ethical polarity informs other elements of the play-script than characterization. It is no accident that Ibsen sets the play in winter, and at Christmastime at that. The characters repeatedly speak of the cold outside, the snow, the "freezing black water" in which Nora intends to drown herself. Inside, we see elements of not only physical but also emotional warmth: the stove, the Christmas tree, a piano, pictures on the wall. The image is one of coziness, intimacy, and protectiveness, which only at the end appears repressive. Nora's house (which, after all, gives the play its title) represents the aesthetic stage of life, upon which she slams the door at the end, to escape to the cold ethical world of independence and duty outside. We added everything the budget would allow to enhance the "aesthetic" quality of the room, using rugs, tablecloths, bric-a-brac, doilies, and over-stuffed furniture, all in warm colors wherever possible. Rather than the proscenium set Ibsen calls for, we used a thrust placed in one corner of the room, with the audience seated on two sides in the form of an L. In a large theatre, this would probably have been a mistake, because a box set would have been necessary there to give the proper sense of enclosure; in our tiny theatre with its low ceiling, however, that feeling was already there, and I thought that a thrust stage would add to the quality of intimacy. The audience would also be close enough to see nuances of gesture and hear shades of meaning that are so important in Naturalism.

Because of the thrust stage, however, we lost a wall on the set, and

thus had to place the window Ibsen calls for on one of the sides of the
living room facing the audience. The actors related to it as if it were
there, and did many exercises in rehearsal to try to project a reaction
to the frozen world outside that would make it vivid when they were
supposed to be looking at it. We also worked hard on every entrance
from outside to make it clear that the characters were coming in from
the cold. They wore coats, hats, gloves, boots; they shivered, blew on
their hands, stamped their feet. The children even came in covered
with snow—no hard task in Canada in the wintertime, since there was
always plenty of it just outside the theatre door! But the loss of the
window was a serious one. Although the actors did respond well to the
imaginary window, the audience should always be able to see a real,
visible window as a reminder of the outside world, forming a constant
background to the play. In general, although working in intimate
theatres of this kind enhances many aspects of Naturalistic drama,
there is inevitably a loss of a visual impression of the outside world.
I have never yet seen an effective solution to this problem, and must
say that I am at a loss to think of one myself.

We also tried to use the set to reflect elements of the past, which are
so important to the action of this play. There was a picture of Nora's
father on one wall (Helmer pointed to it when discussing her father
in the final scene), as well as pictures of Italy and even a general
Italian style of decor throughout the room. A common error in producing Ibsen is to put the play in a typical Norwegian living room
of the period, usually reproduced from some book of period furnish-
ings. But in *A Doll House*, the interior does not represent "Norway";
Norway is the cold, harsh world outside. Norway and Italy, north
and south, are again the aesthetic-ethical polarity (as they are in
many other of Ibsen's playscripts). Norway is the place where Helmer
got sick, where Dr. Rank *is* sick, a severe land of ice and snow, of
money and debts, where people work themselves to exhaustion, where
respectability and devotion to duty are necessities of life. Italy is the
land of warmth, of the tarantella, of music and joy and love. It is also
the place where Helmer recovered his health—perhaps a medical flaw
in the playscript, but certainly not an artistic one. For our setting, we
tried to create an *Italian* interior rather than a Norwegian one. Why
would Nora and Helmer not try to make their living room a constant
reminder of the land that meant so much to them? But, more impor-

tant, the living room in symbolic terms represents the same thing that
Italy does, a refuge of warmth and love.

Nevertheless, within the living room we tried to suggest a polarity
also. The two poles Ibsen gives in the script here are the stove and the
window—warm and cold, aesthetic and ethical. Ibsen has Nora go to
the stove whenever she is emotionally upset, as if it could revitalize
her. It is a cozy corner of the room to which she naturally gravitates
for scenes of love and happiness. When her old friend Mrs. Linde
comes for a visit, for example, Nora says:

> Yes, enjoy ourselves, we'll do that. But take your coat off.
> You're not still cold? (*Helping her.*) There now, let's get
> cozy here by the stove. (P. 48)

In general, we played the emotional scenes, like this one or the one
in which Dr. Rank declares his love for Nora in Act II, by the stove.
Business scenes, like those between Nora and Krogstad or the discussion scene between Nora and Helmer at the end, were played at the
opposite corner of the room, at the window or the table, which was
placed next to it. But of course, being so far from the stove, this area
would *literally* be cold, which the actors could show by putting their
hands in their pockets, buttoning up their jackets, shivering, and so
on. It is a good example of integrated symbolism, in which symbolic
coldness is enhanced by fully plausible, actual cold.

Assigning emotional qualities to various areas of the room made
possible all kinds of parallels and contrasts in the staging. The scene
between Krogstad and Mrs. Linde at the beginning of Act III, which
starts as a cold-blooded discussion about the letter and ends in a mutual
declaration of love, naturally began at the table and ended on the sofa
by the stove. The scene between Helmer and Nora that follows, which
begins with Helmer making love to her and ends in the dissolution
of their marriage, began at the sofa and ended at the table. One of the
chairs at the table was established as Nora's; in the opening scene
she sat there like a child receiving a scolding, while Helmer moved
about the room lecturing her. In the final scene, he sat in the same
chair while she moved in the same pattern and lectured *him*. Similarly, an easy chair with a footstool (on the "cold" side of the room)
was established as Helmer's; Nora sat on the footstool at his feet in

the scenes where he is working on some papers. At the end, in the scene where he "forgives" her, she sat in the same chair and he on the footstool. The action of forgiving was undercut by the weak position in which he had placed himself, as well as reminiscences of the same physical relationship, in reverse, in the earlier scenes. Thus, in the final scene, the staging showed Helmer literally lowering himself, and Nora literally rising, at the same time they were doing so in a symbolic sense.

The audience member of course does not respond consciously to such things, at least the first time he sees the play. But, gradually, subliminally, by accretion, certain emotions become associated with certain spaces and certain patterns of movement and *can be evoked by them.* Performance is then not just something generally "immediate" or "lively," as theatre boosters are always describing it, but expressive of specific thoughts and feelings; the physical reality of the stage becomes *metaphorical as well as tangible,* in the same way that words, in a literary work, become metaphorical as well as literal. This is how effective staging can proceed from the playtext, even when not found in the text surface. When one sees a script not as a dry bit of philosophy or journalism, to which staging must be added to make entertaining, but rather as an emotional complex that implies certain metaphorical staging by projection, one arrives at a production that is not just "correct" in a pedantic way, but more exciting, more powerful, more truly *theatrical* than is possible with the additive process. Proper staging is in the text by implication. This does not mean that there is only one correct way of staging a script, but it does mean that, once variables of stage and actor are established, the script will suggest certain natural staging potentials. It is neither necessary nor possible that these potentials be *completely* realized, but they *should* be looked upon as the primary source of the director's and actors' inspiration.

A process similar to our work with the setting enabled us to arrive at effective costuming for the production. Ibsen already gives one very powerful contrast in costuming: Nora's change from her tarantella costume into her street dress at the end. The change is fully justified in logical, Naturalistic terms—she can hardly go off to make her way in the world dressed as a Neapolitan peasant girl—but it also represents the usual aesthetic-ethical polarity. By extension from this example, we were able to dress the aesthetic characters like Krogstad, the children, and Nora at the beginning in warm colors, while the ethical characters like Mrs. Linde, Helmer at the beginning, or Nora at the end were in cool colors or black. The aesthetic costumes were free flowing and showed (as much as possible for Norway in winter in 1879) a good deal of the body underneath; the ethical costumes were actually constructed a bit too tight for the actors wearing them and hid the body completely except for the face and hands. (This in turn affected the actors' movements in a striking way: the aesthetic characters moved freely and easily, while the ethical characters were stiff and constricted.) The point is that in staying within the requirements of the text, even one as Naturalistic as *A Doll House*, there was still enormous scope for the designer's imagination. The text was actually a stimulus to the designer, rather than a hindrance. Recostuming the play in Nazi Germany or Canada in 1975 would have been unthinkable, not because we were afraid of offending Ibsen purists (if such people even exist), but rather because such possibilities would have seemed terribly drab and unimaginative in contrast with those suggested *by the script.*

The production of *A Doll House* was, in the end, extremely successful. I do not like appeals to the audience's reaction as proof of goodness or badness in the theatre—audiences have been wrong in the past as often as critics or academicians—but, since my view of the text and its production might be dismissed as merely an academic exercise, I should say that we received excellent reviews, that we turned away customers every night, and that many people came back and saw the play twice—and some came as many as five or six times. Treating Ibsen's playscript seriously, attempting to come to grips with its depth and complexity, yields a more exciting and even a more controversial production than would treating it condescendingly, as has become traditional. A noble heroine escapes from an oppressive husband—what is so radical about that, even for 1879? Taking that route in production is quickly boring. Ibsen is far more radical than even his reputation, when it is clear that Nora is walking out, not on oppression, but on *love.*

9

Pinter's <u>The Homecoming</u>

Pinter's *The Homecoming* was produced at the University of Calgary in the early spring of 1972, as an example of a contemporary, "Theatre of the Absurd" playscript. Like *The Cenci*, it was performed in the university's main theatre, on its thrust stage. The actors were, as with both *The Cenci* and *A Doll House*, students in the Drama Department. I offer it here as an interesting example of a Structuralist approach to contemporary material, in which the notion of "deep structure" is often indispensable.

It is well known that Pinter's scripts play better than they read. The impression the reader first gets is of flat, Naturalistic dialogue that winds on aimlessly:

> *Lenny*. Staying the night then, are you?
> *Teddy*. Yes.
> *Lenny*. Well, you can sleep in your old room.
> *Teddy*. Yes, I've been up.
> *Lenny*. Yes, you can sleep there.
>   *Lenny yawns.*
>   Oh well.
> *Teddy*. I'm going to bed.
> *Lenny*. Are you?
> *Teddy*. Yes, I'll get some sleep.
> *Lenny*. Yes I'm going to bed, too.[1]

Punch magazine once published a cartoon showing Pinter, disguised in a dog costume, eagerly transcribing the conversation of two cockneys at a table above him. Indeed, at first glance, his scripts do appear to be a slice of life, carried to the point of inanity. Nevertheless, the impression on the audience in performance—at least with good productions—is quite different. The plays seem highly charged, even melodramatic. The rhythm of the dialogue, when spoken, turns out to be both musical and evocative. (It is no accident, for example, that in the speech above there is a comma after "Yes" in Teddy's final speech, and none in Lenny's reply.[2] The comma is there to suggest a slight hesitation, a reluctance, on the part of Teddy, to which Lenny responds with force and finality.) And beneath the bland façade lurk terror and violence.

Many productions of Pinter do fail, however. There are two prevalent causes of this: The first is to treat his playscripts as if they really were Naturalistic, taking seriously all the elaborate exposition and personal history the characters supply and dealing with the action in terms of psychological motivation. The second is the "Theatre of the Absurd" approach. This phrase was invented by Martin Esslin, in a book of that name, to describe the scripts of a number of playwrights who came to prominence in the nineteen-fifties, such as Beckett, Genet, and Ionesco. Esslin was using the term *absurd* in a very strict sense, in the manner of the Parisian Existentialists, for whom all existence is absurd, including the apparently logical or mundane. That is, Esslin was not talking about zany behavior as such, or absurdity in the popular sense. Unfortunately, however, in the theatre the phrase came to mean, for many directors, crazy plays about crazy people doing crazy things. From this it is easy to infer that the scripts are just "scenarios," having nothing to do with traditional drama, with which the performers can have a delightful holiday. Copyright laws prevent drastic alterations of the script, but productions of this sort will ignore stage directions, rewrite or improvise lines, introduce extraneous elements like masks or flashing lights, and treat dialogue as a meaningless chant. Either approach, the Naturalistic or the "Absurdist," is of course disastrous, once again illustrating the dangers of an extrinsic method of script analysis. In order to make Pinter's plays function effectively in the theatre, it is necessary instead to analyze, in detail, how the scripts themselves actually function.

A genre approach, whether via Naturalism or Theatre of the Absurd, is especially dangerous with Pinter's playscripts, because of the *separation* of the surface and deep structures. With Ibsen, or Shelley, or even Shakespeare, one can often succeed with a surface approach to the text (assuming one works with care and does not rewrite anything), because the deeper meanings are intensifications or extensions of what is on the surface; the Kierkegaardian patterns in *A Doll House*, for example, amplify the play's significance but they are not *opposed* to the surface action of a wife leaving her husband. In a Pinter play, on the other hand, the surface action may be totally unrevealing: Two brothers live together in their family house with the two sons of the elder. A third son comes to visit with his wife. The third son leaves, but his wife remains. The uncle dies, and the father himself has a heart attack. This description explains nothing. While a wife walking out on her husband automatically implies some specific moral questions, the comings and goings in *The Homecoming* could, in outline, provide the basis for almost any kind of play. There is nothing in the outline that automatically implies the furious power struggle going on underneath—yet that struggle is the essence of the play, without which the performance will be either flat and dull or aimlessly confusing.

For our production, we first approached the text via the ratios of Kenneth Burke, looking at the background to the action and the characters, in both a historical and immediate, spatial sense. The script then appears to bear out the first impressions of a slice of life; that is, there are vast and complicated extensions offstage in space, and backward and forward in time. From the father, Max, we learn about his parents, his dead wife Jessie, his sons as they were growing up, a mysterious person named "MacGregor" from Aberdeen, and Max's life as a butcher. From Sam, Max's brother, we learn about his work as a chauffeur, including several specific jobs, and the fact that "MacGregor had Jessie in the back of my cab as I drove them along" (p. 78). From Lenny, one of the sons, who is apparently a pimp, we hear two long and violent stories of how he apparently assaulted two women. We learn about Joey, his brother, in his attempts to become a boxer. We learn about Teddy, the third brother, in his life as a professor, and hear a long story from Ruth, his wife, about her work as "a model for the body" (p. 57). In fact, over 80 percent of the playscript's dialogue is exposition—description of events in the past. Toward the end of the script, however, the discussion starts to shift into the future: Ruth will be set up as a prostitute in a flat on Greek Street, to support the family. Teddy will return to America and his professorial job. Ruth will take over the running of the house in her spare time.

As for space, the living room which we see is carefully described in the opening stage directions, and the characters make many references to it, such as Teddy's description:

> Big, isn't it? It's a big house. I mean, it's a fine room, don't you think? Actually there was a wall, across there . . . with a door. We knocked it down . . . years ago . . . to make an open living area. The structure wasn't affected, you see. (P. 21)

A specific chair is several times identified as belonging to Max. We hear about the bedroom upstairs, the kitchen on the main floor, and a "workroom cum bedroom" that Lenny has next door to the living room. Outside the house, there are the gymnasium where Joey works out, a swimming bath down the road, the butcher shop, Greek Street where Lenny keeps his whores, places like Hampton Court where Sam drives his customers, London Airport where Teddy goes to leave, Italy from which he and Ruth have just come, and America where they have been living. The action is thus thoroughly embedded in space and time, and the feeling of verisimilitude is enhanced by the fact that the scene of the play apparently includes some real, and well-known, places.

Yet nothing could be worse in production than to take this Naturalistic façade seriously, to insist on the actors' making it vivid for themselves and the audience as one would do with an Ibsen play. When one tries to do so, he finds all kinds of difficulties arising in rehearsal: Included among all the perfectly plausible details, for example, are a number of unaccountable ones. What are we to make of Max, for instance, when he speaks of his family's history this way:

> A crippled family, three bastard sons, a slutbitch of a wife— don't talk to me about the pain of childbirth—I suffered the pain, I've still got the pangs—when I give a little cough my back collapses— . . . (P. 47)

Should the actor playing Max, using an emotion memory exercise, relive "the pain of childbirth"? Moreover, some of the "exposition" in the script seems to be an outright parody of traditional Naturalistic description, as when Lenny says:

> You know, I've always had a feeling that if I'd been a soldier in the last war—say in the Italian campaign—I'd probably have found myself in Venice. I've always had that feeling. The trouble was I was too young to serve, you see. I was only a child, I was too small, otherwise I've got a pretty shrewd idea I'd probably have gone through Venice. Yes, I'd almost certainly have gone through it with my battalion. (P. 30)

We *know* that Lenny was not a soldier in the war and was not in Venice from the way he phrases this speech, but the very elaborateness of it (and it is picked up again in the second act, when Ruth replies to Teddy's request that they return to Italy by saying, of all things, that "if I'd been a nurse in the Italian campaign I would have been there before" [p. 55]) makes it *sound* like real exposition. Passages like these serve to call into question *all* the exposition in the play. We are made to realize something that rarely occurs to us in watching Ibsen, which is that every bit of offstage detail could be wrong; the character in making his description could always be mistaken, or confused, or lying, or distorting the truth for his own purpose. The concrete, banal quality of the offstage world is only an illusion; it is actually as noumenal as the offstage world of *The Cenci*. And, in the same way that the banal offstage world becomes mysterious, the mysterious acts we see *onstage* become banal: Sam drops dead in the middle of the living room (from no apparent cause), and the others treat the incident as if it were a minor annoyance, Max complaining about the corpse messing up the clean floor, and Teddy remarking wistfully that "I was going to ask him to drive me to London Airport" (p. 79). Max in an earlier incident punches Joey in the stomach, brains Sam with his walking stick—and then makes small talk with Ruth about her children. Lenny at one point chats about philosophical topics in a tone one would use for discussing football pools: "Come on, be frank. What do you make of all this business of being and not-being?" (p. 52). Instead of being embodied in a conflict

between the offstage and onstage world, as in *The Cenci*, the banal-
mysterious polarity is pervasive; everything banal is constantly turning mysterious, while everything mysterious is constantly becoming
ordinary, commonplace, acceptable. One of Ruth's speeches sums it
up nicely:

> Look at me. I . . . move my leg. That's all it is. But I wear . . .
> underwear . . . which moves with me . . . it . . . captures your
> attention. Perhaps you misinterpret. The action is simple. It's
> a leg . . . moving. My lips move. Why don't you restrict . . . your
> observations to that? (Pp. 52–53)

What we see—the moving leg—does imply many things that we cannot see, and, for a man in the presence of an attractive woman, the
unseen will indeed take more of his attention that what is seen. Yet
what is seen is only a leg, and what is unseen is only—underwear.
As a first approximation of a unifying principle for the script, we
therefore formulated the following: the ordinary becomes strange; the
strange becomes ordinary.

In production this meant, first of all, a commitment to the Naturalistic façade. The room must look like an actual room; the clutter
of Naturalistic detail—the cups, the cigars, the furniture, the whiskey,
the newspapers, the clothing—must all be actual things, with the
patina of use, such as would actually be found in contemporary London. The dialects must be the precise Cockney-Jewish combination
that will give the speeches their natural rhythm and inflection. The
tone of the acting must be relaxed, matter-of-fact, mundane. But this
Naturalism must *not* be allowed to become an end in itself in production. All the Naturalistic elements must suggest other, completely different things beyond themselves. When Ruth takes a glass of water
from Lenny, for example, and says, "Have a sip. Go on. Have a sip
from my glass" (p. 34), it must be as seductive as if she were removing
her clothes. When Max talks casually with Ruth about her children,
it must be seen as the actual climax of what went before, giving
greater injury to Lenny and Sam by ignoring what has just happened
than if he had continued to hit them. When Teddy and Ruth chat
about the relative merits of English versus American swimming pools,
in their scene together near the end of the play, it must be seen as the

final, disastrous breakdown of their marriage, no less definitive than the discussion scene at the end of *A Doll House*.

In other words, it is necessary to approach the script in terms of the "action" of Stanislavski and Fergusson, defining each acting unit in terms of the characters' *objectives*. Underneath all their small talk, Pinter's characters are always desperately in search of powerful objectives, such as power, love, or destruction. Some time ago, when I taught acting regularly, I always found that Pinter's playscripts were the best for driving home the idea of the Stanislavskian objective. I would assign a scene from one of Pinter's scripts to a pair of actors, who would read it out as honestly and meaningfully as they could. The results would be confusing or merely dull. Then I would give each actor an objective: "Mrs. A wants Mrs. B to love her; Mrs. B wants to get rid of Mrs. A." Immediately the scene would spring into relief, like a two-dimensional picture suddenly viewed stereoptically. Each line, each word, would now carry a special nuance. The scene would progress to a distinct climax and resolution. We had found the drama behind the words.

With good actors, it is sometimes only necessary to define their objectives clearly and let them explore the material for themselves. The following scene in *The Homecoming* might seem at first only a casual discussion about clothes:

> *Ruth.* What do you think of my shoes?
> *Lenny.* They're very nice.
> *Ruth.* No, I can't get the ones I want over there.
> *Lenny.* Can't get them over there, eh?
> *Ruth.* No . . . you don't get them there.
> > *Pause.* (P. 56)

This sequence only comes to life, however, when the actors are given an objective like "you want to gain power over him (her) by seducing him (her)." I was able to help out by suggesting this objective and by placing the actors in a suggestive physical relationship, with Ruth sitting on the sofa and Lenny on a footstool in front of her. From this, it was only natural that Ruth should show, not only her shoe to Lenny, but a bit of her leg. Lenny, as he said, "They're very nice," let his eyes travel from her feet up her legs, so that it was not quite clear to which he was referring. Continuing to turn her foot and look at it, Ruth delivered her next line, "No, I can't get the ones I want over there," with a kind of *over*casualness. Then Lenny, in his next line, gave the word *them* a slight overemphasis, suggesting that it was something other than shoes that she was not getting from her husband in America. On her final line, Ruth stopped looking at her shoe and for the first time made eye contact with Lenny, creating an electrical moment of intimacy, which carried over into the pause. It was clear then that they were not talking about shoes at all. There had been a definite progression of sexual excitement; yet, on the other hand, it was all done in a simple and understated manner. It would not have done, for example, to have them actually fondling and kissing during this sequence, so that the ostensible subject of discussion—the shoes— was either forgotten or turned into a bizarre irrelevancy. It was necessary to maintain the tension between the banal and the mysterious; to make the audience constantly aware of both shoes and sex, and gradually shift the emphasis from one to the other.

The same approach was applied to the rest of the play. The omnipresent exposition, for example, was never overplayed. It was not necessary to study maps of London in order to make the offstage world vivid, or to write lengthy character biographies to make the play's prehistory seem graphic. The truth or the untruth of the exposition is simply irrelevant to the play, because in every case it simply exists as raw material for the character to use in pursuit of some tangible goal *in the present*. There is no way of telling, for instance, whether MacGregor actually "had" Jessie in the back of Sam's cab or not. The script does not tell us, and the characters, being fictitious, have no further reality beyond the script to which we can refer. But, on the other hand, we do not need to know; the only thing that *is* important to know is that Sam maintains it happened in order to gain revenge on Max at the particular moment he says it. My work with the actors in production, therefore, was always oriented to the present moment in the performance, stressing the objectives (which always in this play are something a character wants from another, rather than something strictly personal) and "relating," in Stanislavski's sense. That is, I stressed the importance of the actors' focusing on each other, carefully listening and looking in order to gain an advantage. It was less important to relate to the offstage world or to the past, which might be the subject of discussion at any moment; one could never ignore it completely, of course, but one had always to treat it as ammunition rather than as "the truth."

This is the reason for the strange, close interconnection between the bizarre and the mundane in the playscript. The bizarre is always taken for granted, a means to an end rather than an end in itself. (This of course is Esslin's concept of the absurd—absurdity as the *background* to the action, part of the "scene" rather than the action itself. Theatre of the Absurd plays are *not* absurd on their own terms; once the absurdity has been established, as part of the "given circumstances," the plays are perfectly logical and even traditional.) The characters' reactions to circumstances have nothing to do with whether those circumstances are absurd or plausible; they are instead a function of their particular objectives of the moment.

In *The Homecoming*, these objectives all seem to focus on a single, overriding objective, which forms a unifying principle for the playscript: "to dominate." This unifying principle goes deeper than the earlier formulation—"the ordinary becomes strange; the strange becomes ordinary"—because it provides a *driving force* for the play. The shifts from mundane to bizarre and back again are not just technical tricks for dismaying the audience; they are always the characters' basic strategies for achieving dominance. When Max complains about Sam's corpse dirtying up the floor, the understatement is, on the surface, hilarious; but beneath this is Max's final victory over Sam, in a contemptuous put-down. Ruth uses *overstatement* in turning some casual remarks about shoes into an act of sexual aggression; Max uses *understatement* in reacting to Sam's corpse on the floor as if it were a discarded newspaper or a scrap of food. Of course, we do not know *why* the characters always choose this kind of strategy—that remains forever mysterious. But it is a mystery with a clearly discernible pattern, which can be summed up in a final formulation of the unifying principle: "to dominate by treating the ordinary as strange, and the strange as ordinary."

The play is thus a power struggle from beginning to end. It follows a plan for Pinter's playscripts that a student of mine once described as "the home team versus the visitors." His plays always take place in single rooms (which may be part of a larger apartment or house); the inhabitants are menaced by an intruder or intruders, and a struggle ensues; in this struggle, the intruders usually win. In *The Homecoming*, Ruth is the intruder into the family home of the five men; the twist is that she does not appear menacing from the beginning, as the intruder usually does in a Pinter work, but rather appears somewhat intimidated herself. At the end, however, it is clear that she is victorious: Sam is dead, Max is dying, Teddy has been expelled, Joey kneels at her feet with his head in her lap, completely under her spell. Only Lenny seems to retain his old power—and he has just given in to her on the conditions of her "employment" as one of his whores. *Why* this struggle takes place is again something that we can never know—it is merely presented to us, as another "given." There appears to be a "territorial imperative" about it. The repeated references to the house and room, the significance of Max's having his own personal chair—the throne of his little kingdom—and the way different characters appear to stake out private territory, like Max's living room rug, Sam's kitchen, Lenny's "workroom cum bedroom," and, finally, Ruth's flat on Greek Street, support this view. But again there is no real *motivation* supplied; we are given only an objective, which is the vicious drive for domination.

The idea of territoriality was helpful in production. Our set followed the script's description exactly; the fact that it was on a large thrust stage, however, made it possible to establish definite areas around each piece of furniture. Max's chair, in a prominent position up left, was sacrosanct; no one sat in it except him—until the end, when Ruth sat there. In general, in each scene each character would stake out a territory for himself—say, the sofa, or one of the chairs, or the sideboard, in each case with its surrounding area. For another character to enter this area was then to be looked upon as an automatic threat. For a character actually to touch another was looked upon as an extreme threat, even if the action were only one of handing someone a glass of water. This gave a strange but dramatic tension to the play, the excitement varying according to the precise spatial relationships at any given moment. The audience responds powerfully, though unconsciously, to this sort of thing; on the one hand it is precise and clear, but on the other it is subtle and mysterious since it is never spelled out in so many words.

It will be clear that a unifying principle of this type—"to dominate"—is not something that can be applied to a production in overall, general terms like a "concept." It is instead something alive and active. It must be carefully worked out, moment by moment, by the particular actors involved—and its actual working out will vary a bit from rehearsal to rehearsal and performance to performance. The director does nothing but set up the rules of the game, so to speak, and then insist that it be played with commitment and honesty. Ideally, the director's contribution will not even be noticed. This is primarily a playwright's theatre, but secondarily (and close behind) an actors' theatre. Nevertheless, there is still a lot for the director to do, even after the rehearsals are going well. Here is where the director must have a sense of "plot" as discussed in Chapter IV in connection with Aristotle. That is, in addition to setting up the rules and insisting that the actors play strongly, the director must be sensitive to elements like choice, progression, and rhythm—in other words, to the *detailed* working out of the script on the stage rather than its generalities. And, although Pinter's playscripts may appear at first glance to be almost plotless, they are strongly arranged in the deeper meaning of plot. In developing this "plot," the director will again be doing something that will bring him no fame or glory; plot must seem organic, even obvious, so that only the more sensitive audience members will even be aware that the play could ever have developed differently. Nonetheless, it is an extremely important part of directing, and one that few directors ever really master, because of the common prejudice against seeing a script in generative terms.

Choice. Pinter makes such extensive use of everyday objects like cigars and newspapers and glasses of water that their use may seem to involve no choice at all, but merely a recording of real life. But, of course, choice is always involved. In the "shoe" unit discussed above, the subject of discussion might just as well have been gloves or dresses, but for the fact that shoes provided the exact sexual connotation necessary for the moment. Actors need to be reminded, as do readers, that such details must never be taken for granted, as mere accidents. In one of his acting texts, Stanislavski describes a group of acting students who have become bored with an improvisation they have performed hundreds of times. Because of their boredom, their performance has gone flat, and nothing they do seems to restore it to life. They play slow, or fast, or with externally heightened energy, or with various personal acting gimmicks, but continue to fail. Stanislavski (in his persona as "Tortsov," their teacher) starts asking them questions about the given circumstances: What is implied by the fact that one character is mentally retarded? What does it mean to be the brother of such a person? What would a large sum of money do to a family of this sort? By getting the actors to question the circumstances, instead of taking them for granted, he makes them see the scene once more afresh, re-creating the "illusion of the first time." Applying the principle of choice, then, can be useful in keeping a performance "up" over a long run; but it is also important in providing freshness and vitality in the first place.

Consider the following sequence:

Lenny. Just give me the glass.
Ruth. No.
      Pause.
Lenny. I'll take it, then.
Ruth. If you take the glass . . . I'll take you.
      Pause.
Lenny. How about me taking the glass without you taking me?
Ruth. Why don't I just take you?
      Pause.
Lenny. You're joking. (P. 34)

This is obviously another seduction sequence, similar to the one about the shoes. But why a glass? To give the unit its own peculiar quality, it helps to improvise it with various other objects: a pencil, a dish, a handkerchief. It is not necessary to be a Freudian to see that everyday objects can be symbolic; a pencil is not a "phallic symbol" because Freud said it was, but rather because it can point and penetrate. This is quite apparent when one actually works with it on stage; it even suggests a weapon as well—and could actually be used as one. The quality of the scene changes distinctly when a pencil is used—Lenny, rather than Ruth, seems like the aggressor and appears to win the little struggle rather than her winning it. The glass, on the other hand, is a clear female symbol, as are all vessels. (Slang terms for women or female genitals—"sex pot," "box," and so on—tend to suggest vessels, for example.) When it is used, Ruth is clearly the aggressor, though in a mysterious, passive way. But, on the other hand, the glass is still a real glass, which functions as one. All theatre, but especially Naturalistic theatre, makes use of this ambiguity between the symbolic and the real functions of everyday objects, an ambiguity that all of us are at least subliminally aware of. As the actors became conscious of this strange dual nature of the glass, it became a living thing for them, rather than just an accident of Naturalistic detail. Their eyes lingered on it; they became aware of its particular size, shape, color, gleam. The audience in turn responded the same way. The glass thus became part of the play's action, rather than just a prop.

The same principle can be applied to all the background details in the playscript. Because every play must have *some* such details, it is hard at first to question, "Why these particular ones?" But why, for example, is Jessie—Max's wife and the mother of the three boys—dead? What would happen if she were still alive, and Max the dead one? Well, clearly, the house would no longer be an exclusively masculine world, and Ruth would seem less like an intruder. But when we look deeper into this masculine world, we see many examples where it seems specifically to *lack* women. Max's strange line about feeling the pains of childbirth takes on a special significance—it is as if he were trying, ineffectually, to take on the mother's role himself. And his hilarious line about Ruth when she first appears—"I've never had a whore under this roof before. Ever since your mother died" (p. 42)—takes on a special meaning as well. Ruth's ultimate action is to *replace* Jessie. And Joey's two-hour session with Ruth in the bedroom—in which he specifically does *not* have sexual relations with her, yet strangely seems satisfied—supports this view as well. Joey is looking for a surrogate mother, to replace the one who died, and has at last found one. At the end of the play, Joey kneels at Ruth's feet with his head in her lap, in a kind of Pietà; Sam and Max are on the floor, dead and dying; only Lenny remains standing. In the deep structure of the play, there is a passing of generations. The drive for dominance has led to a new family structure, with a new "father" (Lenny), a new "mother" (Ruth), and a new "son" (Joey). All are ersatz figures, compared with their predecessors, who were genuine father, mother, and sons, in both the biological and social sense; one can thus interpret the action as being some kind of statement about the breakdown of the

nuclear family in modern times, but this is one of those resonant meanings that borders on the extrinsic.

Sequence. The script follows the traditional Three Unities of time,
place, and action. The play begins in the "evening" and moves in five
scenes (separated by two blackouts in the first act, the act break itself, and a blackout in the second act) through "night," "morning,"
"afternoon," and "evening" of the next day, thus covering a period
of roughly twenty-four hours. The breaks are of little consequence—
the only thing of importance that happens during them is the two-hour
"love play" of Ruth and Lenny in Act II—so that the action is generally smooth and continuous.

It is important in performing Pinter that this smoothness be pre-
served. Nothing must seem forced or abrupt. The pauses, for which
Pinter is so famous, must not break up the action, but rather must become part of it. The action must continue through the pauses, so that
the audience is not even aware that speech has stopped, through the
use of subtle gestures, glances, eye contact (many of the pauses are
accompanied by the direction "They look at each other"), and movements. Careful examination of the script reveals that Pinter's pauses
are never arbitrary; they are always strongly motivated, even *necessary* for the scene to work. In the following, for example, Joey is
talking to his father about his workout at the gymnasium.

> *Joey.* I've been training with Bobby Dodd.
> *Pause*
> And I had a good go at the bag as well.
> *Pause.*
> I wasn't in bad trim.   (P. 17)

In a poor production, the actor will merely pause mechanically at the
indicated places, and the stage will go dead. The action will lurch
along from speech to speech, with inexplicable stops in between
(which the actor and director can explain away by calling the play
"absurd"). The proper way to play this unit, however, is to have Joey
look desperately at his father during the pauses, in expectation of a
reaction of approval. The pauses are then not stops, but rather a con-

tinuation of Joey's objective (to gain approval) by nonverbal means. As T. S. Eliot put it in the *Four Quartets*, "Words, after speech, reach / Into the silence." In the second pause, Joey might even mime a few punches, as a way of showing off his prowess, or he might just look all the harder at his father, who remains impassive. It often helps, in getting across the idea of an *active* pause to the actor (although it was not necessary here in our production), to improvise the sequence with the silent actor replying during the pauses in the way the speaker would wish. In this case, the result would come out something like this:

Joey. I've been training with Bobby Dodd.
Max. Fine, son, fine. You'll be champion in no time.
Joey. And I had a good go at the bag as well.
Max. Good work, son. You look in great trim.

After playing this version a few times, the actors return to the script; the actor in the role of Joey from that time forward always plays *with the expectation* that Max will respond as he did during the improvisation, but of course Max now remains silent. The pauses will then come startlingly to life—in fact become moments of even greater emotional intensity than the spoken parts of the sequence.

Tempo. The tempo called for in this script is very slow. On the surface, there are very few events to cover the two hours or so of playing time: Ruth and Teddy arrive, Teddy leaves, Ruth stays. Individual units at first seem agonizing—Lenny's stories, for example, seem endless and without point, and sequences like the water-glass unit appear to take forever to accomplish a very trivial action. Nevertheless, the temptation to speed things up must be scrupulously avoided. This is because, below the surface in the deep structure, a great deal is going on—seductions, power struggles, acts of vengence, territorial defenses, the passing of the older generation. To speed up the surface activity is to destroy these deeper resonances and make the play seem *really* slow. The audience must be given time to ponder, to notice subtleties, for the surface of the action really offers them very little by itself. That is, one can rush a play like *Macbeth*, and the audience will still remain interested because there is so much surface activity; they may not be very deeply moved, but at least they will not get bored. With a play like *The Homecoming*, however, there is no sense in rushing or "getting on with the action," since there is almost no surface action to begin with. Rushing is one of the most common flaws in directing today—which is why so many productions seem so slow.

In our production, the actors were required to rehearse *very* slowly —never to proceed without being aware of what was going on behind the action and, in particular, not to rush transitions. Some of the transitions called for in the script are extremely difficult. For example, near the end of the first act, Max, just after having called Ruth a whore and having ordered Joey to "chuck out" her and Teddy, must punch Joey in the stomach and hit Sam on the head with his stick, and then suddenly start talking to Ruth with gentle, familial coziness:

> *Max.* You a mother?
> *Ruth.* Yes.
> *Max.* How many you got?
> *Ruth.* Three.
> > *He turns to* TEDDY.
> *Max.* All yours Ted?
> > *Pause.*
> > Teddy, why don't we have a nice cuddle and kiss, eh? Like the old days? What about a nice cuddle and kiss, eh?
>
> (P. 43)

The acts of violence are physically the most active moment in the play, yet Max must change almost instantly into a blubbering sentimentalist. In the early rehearsals, the actor made this transition very slowly. There is a "Silence" called for before he talks to Ruth, which had to go on endlessly as he collected himself and completely changed his tone. Later, as he got the feel of it, he was able to play the transition much faster—the silence was only a few seconds—but it never became abrupt. There was always a smooth, easy, continuous change from rage to charm, so that the audience saw a process rather than two unconnected states. In this way, the web of continuity, which gives the play its strange quasi-Naturalistic quality, was never broken. The moment seemed both bizarre and not bizarre, almost ordinary, given the strange parameters of the stage world.

There is an analogy here to a piece of music. When a musician must play a difficult passage, he does not rehearse by going over it again and again at full speed. He starts *slowly*, becoming thoroughly familiar with every note and its value before attempting the passage *"a tempo."* Such a procedure is rarely used in the theatre, but it would be very useful in preventing the rushing and blurring that is now so common there. Directors are always calling for "pace" as if tempo were an external thing, not in the script, when actually it is the result of playing a specified set of events in a specified period. If he is working properly, there is no reason for a director ever to call for faster pace from his actors. In this case, it was a matter of telling the actor playing Max that he had to relax and charm Ruth *before* Sam and Joey could recover and strike back at him. (If he had failed to get the idea, I would have had them actually do so.) Pace thus became an *inner* goal, imposed by the circumstances of the playscript, rather than by the director shouting "faster."

Duration. Tempo varies considerably throughout the playscript, despite the general slowness. The violent moment described above is an example of an extremely fast unit. The violence appears to arise with very little provocation—Joey merely calls Max an old man, and Max erupts. The stage directions are as follows:

LENNY *walks into the room, in a dressing-gown.*
He stops.
They all look around.
MAX *turns back, hits* JOEY *in the stomach with all his might.*
JOEY *contorts, staggers across the stage.* MAX, *with the exertion of the blow, begins to collapse. His knees buckle. He clutches his stick.*
SAM *moves forward to help him.*
MAX *hits him across the head with his stick.* SAM *sits, head in hands.*
JOEY, *hands pressed to his stomach, sits down at the feet of* RUTH. *She looks down at him.*
LENNY *and* TEDDY *are still.*
JOEY *slowly stands. He is close to* RUTH. *He turns from* RUTH, *looks round at* MAX.
SAM *clutches his head.*

MAX *breathes heavily, very slowly gets to his feet.*
JOEY *moves to him.*
They look at each other.
Silence.   (Pp. 42–43)

All this, including the silence, takes no more than ten seconds to perform, which is all the more odd in a play in which, for example,
Lenny's story about the lady with the "iron mangle" whom he assaulted (pp. 32–33) takes nearly five minutes to tell. Similarly, Teddy
and Lenny take a dozen lines (including three pauses) to decide that
it must be a clock that has caused the tick that has been keeping
Lenny awake (p. 25). When Ruth asks Lenny for a drink in the second act, it takes perhaps three times longer than would be strictly
necessary:

> *Ruth.*   I'd like a drink. Did you get any drink?
> *Lenny.* We've got drink.
> *Ruth.*   I'd like one, please.
> *Lenny.* What drink?
> *Ruth.*   Whisky.
> *Lenny.* I've got it.
>   *Pause.*
> *Ruth.*   Well, get it.   (P. 60)

Lenny at last goes to get the whisky, but the unit does not end there;
further discussion ensues about the glass in which the whisky is
poured, and Ruth's preferences as to soda and ice. If Pinter had wanted
to, he could just as easily have advanced the action by writing something like the following:

> *Ruth.*   I'd like a drink.
> *Lenny.* What drink?
> *Ruth.*   Whisky.
> *Lenny.* I've got it.   (*Goes and pours.*)

Pinter's technique, then, is here one of extension, just as in the unit
of violence his technique was one of compression. In general the pattern is that *important events are compressed, while trivial ones* (on

the surface) *are extended*, often to the point of inanity. This is part of Pinter's method of burying the playscript's true action in the deep structure. When the conflicts in the deep structure do rise to the surface, it is always in the form of an eruption. Max's hitting of Sam and Joey, his earlier spitting on Lenny, Teddy's announcement that he deliberately stole Lenny's cheese roll, and Sam's dropping dead as he announces Jessie's infidelity in a single, short line, are all brief and understated. On the other hand, they are always thoroughly motivated and serve as pointers into the more extended, apparently banal scenes, indicating what is actually happening during them. The wordy scenes of banality serve to bury the moments of violence, but the moments of violence in turn give coherence and excitement to the scenes of banality. Like a dormant volcano, violence is always ready to erupt into the everyday action of the play, and the audience must always be aware that the volcano is there.

This means that, in rehearsal, the moments of violence must receive special attention. It is not enough to rehearse the scenes with the explosive elements treated as part of the general flow. We isolated the moment when Max hits Sam and Joey, and rehearsed it hundreds of times, until it was choreographed with the precision of a ballet. Only then did we re-integrate it into the scene, working on the transitions in and out of the unit as I described earlier. Again, the opposite extreme to producing Pinter as an "absurdist," with the action leaping about erratically and incoherently, is to treat him too Naturalistically, playing with a uniform sameness that avoids the peaks and valleys. In a speech like this one of Teddy's,

> You can help me with my lectures when we get back. I'd love that. I'd be so grateful for it, really. We can bathe till October. You know that. Here, there's nowhere to bathe, except the swimming bath down the road. You know what it's like? It's like a urinal. A filthy urinal!
> *Pause.*
> You liked Venice, didn't you? It was lovely, wasn't it? You had a good week. I mean . . . I took you there. I can speak Italian.
>
> (P. 55)

it is all too easy for the actor to get carried away with the lulling tone

at the beginning and after the pause, leading him to ignore the ex-
clamation mark. Nevertheless, the phrase "A filthy urinal!" must be
completely different from the rest, a cry of anguish and rage. For an
instant, Teddy drops his mask of sweet reasonableness and displays
his true emotions; then, so quickly and naturally that we wonder if it
really happened, he puts it on again. But that single brief moment
informs not only the speech but also the entire scene, as well as the
three-way struggle among Lenny, Ruth, and Teddy throughout the
entire play.

Rhythm. Pinter is better understood, and better performed, as soon
as one recognizes that he is a poet. I do not mean this in the usual
vague sense, in which playwrights are called "poetic" because of their
temperament or sensitivity or rebelliousness, but in the literal sense of
being a versifier. By rewriting his prose passages in the form of verse,
this becomes immediately clear:

> They often ruminate,
> Sometimes singly,
> Sometimes in groups,
> About the true facts
> Of that particular night—
> The night they were made
> In the image of those two people *at it*.

> It's a question long overdue,
> From my point of view,
> But as we happen to be passing
> The time of day here tonight
> I thought I'd pop it to you.   (P. 36)

The short phrases, the colloquial tone, the shifting yet vigorous
rhythms, the repetitions, the doggerel rhymes, as well as the subject
matter with its simultaneous vulgarity and profundity, all recall the
poetry of T. S. Eliot, particularly in the unfinished playscript,
Sweeney Agonistes (although not, alas, in the completed dramas
where Eliot generally preferred an abstract decorum to vigor):

Birth, and copulation, and death.
That's all the facts when you come to brass tacks:
Birth, and copulation, and death.
I've been born, and once is enough.
You don't remember, but I remember,
Once is enough.[3]

The literary influences on *The Homecoming*, however, are less important than the implications of Pinter's poetic style for performance. The actors must be taught to reproduce this kind of flexible verse, with its subtle patterns. (Perhaps the reason Eliot never completed *Sweeney* was that, at that time, he could not find actors who could speak it properly. The only verse that English-speaking actors are generally taught to speak is that of Shakespeare, and, while Shakespeare certainly drew on colloquial speech, it was a language far less disjointed and brutal than that of our century.)

One should recall that the conventions we have come to take for granted in printed poetry, such as the division into lines (with each capitalized at the beginning) or the division into stanzas, originally existed as signals to the person reading them *aloud*. Pinter's scripts are no less poetic for employing a different set of signals, since the audience, of course, cannot be sure how the speeches were originally set down on the page. In general, Pinter has chosen to signal the actors through punctuation marks, particularly the comma and ellipsis (...), as well as the stage directions "slight pause," "pause," and "silence." These all denote hesitations of increasing length, "silence" being longest of all, and thus generate rhythmic patterns in the same way that line and stanza distinctions do in printed poetry of the traditional kind. They must be scrupulously adhered to. In our production, we took days out from rehearsal to work on speech rhythms alone, not only at the beginning of the rehearsal period, but throughout (two days in a row were devoted to it just before dress rehearsal, for example). The most difficult thing turned out to be not doing the pauses themselves, but rather *avoiding* pauses where they were not indicated. Sloppy productions of Pinter's plays take the frequent stage directions for pauses and silences as a license for as many additional pauses as the actors feel like adding. The result is like adding extra rests to a piece of music. As I noted earlier, the pauses in a Pinter script are never random;

they represent a continuation of the action by nonverbal means and are always psychologically motivated. In fact, they are usually the culmination of a clear progression:

> *Ruth.* I haven't quite finished.
> *Lenny.* You've consumed quite enough, in my opinion.
> *Ruth.* No, I haven't.
> *Lenny.* Quite sufficient, in my own opinion.
> *Ruth.* Not in mine, Leonard.
>   *Pause.*
> *Lenny.* Don't call me that please.   (P. 33)

The pause here is, typically, the culmination of a power struggle in which, as evidenced by Lenny's line after the pause, Ruth is victorious. If the lines leading up to the pause are not delivered in staccato fashion, with no hesitations except the tiny ones implied by the punctuation, the growing tension and release implied in this sequence will be weak and unfocused.

This example shows how the surface rhythms, implied by such technical means as punctuation and stage directions, are related to the deeper performance rhythms implied by the script. The pattern of tension/release/new tension, which is the rhythmic norm in the script, is generated by the deeper pattern which can be approximated by the unifying principle of banal/bizarre/banal.

Progression. The slow pace of continuous action is not without progression. Even when there is an eruption, as in Teddy's speech about the swimming bath, it is an eruption only in terms of the surface action. Teddy's resentment at the growing flirtation between Lenny and Ruth, as well as his intellectual contempt for his family, have all been well established up to this point. Furthermore, the swimming-bath speech, for all its surface calm, resonates with images of sex, power, and hostility. "You can help me with my lectures when I get back" reflects Teddy's desire for power over Ruth, as well as being a statement of his intellectual superiority; unlike lesser creatures, including Ruth and the family, Teddy "lectures." The reference to bathing carries a sexual connotation (which Ruth picks up shortly thereafter, in recalling a time she modeled nude at a lake), while the references to a urinal are both sexual and hostile. Emotional outbursts in the play, then, are paradoxically both eruptive and carefully prepared. The actor must suggest, beneath a surface calmness, a *growing* emotional force. In this case, the actor became more and more casual as he proceeded through the speech—quieter, slower, until he was *overly* calm. There was thus a progression into the emotional outburst, but it was a reverse progression.

Reverse progression is common throughout the playscript. Whenever the script contains a bizarre element, it progresses into the bizarre by becoming more *natural*. In the water-glass unit, for example, Ruth's remarks could at first be interpreted as perfectly normal:

> *Ruth.* Have a sip. Go on. Have a sip from my glass.
> *He is still.*
> Sit on my lap. Take a long cool sip.
> *She pats her lap. Pause.*
> *She stands, moves to him with the glass.*
> Put your head back and open your mouth.
> *Lenny.* Take that glass away from me.
> *Ruth.* Lie on the floor. Go on. I'll pour it down your throat.
>
> (P. 34)

"Have a sip" could be interpreted as a simple expression of friendliness. With "Sit on my lap" Ruth becomes overtly sexual but is still within the bounds of credible human behavior. The line "Lie on the floor. Go on. I'll pour it down your throat," however, is bizarre, zany, inexplicable. We see a whole new side of Ruth and realize that her weakness is an act, that even her seductiveness is not an expression of simple desire, but of something darker and more powerful. We have left the bounds of Naturalism; Ruth is no longer just a housewife but a witch or sorceress. But Pinter has led us into this mysterious condition so gradually that we hardly notice the boundary.

The banal/bizarre rhythm of the script, then, is characterized by a gradual progression rather than quick alternation. The entire playscript, considered as a whole, can be seen in this way. At the beginning, we see what appears to be a Naturalistic play, with a solid, detailed setting in a real city. There is a family with well-rounded characters and complex interrelationships. They have problems and fears and hopes: a father worries about getting old, a son dreams of becoming a boxer, another son has become a professor and feels alienated from his lower-class origins. It sounds like something by Clifford Odets. By the end, however, we have a middle-class housewife taking on a job as a prostitute as casually as if she were becoming a typist to earn some extra money for her family; an uncle dropping dead on the floor and being ignored; a husband who watches unperturbed while his wife has sexual relations with his brothers, and then simply goes home to take care of the children. Pinter's genius is that he has taken us from one state to the other in a seamless progression. He is a magician who forces us to accept the impossible. In this way, of course, he forces us to see the bizarre in our own lives, to see that all existence is odd, absurd. It is only because we are immersed in our existence, with nothing to compare it to, that it seems "normal."

We have thus come full circle and are back to thinking of this script in genre terms, as an example of "Theatre of the Absurd." But the absurdity is a quality embodied in the playscript, rather than being an external philosophical judgment about it. It is also a quality that must be projected into a performance in a precise and detailed way if it is to have real dramatic impact. The same can be said about the important qualities of any good playscript.

10

Afterthoughts

In the last three chapters, I have found myself more and more shifting back and forth from what is, strictly speaking, supposed to be dramatic criticism to what is supposed to be directorial technique. The very idea of an essay containing, say, a discussion of both poetic imagery and actors' improvisations seems quite odd. Yet the more one does it, the more natural it appears. I have for a long time been interested in the area where dramatic criticism and theatrical production overlap; the more I study the problem, both as a critic and as a director, the larger the area seems. Perhaps the mistake is in seeing them as separate in the first place.

With the growth of university theatre departments, there has come greater and greater compartmentalization. People are almost forced to choose between criticism and directing; those who want to do both are in danger of being typed as "generalists," which in today's universities falsely connotes the second-rate. Critics and directors teach different classes, attend different conferences, write for different journals. In fact, I know of no journal now publishing that is devoted to the script in performance. There are literary journals that publish articles on playscripts, with no particular recognition of their performance potential; and there are performance journals that want little to do with script interpretation, some even regarding playscripts with loathing. The middle ground has been abandoned.

I hope that my interpretations of *The Cenci*, *A Doll House*, and

The Homecoming in production terms will demonstrate what a loss that is. Whether or not my particular formulations have been successful, they should still indicate the great possibilities for a "dramaturgical criticism." Future scholars and theatre practitioners can learn from my explorations, even at points where they disagree. (There should be many such points; no critical essay of any sort should ever be considered as a fixed and final statement.) And, I hope, they can publish their own dramaturgical findings, to carry on the dialogue.

Many have despaired of trying to combine criticism and performance. G. Wilson Knight once wrote: "My experience as actor, producer and play-goer leaves me uncompromising in my assertion that the literary analysis of great drama in terms of theatrical technique accomplishes singularly little."[1] Knight is not writing as a literary snob; his experience as actor, producer (i.e., director), and playgoer is extensive, and he has even written a book on Shakespearean production. There are two good reasons for his negative tone here: First, most "analysis of great drama in terms of theatrical technique" tends to be the director's notes kind of thing, the "how I did it" essay that lets us in on the director's working methods for a specific, celebrated production. This usually tells us a lot about the particular director, but precious little about the playscript itself. Second, the techniques of theatre journals, as they have developed over the past two decades, have been inimical to close textual study, as well as to close study of the performance. It is much easier to publish a production concept than its execution; daring photographs of Hamlet sitting in a wheelbarrow, or flashy titles like "King Lear in Spanish Harlem," catch the reader's attention but necessarily provide a static, generalized view of the play, which may have been very boring in the flesh. Dramaturgical criticism, on the other hand, necessarily requires a lengthy, careful, often unexciting kind of essay, the sort that editors, with an eye to circulation, are reluctant to publish. Thus, very little criticism "in terms of theatrical technique" of a caliber that Knight could approve ever even appears.

One exception has been the approach through historical productions, as practiced by critics like John Russell Brown, in which one learns about playscripts (usually Shakespeare's) by examining how different directors and actors have performed them over the years. This method has often been very valuable and needs to be continued and expanded.

But there is still a need for two other kinds of critical essays: first, those employing the method, suggested in passing by Richard Schechner, by which the critic learns about a script from directing it himself, or from being closely involved with a production as *Dramaturg*, and reports his findings for the use of future producers of the script; and, second, the kind of essay, more hypothetical, that deals with a script in terms of its performance potential, not spelling out *how* it must be performed but rather channeling the imagination of theatre practitioners, by pointing out patterns that they "might otherwise have missed." Dramaturgical criticism of these kinds is very rare. I have tried to show that it is at least possible; and I believe that it is potentially very valuable to our theatre.

Notes

Preface

1. Kenneth Burke, *A Grammar of Motives* (Berkeley: University of California Press, 1969), p. 262.

Structuralism

1. Ernst Kris, "Prince Hal's Conflict," in *Psychoanalytic Explorations in Art* (New York: Schocken, 1964), pp. 273–288.
2. Ibid., p. 278.
3. Cleanth Brooks, "The Naked Babe and the Cloak of Manliness," in *The Well-Wrought Urn* (New York: Harcourt, Brace & World, 1947), pp. 22–49.
4. G. Wilson Knight has written a book called *Shakespearian Production* (2d ed.; London: Routledge, 1968), which is indeed valuable for the *visual* aspects of production, but for little else.
5. Cleanth Brooks and Robert B. Heilman, *Understanding Drama* (New York: Holt, 1959), p. 28.
6. Ibid., p. 29.
7. William Flint Thrall, Addison Hibbard, and C. Hugh Holman, *A Handbook to Literature* (New York: Odyssey, 1960), p. 199.
8. Jean Salles, in Racine, *Phèdre* (Paris: Bordas, 1972), p. 117; my translation.
9. Roland Barthes, *Sur Racine* (Paris: Éditions du Seuil, 1960), p. 122; my translation.
10. Ibid., p. 9.
11. *Six Plays of Strindberg*, trans. Elizabeth Sprigge (Garden City, N.Y.: Doubleday, 1955), p. 84.

12. Jacques Barzun, "Biography and Criticism," *Critical Inquiry* 1, no. 3 (March 1975): 483.
13. Kenneth M. Cameron and Theodore J. C. Hoffman, *The Theatrical Response* (New York: Macmillan, 1969), p. 239.
14. The notion of interpreting "into" a text may cause confusion because of the common phrase "reading in," meaning the kind of false interpretation that sees things in the text that are not really there. But, actually, reading "in" is exactly what a critic *should* do; false interpretation of the overly fanciful sort might better be called "reading *out.*"
15. L. C. Knights, "The Question of Character in Shakespeare," in *Approaches to Shakespeare*, ed. Norman Rabkin (New York: McGraw-Hill, 1964), pp. 61–62.
16. John Gassner, *Dramatic Soundings* (New York: Crown, 1968), p. 210.
17. Roger Gross, *Understanding Playscripts: Theory and Method* (Bowling Green, Ohio: Bowling Green University Press, 1974), pp. 150–151.

Current Performance Theories

1. Francis Fergusson, Introduction to *Aristotle's Poetics* (New York: Hill & Wang, 1961), p. 9.
2. Horace, "On the Art of Poetry," trans. T. S. Dorsch, in *Classical Literary Criticism* (Harmondsworth, England: Penguin, 1972), p. 90.
3. "*Verfremdung,*" sometimes translated instead as "estrangement."
4. Bertolt Brecht, "Short Description of a New Technique of Acting Which Produces an Alienation Effect" (1940), in *Brecht on Theatre*, trans. John Willett (New York: Hill & Wang, 1964), p. 145.
5. Constantin Stanislavski, *An Actor Prepares*, trans. Elizabeth R. Hapgood (New York: Theatre Arts, 1948), p. 38.
6. Ibid., p. 252.
7. Willett, in *Brecht on Theatre*, p. 42.
8. Ibid., pp. 200–201.
9. Antonin Artaud, *The Theatre and Its Double*, trans. Mary Caroline Richards (New York: Grove, 1958), p. 24.
10. Ibid., p. 25.
11. Ibid., p. 31.
12. Ibid., pp. 123–124.
13. Ibid., p. 39.
14. Ibid., p. 78.
15. Ibid., p. 100.
16. Charles Marowitz, Introduction to *The Marowitz Hamlet and the Tragical History of Doctor Faustus* (Harmondsworth, England: Penguin, 1970), pp. 13–15.
17. Ibid., p. 10.

18. Richard Schechner, "Approaches," in *Public Domain: Essays on the Theatre* (New York: Bobbs-Merrill, 1969), p. 44.

19. Ibid., pp. 51–52.

20. Ibid.

21. Ibid., p. 67.

22. Ibid., p. 91.

23. Ibid., p. 64.

What Aristotle Might Have Said

1. All references are to Book and Section in *Aristotle's Poetics*, trans. S. H. Butcher (New York: Hill & Wang, 1961).

2. Gerald F. Else, *Aristotle's Poetics: The Argument* (Cambridge, Mass.: Harvard University Press, 1957). A valuable anthology on the influence of Aristotle is *Aristotle's Poetics and English Literature*, ed. Elder Olson (Chicago: University of Chicago Press, 1965). Others who have written excellent commentary in recent years on Aristotle are Kenneth Burke, O. B. Hardison, and, as already mentioned, Francis Fergusson.

3. Tennessee Williams, *Memoirs* (New York: Bantam, 1976), p. 212.

4. I shall capitalize this word to signify Style in the classificatory sense, as widely used in university theatre courses (e.g., "Styles of Acting," "Period Styles"), to distinguish it from style in the sense of manner or tone.

5. Burke, *Grammar of Motives*, p. xvi.

6. Susanne Langer, *Feeling and Form* (New York: Scribner's, 1953), p. 99.

7. Michel St.-Denis, *Theatre: The Rediscovery of Style* (New York: Theatre Arts, 1960), p. 26.

8. Alfred Harbage, "Shakespeare's Technique," in *William Shakespeare, The Complete Works*, ed. Alfred Harbage (Baltimore: Penguin, 1969), pp. 34–35; emphasis added.

9. *Oedipus the King*, trans. David Grene, in *Sophocles* I, from the edition of the complete Greek tragedies, ed. Lattimore and Grene (Chicago: University of Chicago Press, 1954).

10. Langer, *Feeling and Form*, p. 307.

11. Ibid., pp. 126–127.

12. *Shaw on Theatre*, ed. E. J. West (New York: Hill & Wang, 1958), p. 158.

Text and Performance

1. Norman Holland, *The Shakespearean Imagination* (New York: Macmillan, 1964), p. 325.

2. Langer, *Feeling and Form*, p. 139.

3. Gross, *Understanding Playscripts*, pp. 17–18.

4. Bernard Beckerman, *Dynamics of Drama* (New York: Knopf, 1970), p. 254.

Critical Methods and Metamethods

1. Gross, *Understanding Playscripts*, pp. 150–151.

2. Burke, *Grammar of Motives*, p. 3.

3. Ibid., p. 5.

4. Ibid., p. xviii.

5. Paul M. Levitt, *A Structural Approach to the Analysis of Drama* (The Hague: Mouton, 1971), p. 21.

6. Ibid.

7. Francis Fergusson, *The Idea of a Theatre* (Garden City, N.Y.: Doubleday, 1949), p. 48.

8. Ibid., p. 62.

9. Ibid., p. 117.

10. Ibid., p. 119.

11. Ibid., p. 117.

12. Ibid., p. 119.

Shelley's *The Cenci*

1. The edition used was Percy Bysshe Shelley, *The Cenci*, ed. Roland A. Duerksen (Indianapolis: Bobbs-Merrill, 1970). Subsequent references to the script will be made in the text.

2. "Preface," ibid., p. 9.

3. Reported in Stuart Curran, *Shelley's "Cenci": Scorpions Ringed with Fire* (Princeton: Princeton University Press, 1970), p. 249. This valuable book provided a good deal of information about the playtext and its history. That an entire book should be written about a single playscript, which is rare except with Shakespeare, is an encouraging sign for dramatic criticism.

4. Antonin Artaud, *The Cenci*, trans. Simon Watson Taylor (New York: Grove, 1969), p. vii.

5. Ibid., p. 31.

6. Curran, *Shelley's "Cenci"*, p. 66.

7. Ibid., p. 101 n.

8. Constantin Stanislavski, *Creating a Role* (New York: Theatre Arts, 1961), pp. 184–185.

Notes

Ibsen's *A Doll House*

1. Henrik Ibsen, *A Doll House*, trans. Rolf Fjelde, in *Ibsen: Four Major Plays* (New York: New American Library, 1965), p. 94. Subsequent page references will be made in the text. In his Foreword (pp. xxv–xxvi), Fjelde gives compelling reasons for the title *A Doll House*, which I have used throughout this book, in preference to the more usual *A Doll's House*.
2. Søren Kierkegaard, *Either/Or*, trans. David F. Swensen and Lillian Marvin Swensen (Garden City, N.Y.: Doubleday, 1959), I, 25.
3. Ibid., II, 259.
4. Henrik Ibsen, *Brand*, trans. Michael Meyer (Garden City, N.Y.: Doubleday, 1960), p. 96.

Pinter's *The Homecoming*

1. Harold Pinter, *The Homecoming* (London: Methuen, 1970), p. 26. Subsequent page references will be made in the text.
2. Pinter has published several versions of the playscript, which differ slightly from each other, reflecting meticulous revisions. Earlier versions have a comma after the "Yes" in Lenny's final speech in this section.
3. "Fragment of an Agon," in *The Complete Poems and Plays of T. S. Eliot* (London: Faber and Faber, 1969), p. 122.

Afterthoughts

1. G. Wilson Knight, *The Wheel of Fire*, 5th ed. (New York: World, 1957), p. viii.

Index